Butterfly of the Night

Palewell Press

Butterfly of the Night

by Haydar Karataş
translated by Caroline Stockford

Butterfly of the Night
First edition 2021 from Palewell Press,
https://palewellpress.co.uk
Printed and bound in the UK
ISBN 978-1-911587-48-4

All Rights Reserved. Copyright © 2021 Caroline Stockford. No part of this translation may be reproduced or transmitted in any form or by any means, without permission in writing from the translator. The right of Haydar Karataş to be identified as the author and of Caroline Stockford to be identified as the translator of this work has been asserted by them in accordance with the Copyright, Designs and Patents Act 1988

The original of the front cover image was downloaded from www.canva.com, is Copyright © 2021 Mustafa Horus
The cover design is Copyright © 2021 Camilla Reeve
The photo of Caroline Stockford is Copyright © 2021 Caroline Stockford
The photo of Haydar Karataş is Copyright © 2021 Haydar Karataş
A CIP catalogue record for this title is available from the British Library.

Acknowledgements

First published by İletişim Publishing, Istanbul in 2010

Historical Introduction

Haydar Karataş, the author, of *Gece Kelebeği – Perperık-a Söe* (Butterfly of the Night) has been living in exile in Zurich where I taught for many years at the University, however without knowing him. The book's original edition has long been untouched in our private library. Only, when Caroline Stockford asked me in April 2021 to preface the book's English edition, I finally read *Butterfly of the Night* within a few days, alternately in the original version and in the new, precious English translation. As a historian, I have written about misery, suffering and extreme violence. But still, I read the novel with a fresh mind and was deeply impressed by the all-too-true story it tells. Its child-narrator – Haydar Karataş's mother – moved me into an intimate proximity to a historical event that I knew from research, but whose individual experience this work reveals in a unique way. The following pages are supposed to orient readers of *Butterfly of the Night* and to give them the means to historically understand the novel in the context of Kemalist Turkey in the 1930s.

* * *

Between March 1937 and September 1938, non-state-controlled parts of the Turkish province of Tunceli (formerly known as Dersim) were subjected to a military campaign that resulted in a particularly high death toll; many thousands of civilians fell victim to the violence. Contemporary officers called it a "disciplinary campaign" (*tedip harekâtı*, a term also used by the official military historian, Reşat Halli, in his 1972 account) 1; politicians and press, a Kemalist "civilising

---

1 Reşat Halli, *Türkiye Cumhuriyetinde ayaklanmalar (1924–1938)*, ed. by the Directorate of the General Staff for Military History, Ankara: Genelkurmay Basımevi, 1972.

mission."2 In contrast to the 1925 repression of the Kurdish Sheikh Saïd rebellion and the 1921 Kurdish-Alevi uprising in Koçgiri, it took place when the Republic of Turkey had already been consolidated. The campaign of Dersim was not a short-term reaction to a concrete uprising; it had been prepared well in advance. Mustafa Kemal Atatürk, the state president, personally stood behind it and died soon after it ended.

The Republic of Turkey was founded after the 1923 Treaty of Lausanne, which had recognised the Turkish nationalist movement as the country's sole legitimate representative and admitted its victory in Asia Minor. The new Republic implemented revolutionary changes from above, including the abolition of the Caliphate in 1924, and the introductions of the Swiss Civil Code in 1926 and the Latin alphabet in 1928. Broadly acclaimed as a successful modern Turkish nation-state, the Republic rebuilt its international relations. However, the ideological climate of the 1930s was tainted by the racist undertones of radical Turkism (Turkish ethno-nationalism); cosmopolitan Ottomanism and multicultural traditions, including non-Turkish languages, were erased.

The region of Dersim in Northeastern Anatolia, renamed Tunceli in 1935, stood markedly at odds with the politico-cultural landscape of 1930s Turkey. In a 1926 report, Hamdi Bey, a senior official, called the area an abscess that needed an emergency surgery from the Republic.3 In 1932, journalist Naşit Uluğ, who acted as deputy from 1931 to 1935, published a booklet entitled *The Feudal Lords and Dersim,* which concluded by questioning how a "Dersim system" marked by feudalism and banditry

---

2 Naşit H. Uluğ, *Tunceli Medeniyete açılıyor*, Istanbul: Kaynak, 2007 (first ed. 1939).

3 Halli, Türkiye Cumhuriyetinde ayaklanmalar, 375.

could be destroyed.4 After Hamdi, General Inspector Ibrahim Tali, Marshal Fevzi Çakmak and Minister of the Interior Şükrü Kaya all collected information on the ground and wrote reports concluding the necessity of introducing "reforms" in the region.5 The need for such reforms, together with military campaigns to implement them, had been a postulate since the 19th century Ottoman *Tanzimat*. Several military campaigns had taken place at the time but had brought only limited successes. In the second third of the 19th century, parts of Dersim – along with other eastern parts of the Ottoman Empire that since the 16th century had been ruled by autonomous Kurdish lords – came under direct rule of the central state. In the republican era, this still depended upon the cooperation, i.e., co-optation, of the local lords. The central parts of Dersim, by contrast, resisted both co-optation and direct rule until the 1930s.

Dersim is a mountainous region between Sivas, Erzincan and Elazığ (renamed from Elaziz in 1937; Turkification of local names began during World War I). Covering an area of 90 km east-west and 70 km north-south, its population in the 1930s, according to official contemporary estimates, counted nearly 80,000 people; one-fifth of them were men considered able to bear arms.6 Dersim's topography was well-suited to cattle breeding but only to limited agriculture. Its valleys, caves, forests and mountains offered many places for refuge and hiding. They had been vital for the survival of Dersim's Alevi population, a Kurdish-speaking minority group that venerated the

---

4 Naşit H. Uluğ, Derebeyi ve Dersim, Istanbul: Kaynak, 2009 (first ed. 1932).

5 M. Kalman, Belge ve Tanıklarıyla Dersim Direnişleri, Istanbul: Nujen, 1995, 135-68; Hüseyin, Dersim 1938 ve zorunlu iskân, Telgraflar, dilekçeler, mektuplar, Ankara: Dipnot, 2009, 57-89.

6 Jandarma Umum Kumandanlığı Raporu, Dersim. Jandarma Umum Kumandanlığı raporu, Istanbul: Kaynak, 2010 (first ed. 1932: 59).

Prophet Muhammad's son-in-law, Ali. When the Ottoman state embraced Sunni orthodoxy, they refused the Sharia and remained attached to unorthodox Sufi beliefs and practices widespread in Anatolia before the 16th century; their beliefs were mostly linked to the 13th century Anatolian saint Hacı Bektash. Since many of the Alevis had sympathised with Safavid Persia in the 16th century, they were lastingly stigmatised as heretics and traitors. Dersim was the location of many important places of Alevi religious pilgrimage, partly shared with local Armenians. Its "Seyyids" claimed descent from Ali and entertained a network of dependent communities in and outside of Dersim.[7]

In 1921, an uprising took place in Koçgiri, an Alevi region on the western border of Dersim. This was the first rebellion that had been shaped by Kurdish nationalism. The first language of the "Dersim Kurds," as they were called by contemporary observers, was not Turkish but Zaza (the main language) or Kurmanji. Kurdish nationalism had been influencing a number of Kurdish leaders since the early 20th century. Adopting President Woodrow Wilson's post-World War I principle of self-determination, they had linked the claim to self-determination with Kurdist activism, as General Fevzi Çakmak complained in his report of 1930. Çakmak therefore demanded the removal of functionaries of "Kurdish race" in Erzincan.[8]

Dersim was the only place more or less safe for Armenian refugees during and after the genocide of 1915, which mainly took place in the eastern provinces. In 1916, a Bektashiye leader had tried in vain to win over the chiefs of Dersim to fight side-by-side with the Ottoman army against

---

[7] Erdal Gezik, Alevi Kürtler: Dinsel, etnik ve politik sorunlar bağlamında (Ankara: Kalan, 2004), 141-76; Hans-Lukas Kieser, A quest for belonging. Anatolia beyond empire and nation, Istanbul: Isis, 2007, 166.

[8] Halli, *Türkiye*, 351-52.

the invading Russians. As a result, two limited rebellions broke out, with armed groups harassing the Ottoman army. The Young Turk rulers during World War I and the leaders of the National movement co-opted the Bektashiye, before 1918 and after 1918 respectively.[9]

On 21 June 1934 a Law of Settlement generally legitimized the depopulation of regions in Turkey for cultural, political or military reasons. This law was conceived in order to complete the Turkification of Anatolia in the context of the new focus on Dersim in interior politics. According to Minister of the Interior Kaya's statement, the intent was to create "a country with one language, one mentality, and unity of feeling."[10]

Following several incidents that culminated in tribal attacks against the new infrastructure in Pah and a police station in Sin in eastern central Dersim on the nights of 20-21 and 26-17 March 1937, the military campaign was launched. Having accumulated 8,623 men, artillery and an air force, it was, by early May, vastly superior in numbers and materiel to the forces of the insurgents. On 4 May 1937, the Council of Ministers, including Atatürk and Chief of General Staff, Fevzi Çakmak, secretly decided on a forceful attack against western-central Dersim; the aim was to kill everyone who was using or had used arms, and to remove the population settled between Nazimiye and Sin. On the same day, planes dropped pamphlets promising that in the case of surrender,

---

9 Nuri Dersimi, *Hatıratım*, Stockholm: Roja Nû, 1986 (first ed 1952): 100-103; Halli, Türkiye, 1972; 373-74; Kieser, *Der verpasste Friede. Mission, Ethnie und Staat in den Ostprovinzen der Türkei (1839-1938)*, Zürich: Chronos 2000, 396; Hülya Küçük, *The role of the Bektashis in Turkey's national struggle*, Leiden: Brill, 2001: 212–23.

10 Erol Ülker, "Assimilation, Security and Geographical Nationalization in Interwar Turkey: The Settlement Law of 1934," *European Journal of Turkish Studies*, 7 (2008), Online since 11 December 2008, https://journals.openedition.org/ejts/2123, 8 (visited 20 March 2021).

"no harm at all would be done to you, dear compatriots. If not, entirely against our will, the [military] forces will act and destroy you. One must obey the state."[11]

In the following months, the army successfully advanced against fierce resistance and ever-changing tribal coalitions that were led by Rıza, a talented poet-activist named Alişer, as well as allied tribal chiefs. Unity among the rebels was far from achieved; only a few tribes formed the hard core of the resistance. On 9 July, Alişer and his wife were killed by their own people, and their heads sent to Alpdoğan. In July, Rıza sent a letter to the prime minister in which he vividly described what he saw as anti-Kurdish politics of assimilation, removal and, ultimately, a war of destruction. Via his friend Nuri Dersimi, who had gone into exile in Syria in September 1937, he also sent a despairing letter to the League of Nations and the foreign ministries of the United Kingdom, France and the United States, all of which remained unanswered. On 10 September, he surrendered to the army in Erzincan. Messages of congratulation were sent to Alpdoğan by Atatürk, Interior Minister Şükrü Kaya and Prime Minister İnönü, who had visited Elazığ in June. Shortly before Atatürk's visit there, Rıza, along with his son Resik Hüseyin, tribal leader Seyit Haso and the sons of a few tribal chiefs, were executed. The executions had been hastily organised by Ihsan Sabri Çağlayangil, who later became foreign minister.[12]

Despite the setbacks of 1937, Dersimi groups resumed attacks against the security forces in early 1938, declaring that they all would perish if they did not resist.[13] The military campaign took on a new and comprehensive

---

11 Halli, *Türkiye*, 390-91 and 491.

12 İhsan Sabri Çağlayangil, "Kader bizi una değil, üne itti," *Çağlayangil'in anıları*, ed. Tanju Cilizoğlu, Istanbul: Bilgi Yayınevi, 2007, 69-73; Kieser, *Quest*, 249-51.

13 Halli, *Türkiye*, 412.

character as the government embarked on a general cleansing that aimed, as Prime Minister Celal Bayar stated in parliament on 29 June 1938, "to eradicate once and for all this [Dersim] problem."14 In June 1938, units began to penetrate parts of Dersim between Pülür (Ovacık), Danzik and Pah that had refused to surrender. Between 10 August and early September, a large campaign of cleansing and scouring (*tarama*) took place, costing the lives of many thousands of men, women and children, including members of the tribes that had cooperated with the government.

According to the official statements, the military campaign of 1937 was aimed at bandits and reactionary tribal and religious leaders who misled innocent people. Clandestinely, however, parts of the general population of Dersim had been targeted from the beginning, at least for relocation in accordance with the 1934 Law of Settlement. This was especially true following the decision of the Council of Ministers on 4 May 1937. As had been the case in Koçgiri in 1921, those targeted feared that they would all perish like the Armenians if they did not resist.15 The campaign of spring 1937 targeted the regions between Pah and Hozat in which most clashes had occurred. This included the disarmament of villages and the removal of people, though most of the violence was directed towards armed groups. Halli, who amply cites military documents, scarcely uses the word *imha* (annihilation) for this period. This changed with the campaign of summer 1938, during which the population of Dersim, including in parts that had surrendered and had not been declared prohibited zones under the Law of Settlement, was subjected to extreme violence. On 6 August 1938, the Council of Ministers decided that 5,000-7,000 Dersimis had to be moved from the

---

14 Akgül, *Yakın tarihimizde*, 155.

15 Hüseyin Aygün, Dersim 1938 ve zorunlu iskân, Telgraflar, dilekçeler, mektuplar, Ankara: Dipnot, 2009, 72.

prohibited zones to the west. "Thousands of persons, whose names the Fourth General Inspectorate [under Alpdoğan] had listed, were arrested and sent in convoys to the regions where they were ordered to go."16

Those targeted for relocation included numerous families living outside of the prohibited zones or those living in areas outside of Dersim that were considered to be members of Dersimi tribes. Several notables living outside Dersim were killed in summer 1938, as were some young Dersimi recruits. For the killing of surviving "bandits," the prime minister, along with the interior minister, the Minister of Defence and the Military Inspectorate proposed to implement the notorious "Special Organisation" (Teşkilat-ı Mahsusa/ Özel Teşkilat), which had gained its infamy during World War I for its role in the mass killing of Armenians and, particularly, of targeted personalities.17

The first week of cleansing took place between 10 and 17 August 1938. According to the official military historian Halli, "thousands of bandits" were annihilated during this phase alone.18 While Halli mentions no comprehensive number for the whole campaign, his detailed narrative does provide some precise figures; it also mentions dozens of incidents during which a "large number" of persons were killed. Based on this information, the number of deaths is likely to have been considerably higher than 10,000. An unpublished report by Alpdoğan's Inspectorate, quoted in Turkish newspapers, mentions 13,160 civilian deaths and 11,818 deportees (*Radikal*, 20 November 2009).

---

16 Halli, *Türkiye*, 463.

17 Halli, *Türkiye*, 465. Cf. Oktay Özel, "The Role of Teşkilat-ı Mahsusa (Special Organization) in the Armenian Genocide," in Christine Pschichholz (ed.), *The First World War as a Caesura? Demographic Concepts, Population Policy, and Genocide in the Late Ottoman, Russian, and Habsburg Spheres* (Berlin: Duncker & Humblot, 2020), 81-108

18 Halli, *Türkiye*, 463.

The high number of deaths, along with other ample evidence prove that the killings were not limited to the insurgent tribes. A comparison of the censuses of 1935 and 1940 shows that the district of Hozat, with a loss of more than 10,000 people, was the most seriously impacted.19 A proposed number of 40,000 fatal victims seems, however, implausibly high.20

According to several sources, including Çağlayangil's authoritative testimony, the army used poison gas, imported from Germany, to kill people who hid in caves.21 Many others were burned alive, whether in houses or by spraying individuals with fuel. Even people who surrendered, were exterminated. In order "not to fall into the hands of the Turks," girls and women jumped from great heights into abysses, as many Armenians had done in 1915.[22] The suspicion of having lodged "bandits" or – according to witness accounts of soldiers – military units' desire for vengeance, sufficed as justification to annihilate entire villages. Soldiers confirmed that they were ordered to kill women and children. One has to bear in mind that the Dersimis were seen – and declared by officers – to be Alevi heretics or crypto-Armenians. When gendarmerie posts were established in the 1930, gendarmes even exercised control over whether or not local young men were circumcised. "Was he perhaps a giavour [unbeliever, i.e., non-Muslim], an Armenian?"[23] – i.e., the signature enemy and traitor that the

---

19 Aslan, *Herkesin*, 411.

20 David McDowall, *A modern history of the Kurds*, London: I.B.Tauris, 2000, 209.

21 *NTV Tarih*, December 2009, 61.

22 Dersimi, *Hatıratım*, 318-320.

23 İlhami Algör, *Ma sekerdo kardaş? "Dersim 38" tanıklıkları*, Istanbul: Doğan, 2010, 159; Faik Bulut, *Belgerle Dersim raporları*, Istanbul: Yön, 1991, 299-301.

Young Turk party-state had stigmatized and persecuted in the 1910s. The Dersim was not only a place of age-old Armenian-Kurdish coexistence, as we have seen, and of common Armenian-Alevi pilgrimage places and song and music traditions (*saz ve söz*), but it had also offered the most important asylum in Asia Minor during the genocide. Thus, many Armenians survived and remained there, finally suffering the onslaught in 1937-1938 together with the other Dersimis.

Military, governmental and private Dersimi archives are documenting the exterminatory onslaught. Important material is located in the military archives in Ankara (ATASE), that is closed to independent research. This is true also for the relevant documents of the civil offices, which have largely remained under control of the respective ministries and have not been transferred to the Republican Archives (BCA). However, a number of official reports have been leaked. They, along with Halli's soldiers' testimonies, and witness accounts from survivors all agree that systematic massacres took place; soldiers and survivors specifically added that the targets included civilians, women and children.[24]

Accustomed to looking up to the state and army as omnipotent entities, most soldiers feared speaking about their experiences even decades after the events. "When we came to the headquarters, we learnt that discussions had taken place between the officers. A few said that that these people [women and children in Hozat who had not given information on the whereabouts of the men] had to be annihilated, others said that this was a sin. [...] They [finally] ordered us: 'Annihilate all you can apprehend.' [...] And that day we soldiers, in a horrific savageness and craziness, gathered the women, girls and children in a mosque – it was

---

24 Bulut, Belgerle, 183-206, 299-304; "Dersim Katliamı'ndaki askerler konuştu," CNN Turk of 3 May 2011.

in fact not like a mosque but rather like a church – closed it, sprayed kerosene and easily burnt them alive."25

In the second half of the twentieth century, Dersimis started collecting documents; conducting interviews and finally creating Internet sites.26 Intensified work has added further material in the early 21st century.27 Others made insightful documentary films.28 A central archive dedicated to the documentation of the Dersim massacre, however, does not yet exist.

Hans-Lukas Kieser
Basel, May 2021

---

25 Soldier Halil Çolak, in Bulut, Belgerle, 300-301.

26 Algör, Ma sekerdo; Kalman, Belge; Bulut, Belgerlerle.

27 Notably Hüseyin Aygün, *Dersim 1938 ve zorunlu iskân* (Istanbul: Dipnot, 2009) and idem, *Dersim 1938: Resmiyete karşı hakikat* (Istanbul: Dipnot, 2010); Cemal Taş, *Dağların kayıp anahtarı. Dersim 1938 anlatıları*, Istanbul: Iletisim, 2010.

28 Notably Kâzım ve Nezahat Gündoğan, *İki tutam saç – Dersim'in kayıp kızları* (2010) and *Hay Way Zaman: Dersim'in Kayıp Kızları* (2014), both films on the destiny of girls targeted by violence, intimidation and a systematic child transfer that served the destruction of Dersim's autonomous culture. Both films are based on documentation collected in idem, *Dersim'in kayıp kızları: "Tertelê Çêneku" (Kızların kıyımı)* (Istanbul: Iletisim, 2012). Nezahat Gündoğan's third related documentary *Vank'ın çocukları* (2015) focuses on Armenians who survived in Dersim; it includes the massacres of 1895-96 and the genocide of 1915. Kâzım Gündoğan has published the relevant research in *Keşiş'in Torunları: Dersimli Ermeniler* (Istanbul: Ayrıntı, 2016).

Translator's Note

It is eight years since I first read Haydar Karataş's remarkable book, Butterfly of the Night. In order to write this translator's note, I found my original copy, given to me by Haydar when I visited him and his family in Zürich. It is dated 12 May, 2013 and the dedication reads,
> *Most adults grow to miss the past, as we age, but some people become familiar with this vanishing loss as children and they continue to seek that which disappeared, just like the people in this book.*

The book is the true story of seven years in the life of his mother and grand-mother after they were exiled from their village of Weroz, Dersim. The narrator, his mother Gülizar, was five or six years old as the story begins.

Author Gün Zeli's words on the back of the book read: *"All I can tell you about the book in your hands is: buy it and read it. There are only three books that have ever made me cry. Steinbeck's 'Grapes of Wrath', Sabatier's 'The Safety Matches', and this book you hold in your hands, Karataş's 'Butterfly of the Night'."*

A book of this length should take a year to translate, working full time. And yet it took nearly four years. Throughout this time, Haydar was patient and displayed generous humility.

"I know, that in your mind, you are going through what they went through and that you feel it", he would say. *"Take as long as you have to. The most important thing is that you tell the story well."*

I visited Haydar and his family three times in Zurich during the course of the translation. Haydar and I went for long walks around the city and visited writers' cafes, discussing his books and the Kurdish culture of the Dersim region.

During the translation process, back at home in Wales, I would frequently stop for weeks on end. Had this been a fictional novel I would not have connected so deeply with the characters, I'm sure. Yet, this is a true account of their lives and there seemed to be no let-up in the suffering of the mother and daughter. I felt compelled to tell their story and soon, a terrible guilt began to grow. I began to have blocks against going back to the sadness of the narrative unfolding in front of me.

When I stopped for a meal, all I could think about was the women, trying to mill acorn flour and boiling up poisonous weeds for the scum on top of the broth, which could itself be dried into flour. When I made an internet search, just six pages into the translation, I was shocked to see archive photographs of some of the characters. Notably, Sahan Ağa, whose severed head was shown displayed on the earth, between the knee-length boots of two military police.

The Dersim massacre is still not openly acknowledged by everyone in Turkey. It remained a taboo subject in the country until Haydar wrote the account his family's story. *"I wrote the book in order to come to terms with what had happened to them"*, he told me.

Haydar wrote this book, along with others, over a ten year and four-month period in prison in Turkey. At the age of nineteen he received a life sentence for leading a student rebellion whilst at university in Istanbul. After ten years in different prisons in Turkey, Haydar escaped and boarded a plane for Zurich with false papers that had been prepared for him.

"It was only when the plane was in the air that I knew I was safe," he said. *"As a student I was involved in and led revolutionary groups. When I look back on my life, it was the pain of the history of my family that led me to resist to that degree."*

He wrote the book's manuscript in Yozgat prison. During a transfer to another prison, the guards confiscated and destroyed all his notebooks. However, they missed the fifth of eight notebooks, as it was hidden inside the cover of another book. The fifth notebook told the story of Butterfly of the Night.

The original Turkish manuscript was published by İletişim Publishing in Istanbul in 2010 and was an instant success. A great number of articles were written in relation to the book, discussing the need for acknowledgement of the terrible events of Dersim in the first quarter of the last century. Butterfly of the Night, or *Gece Kelebeği* as it is known in Turkish, sold in excess of 200,000 copies.

In collaboration with the author, some of the dialogue in the last third of the book has been edited as there were instances of repetition.

Haydar explains, *"The repetition of the dialogue between Fecire, Çöyder, Perhan and Musa; the characters' repeatedly going over the details of their situation is there because they are in a dead end; a blind alley. They cannot get out of the situation they are in and all they can do it to reiterate it constantly."* We took the decision with Haydar to remove some of the repetitions so that the narrative did not lose its impetus.

The folk stories in the book were recounted as Gülizar remembered them and do not always resolve in terms of narrative. We have edited them in collaboration with the author.

In the text, we have retained the original spellings of the place names and characters.

In Turkish, the letter ç is pronounced 'ch'
c is pronounced 'j' (Fecire is pronounced Fejihre)
ş is pronounced 'sh'
ö as in the 'I' of 'girl' - purse lips for 'o' but say 'e'
'ü' as the 'u' in 'cute' - purse lips for 'o' but say 'i'
and the i without a dot, ı, is pronounced as the 'ea' of earth.

The soft g or ğ is silent and lengthens the vowel in front. So dağ is pronounced 'daah.'

Haydar, who lives in Zurich with his wife and children, has been a great help and good friend during the lengthy translation process. We are grateful to Professor Hans Kieser for his Foreword, which accurately locates this text historically and provides a solid grounding in the events leading up to this dark point in history. As author and translator, Haydar and I express our thanks to Camilla Reeve of Palewell Press for publishing this important, true account of the lives of the women and children of Dersim in the late 1930s.

The book's protagonist, his mother Gülizar, is still alive, in Istanbul. She is 94 years old at the time of writing. Her son cannot return to visit her and she is now too frail to travel to see him. The deeply painful theme of exile and separation continues.

Caroline Stockford
Bristol, 2021

Butterfly of the Night

Eno tuver Sahan si merd?'

Neno miver...'

'Do you remember the killing of Sahan?'

'No, I do not remember...'

I

This is how my mother would describe those days. One afternoon they saw a man running down Balıkan Mountain. He was one of my Uncle Sahan's bandits and was screaming my mother's name as he ran; tumbling through the oak scrub and streaming with sweat.

'Fecire Hatun! Fecire Hatun!'

He began to climb the slope to our house but was hurrying so much that he rolled backwards twice and scrambled up the slope on all fours. He collapsed on his knees in front of our door, his face contorted as he shouted,

'Fecire Hatun! Fecire Hatun!'

He was coursing with sweat, repeating my mother's name and he might well have died there on the spot had my uncle Veysel not called for a dish of water. Water was brought and Veysel dipped the copper dish in the bucket, giving it to the man who was fighting for his breath. The man took it with shaking hands, spilling half of it as he drank. Then he began stammering once more, 'Fecire Hatun... Fecire Hatun... Hıdır Efendi, get news to Hıdır Efendi...'

That was all that he could say. Suddenly the whole village, man, woman and child came out onto the Balıkan

Mountain Road. The news had spread and the Bactrian villagers could not believe what they were hearing.

On the bare peaks of Sıncık Mountain the news reached my father. Sıncık mountain, where horses neighed and raised up clouds of dust to the ringing of their iron shoes.

When my mother arrived at the cave on Balıkan Mountain blood was still flowing from where Sahan had been beheaded. The blood ran in a thin path from the mouth of the cave to where she stood. Sahan Ağa's two bandits were rooted next to the body of their chief, almost as if he were still living and they were standing guard.

'The women, where are the women?' asked my mother. They'd gone. Pirço had killed Sahan Ağa as he slept. He'd cut off his head and taken it to General Alpdoğan at the Hozat regimental base.

Pirço was a very short man who wore a conical helmet and headed a group of forty armed men. All forty of them were as short at Pirço himself. The story behind his conical helmet, that looked for all the world like a triangle when viewed from a distance, went back as far as Pirço's great-great-grandfather and namesake. Grandfather Pirço, along with his men, had escaped from the Bronze Army [29] and had taken refuge in Inner Dersim. The Pirços proliferated behind these mountains. They owned no land and were known for making their living as highwaymen. They were brave, too.

The latest in the line of Pirços wore this conical helmet strung over his back with a cord round his neck. Whenever this helmet was on his head and not slung on his back people would say, 'Here we go, Pirço is off raiding again!' He'd carry out raids as far away as Erzurum, Sivas and even travel to the regions of the Black Sea where he would attack the various military police headquarters and villages before bringing back the spoils.

---

29 The name given to the Hun army when it entered Inner Dersim

As for my mother, she was the daughter of Süleyman Salih Bey. She was a beautiful woman; tall and slim with green eyes that harboured a hint of blue. Her first marriage had been to a man called Munzur from near Ovacık. From this marriage she had three sons, Baki, Hasan and Ali Rıza and also a daughter who was named Fecire, just like herself. In the Zazaki language Fecire means 'daybreak.'

When her husband Munzur died in the plague epidemic my mother returned with her four children to her father Süleyman Salih Bey's house in Zeranik. However, her father also died soon after and my mother was left alone with her small children. Upon the death of her father my mother found herself at the heart of a huge argument. Her uncles did not believe that a woman could have the right to her father's lands. My mother's only brother, Kahraman Salih Bey always tried to keep out of these family altercations. He hardly supported her at all on the matter. Then, there followed several attempts at abducting my mother by men who knew that whoever married her would become heir to all her father's lands. Those people around my mother advised her to send word to Kopo Rayber (30) to protect her from these repeated attempts to abduct her. My mother sent a man to ask Kopo Rayber for help but instead the man went to one of the men who wished to abduct her. They then tricked her into mounting a horse by telling her they were taking her to Kopo Rayber. They took her, instead, to the house of an outlaw by the name of Sevkan.

At the time my mother's brother, Kahraman Bey, was a barrister at Erzincan. He sent word from there to Yusuf Ağa to tell him his sister had been abducted and asking him to rescue her. Yusuf Ağa was a friend of Kahraman Bey. He raided the village of Sowge with his men, rescued my mother and took her to his own house.

---

30 Rayber was the title given to men in the region of Dersim who were a person of local authority

Yusuf Ağa was Olbeg Bey's son. When a land dispute among the Bactrian tribes caused infighting and led to the killing of over thirty men, the tribes of Dersim gathered together to try to make peace among the varying factions. However, they could not get past the fact of these killings, and so they thought perhaps Olbeg Bey, who had studied law near Erzincan, might be able to assist in finding a solution. Olbeg Bey was Turkish and yet not an Alevite. The men of the tribes involved went to fetch him from Kemah and brought him to Weroz in the belief that he would seal a peace between the tribes. And so it turned out, Olbeg Bey set up a court and achieved peace between the tribes. Following this, the Bactrians wanted Olbeg Bey to stay with them and become their tribal leader. They helped Olbeg Bey to build a fine residence at Torut. It was a two-storey house built on a hill and had double-fronted windows and was later set on fire during the Russian war. Even so, its walls remained standing for many years afterwards.

The houses in Dersim were made of dressed stone and were two-storeys high, with room for animals to be kept on the ground floor, with the first floor being used as living quarters. These houses were solidly constructed around an ornate alder support with the upper beams of the first floor meeting the central support in a cartwheel shape. Wooden floorboards were then laid on top as flooring for the upper level. The lower part of the residence consisted of herringbone parquet. In those times there were specialist Armenian stonemasons in Dersim. Discerning people in the locality employed the Armenian master stone masons to construct their houses. These stone walls that were constructed without mortar looked magnificent from the outside. The central alder support of the house would be brought by ox-cart from Harput.

A branch of the Silk Route passed from Erzincan and Lower Torunoba through the area known nowadays as Geçitkaya. The road then passed over Orta Mountain and came all the way to Hozat. The other branch, meanwhile went from Harput to Hozat.

These were the roads along which the ox-carts passed. The people of Dersim destroyed these roads during the Armenian incident to stop the state from reaching the Armenians of Inner Dersim. They destroyed the mountain passes and filled the roads with large rocks.

The wood and central beam for Olbeg Bey's fine residence was also brought by ox-cart from Harput. The house was built and Olbeg Bey took up residency. The Alevite religious ritual, the *cem,* was being celebrated but was kept secret from Olbeg. When he heard about this, he too joined the gatherings and converted from Sunism to Alevism.

In the time of Olbeg's son Yusuf Ağa, this house was attacked several times and set on fire by soldiers. Each time it was built anew. The final residence was built at Pakire but, when that house too was burned down by soldiers, Yusuf's son Hıdır built his new home at Weroz.

When Yusuf Ağa heard that the barrister Kahraman Bey's widowed sister and mother of four children had been abducted and taken to Sowge village, he attacked the place with his men, took my mother and brought her to this house in Weroz. Yusuf Ağa had allowed my mother to stay for some time as his guest. Then, after obtaining the permission of her brother Kahraman, he married her to his son Hıdır.

My father, Hıdır, had studied for ten years at Ankara using the Ottoman writing system. My mother told me that his grandfather Olbeg had been a Turk. The house in Weroz where I was born was also made of dressed stone, with a central support. Its upper floor was made of wooden floorboards and the lower one of herringbone parquet. It had three big rooms. The inner rooms had walls made from sun-dried bricks and were connected by way of carved walnut doors. My memories of this house are vague. I remember the walls were of white decorative plaster. As you went in through the door you were met by a picture showing the Prophet Abraham standing next to two winged rams as he blindfolded Ishmael. The knife in Abraham's hand almost sparkled. There was a picture of two mountain goats on the mantlepiece above the fireplace and between the two windows was a picture of the Prophet Jesus hanging on the cross and Moses grazing his sheep. The wooden ceiling was painted with pictures of the Twelve Imams. This large house was built on a high valley with Sıncık Mountain at its back and from the front the peaks of Hozat could just be made out in the distance.

After the Armenian incident my father and his brother Sahan took over the administration of the Bactrian tribes from their father Yusuf Ağa. They, and the armed men they had gathered to their side, were responsible for security in the Bactrian region. They also wanted to bring to this household my mother's four children by her earlier marriage. These were times when clashes were frequent and increasing.

At the time in the Bactrian region there were the armed bands of Yusuf Ağa's two sons, Sahan and Hıdır and also the armed band led by Pirço. Pirço's outfit was extremely brave and were dressed from head to toe in armour taken from the Bronze soldiers. The Bronze Army attacked Dersim on two occasions from the direction of Erzincan but were never able to fully invade. When the soldiers of 1938 entered Dersim the armed bands of my uncle Sahan and my father Hıdır joined forces with that of Pirço.

They set off to bring my mother's children from her first marriage to Weroz. Baki, who was working in a salt mine in Kemah was now fourteen years old and Ali Rıza was eleven or twelve. Their little brother Hasan, eight, was also with them. Soldiers had raided the village of Eniesit where they had been living and marched the entire village off into exile somewhere beyond Erzincan. Those who managed to escape fled to the Bactrian region. When my uncle Sahan, my father and Pirço heard that two children had been taken along with the villagers, they set off after the soldiers. They came as far as Kemah. There, they managed to overtake the soldiers in a valley near a former Armenian refugee village[31] that had been emptied of all inhabitants during the Armenian incident. They confronted the soldiers and there followed a heavy clash in which the forces of my uncle, father and Pirço killed many soldiers and took possession of their guns, horses and provisions. However, they failed to find the captives who were being marched into exile from Ovacık and therefore had to return to the village of Eniesit.

There they found out that the men and boys, who formed the line being marched into exile, had all been executed along the way. Baki had been in that group. As they put a manacle around his neck and led him off on the road, his brother Ali Rıza had managed to escape and had followed the column of captives as far as the refugee village. The villagers told my father that the soldiers had set up camp just below the village, along with the group of men they were marching into exile. Apparently, they'd handed the captives over to another regiment as the day was drawing to a close. Towards morning, screams were heard. The villagers couldn't understand what had happened. They discovered that the entire group of captives had been bayoneted.

The place where the group of men and boys being marched into exile were killed was a flat crop field. The next day, soldiers on duty spotted Ali Rıza who had been following the group. The child ran off in the direction of the refugee village and, if what the villagers said was true, those now living in the village hid Ali Rıza. The soldiers searched the village and gathered all the inhabitants in one place but they still could not find the child. When Ali Rıza looked out of the window of the house he was hiding in, to see what was going on, he was spotted and taken captive by the soldiers.

---

[31] The refugees were those migrants who came from the Balkans following the war of 1893

The man who was hiding him in his house said that he'd taken him in with the intention of making him his shepherd. The commander in charge of the soldiers claimed that the boy was an Armenian. They gave his clothing to my father. There were two bayonet holes in Ali Rıza's shirt. One had pierced his stomach at the front and had pricked a hole in the material on the other side where it exited, the other wound was where they'd stabbed him in the liver.

My uncle and father hid the deaths of Baki and Ali Rıza from my mother, and for a long time she believed that Baki had taken Ali Rıza to Kemah and that they'd both found work and been spared.

After my father died his place at the head of the armed band was taken by a man called Doğan. One day Doğan told my mother the truth about the line of captives. However, even if my mother believed it at first, she soon took to denying it had happened. She kept fantasising that her children would be coming to join her. As these hopes of hers grew with each passing day, Doğan, who by now was my mother's third husband, took her to the village where it had happened. The villagers there told the story, once more, to my mother.

The place where Baki had been killed was a flat wheat field. My mother told me that the crop there had grown as high as a man and that it swayed in the cool and gentle breeze like the blonde hair of a girl. The dead were buried under this field, where a dozer had dug a mass grave. As for Ali Rıza, the villagers had buried him on a hill right next to the village cemetery. My mother was more upset that Ali Rıza was lying on that hill all alone, than she was about his death.

Every time my mother told me the story of what happened to Baki and Ali Rıza she would follow it by mumbling a prayer in Zazaki. She never found out what had happened to her daughter, Fecire.

II

I vaguely remember the killing of my father. The whole village was filled with sounds of guns going *trrrrr, takkarr takkarr trrrr* and bullets whistling. The windows of our house were shuddering. My mother didn't know what to do. First she grabbed me by the arm and hid me under a wooden seat. Then she took me and pushed me behind a metal bin that we used to store the grain.

She ran out, she ran back in, she screamed and shouted. I shouted too, wondering why my mother had pushed me behind this metal bin. Where was she going?

'Mummy! Muuummy!' I shouted.

My mother was screaming for help, shouting the name of Çöyder, a local bandit...

'Çöyder! Yusuf Ağa has been ambushed!' She ran back in and came to where I was, took me by the arm and pulled me out from behind the metal bin. She took me upstairs and hid me underneath some seating before she ran off in the direction of the nearby river. Then she returned and began pacing around the house.

'Oh! May his chimney and hearth catch fire, oh, oh...!'

The gunfire seemed to have stopped but then it began again, *trr, trr, trr, trrrrrt, trrrrrt* on and on it went. A bomb went off making a terrible loud noise. My mother began screaming as if she had been shot.

'Çöyderrrrr! Çöyder!!!'

More gunfire followed and the air was full of the metallic smell of gunpowder. Then silence. Silence everywhere. It became so quiet that, had a sparrow perched on the branch of an oak tree, it would have sounded like thunder.

Then I heard my mother's voice, 'Ohh, mother of mine! Get news, get news to all of Dersim! The scholarly Hıdır Efendi, most helpless little grandson of Olbeg Bey, son of Yusuf Ağa has been shot. Oh, my mother! Ohhhh, get news to Demenan, to Laçinan! Tell the people of Yemen to tell the people of Seymansh. Let it be told from Fizzan to Hizzan. Tell them he's been shot, oh my mother... ohh... tell the Deaf Sultan, tell him the world has burned!'

He'd been shot. My father had been shot. They'd cut off his head and taken it away with them just as they'd done to my Uncle Sahan,

III

The killing of my father was of great consequence. The villagers were in shock. My father, the only person who had led them, and told them what to do, had been shot. By this time most of the forced exile marches had already taken place in the other areas and were only continuing here in Dersim. The Bactrian villages were situated over a wide-ranging area of forestry and mountainous terrain that was difficult for the soldiers to penetrate. However, once my father and another five men who led the armed mountain bandits had been killed, fear began to enter the hearts of the local people. The villagers, who once held my mother in highest esteem, began to keep away from her as if she were cursed.

The whole village would walk off in the evening to spend the night in the woods and return to their homes in the daytime to go about their usual business. However, the villagers didn't want my mother to go with them to the forest in the evenings. They were afraid. If the soldiers were to find their hideout in the woods, they didn't want to be caught in the company of the wife of a bandit leader. There had been a lot of rumours too, and my mother didn't know what to do in the face of them. They were saying that she should take her daughter and go over to Erzincan. It seems that venturing off like this was something that my mother really didn't want to do. My mother had said that she was afraid of the roads. It seemed impossible that a woman should set off alone over the high mountains with her little girl; without so much as a pack animal.

In the evenings, as the villages were setting off in small groups to spend the night in the forest, my mother would take me on her back and carry me down Balıkan Mountain and into the thick oak woods, to a river bed that dried out in the summertime.

As the sun began to set behind Balıkan Mountain, the villagers, in ones and twos, would start walking to the forest. My mother and I would sit at the foot of a huge rock that was near our house and we'd watch them go. Everything had changed so quickly. Now, we were completely excluded. I would look at my mother. She appeared not to know what to do. Perhaps she wanted to cry or to shout out in protest. But she was silent. I knew her so well that I knew I mustn't cry or ask why we couldn't go with the others. I knew I shouldn't ask.

It hurt me so much inside to see the whole village go off and leave us sitting at the foot of that rock. I used to think that at least uncle Veysel's daughter, Gülendar, a girl not much older than me whose house was right next to ours, must have been upset at leaving us behind. Later, I realised what my mother must have felt and why she sat in that place. It was our secret. We'd let the villagers think that we would just sit there. And yet it was painful seeing them turn to look back as they walked away. I'd wish that the sun would hurry up and leave the valley and disappear behind Balıkan Mountain. Occasionally, I would tug at my mother and say that we should go too.

When it became dark, we'd get up from our sitting place and go to an oak scrub near the house. I think my mother used to hide her money among the oaks. She would go into the branches and feel around for something with her hands. When she found what she was looking for we would start walking up past where a river bed that dried out in summertime ran down through the thick oak woods. I remember that river bed so well. Almost imperceptible trickles of water on the floor of the parched river bed played hide and seek between pebbles and dry oak leaves.

We would walk up along this dry river bed in the dark and enter a hollow where the water carved trails on the floor like the spokes of an umbrella and where oak roots hung down like vines overhead.

I think my mother and I hid for a long time under the roots of these oaks. I felt safe there. It was a safer place than that rock against which we'd lean our backs and watch the villagers depart. I got used to that little home of ours under the oak roots, where flood waters had carved a pattern on the floor. In the mornings, the sun would filter in through the roots, and the shadows of the oak leaves would dance like fish scales on the sparse waters. I would sit and guess at the shapes made by the roots that hung down like snakes and the oak branches that swayed in the sunshine.

I really got used to our home there. But suddenly, one night, my mother took me on her back and carried me off between the crop fields and past the river bed where my father had been shot. She carried me to an oak wood behind a hill in the direction of Hozat. The oak trees here were shorter than the ones in our previous shelter. The oak trees were a dwarf species and that enabled us to have a good view of our surroundings. Despite this, I didn't like our new home very much. Strange sounds came out of the woods all night long. In our old house under the oaks, all I would hear at night was the slow leaking of the water making a thin, dripping sound as if fell from the roots of the trees over our heads.

I would cry to go back to our old home until eventually one night my mother picked me up and took me back to our safer home in the hollow. But before day dawned we got up and headed up to a rocky formation hidden in the woods. Then without hiding our movements for the first time we walked down the slope behind our house to the village.

Everyone turned their back on us. They looked at us as if we were the reason they had to go off to the woods at night. They were full of hatred, as if speaking to us would be some kind of disaster for them. Perhaps they were upset too, but their attitude was it felt like they were saying, 'Leave! Get out of here and go!'

These looks we received began to have an effect upon me. I, too, would say, 'Come on, mummy, let's go.' But I didn't know where we were supposed to go. The only place I knew was our hiding place where we hid in the river bed with our roof of oak roots.

Eventually my mother and I found a safer place. Our new home was in a willow grove. My mother spread oak branches on the ground and a kilim woven from goat hair that she'd brought from our real house. Some days we didn't even put our heads outside our new nest. My mother plaited two thin willow shoots together and made a doll for me. It was a beautiful doll. She had leaves for clothes and weeds for her hair. We made a skirt for her out of two oak leaves that had yellowed to resemble tobacco leaves. My mother talked to the doll exactly like she spoke to me. We were thinking of a name for her. In the end we gave her the name 'Perperik-a Soe' which means 'Butterfly of the Night.' In our new home in the willow grove my mother told a lot of stories. As my mother was telling a story I'd look at Butterfly of the Night and was amazed to see how keenly she listened.

The best story that my mother would tell was of 'Alik and Fatik.' I think she told it to me every single day, perhaps more than once on some days.

She would start the story by saying, 'My beautiful Butterfly of the Night', and, if she didn't start the story like this, I would stop her and say, "You forgot 'Butterfly.'" At which my mother would stroke Butterfly of the Night's hair and begin the story again.

'Beautiful Butterfly of the Night. Once upon a time there were a brother and sister called Alik and Fatik. They were both little children and they had a mother who loved them very much. One day their mother grew ill and their father came to them and said, 'Dearest children, your mother is dead and I do not know how to prepare food, or to clean your clothes or to sew them when they must be repaired. What would you say if I were to bring you a new mother?'

Alik thought of the tasty food her mother used to made and said, 'Alright.' Fatik however said, 'Father, as long as the woman you are bringing does not treat us like step children, but like her own, then bring her. But we too should meet her first.' The father was very pleased that his daughter, who was still only seven years old, had spoken so wisely.

'You are quite right my daughter', he replied, 'If the woman I intend to take as my wife can be a real mother to you then I will go ahead and marry her. I will invite her to stay for one week and if she cannot be a mother to you in that time, if she cannot make you delicious food, then I will not marry her.'

The doll my mother had made was so beautiful. She would take Butterfly of the Night's hand and talk to her. I don't remember how many days we stayed in this new house. My mother said everything to me through the doll, as if she were telling a story.

I really forgot about the outside world as I watched my mother weaving the doll from willow shoots and how she would whisper sweet little words in the doll's ear.

One evening, my mother folded up the goat-hair kilim on the floor and placed it in the branches of the willow trees. We're leaving, I thought, we're leaving to find a new home.

We left the shelter of the willows and walked through burnt fields towards the hill against which our old house had been built. Smoke was still rising everywhere. Our house, too, was on fire and burning steadily.

I clung tightly to the doll my mother had made. My mother was running around the outside the house, slapping her knees with her hands as she ran back and forth. She was trying to pull at something just visible under one of the broken-down walls. We went and sat at the rock from which we used to watch the villagers trail off into the forest. The whole place was deserted. Uncle Veysel's house had been the nearest to our own, and from this burnt-out ruin we saw a cat emerge. The cat stopped and stared at us, gave out a miaow or two and seemed to be stuck there, unsure whether to come over to us or not. He must have realised that we had not a single crumb of food to offer him and disappeared again among the piles of stone debris.

I think Uncle Veysel's daughter, Gülendar, was a year or two older than me. I remembered when she had stood there, just like the cat, looking at us but never coming near. And now, everything was gone. Crops, houses, trees... As for the people, they'd all been marched away. If they hadn't been killed somewhere along the way, then their fate would be exile in unknown lands. With their departure, the hopes of survival for those in hiding, like my mother and I, went up in smoke.

And so, we left our village of Weroz, when every house had been burned down and every villager was gone. My mother took me on her back and we began to climb the rise towards the hill that ran parallel with Sıncık Mountain. We were heading in the direction of Ovacık to my Uncle Kahraman Bey's village of Zeranik.

As the trees began to thin out, we stopped and sat down at the foot of a bare, shingle-covered hill, looking down through the forest to our house. Our beautiful home was still burning. The smoke rising up from the ruin looked just like a chimney plume in the distance. The river bed that twisted and coiled like snake was twinkling in the evening sun. I was thirsty. 'Water', I said. 'Mummy, water.' There was no water. My mother took out her breast that had long since been dry of milk and put it to my mouth.

At the crest of the hill, we came across a few barbel plants. Someone had thought to encourage them to grow up on the mountain, away from the goats and the soldiers. I was still wearing the green nylon shoes that my father bought me. Even so, it was difficult to walk on the never-ending shaly stretches of mountain in those rubbery shoes. The volcanic pebbles cut my feet like little blades. The sandals my mother usually wore had long since torn and she was now walking barefoot. Despite this she didn't put me down from her back. Instead, she kept telling me about the wonderful dishes we would eat when we arrived at her brother Kahraman Bey's house. The only thing I had to do, to be able to eat all that lovely food, was not to cry.

Even so, after a short while I forgot about the wonderful food awaiting us at Kahraman Bey's house and I began to cry. It was hard to explain the vision of that faraway food to my hungry belly, and I no longer wanted to eat the crushed-up, bitter roots that my mother had been feeding me. Our road was made even harder by the biting wind that now and then lashed our faces. It was less of a problem when it blew from behind, but when it blew at us head-on it made it more and more of a struggle to take every step. At times like that we would squeeze in between the rocks and wait for the wind to die down.

I can't remember how many days we walked in the mountains. When I look back now, and try to estimate the distance between Weroz and Ovacık, I would guess that it is a journey of three or four days on foot. There was a forest path to Ovacık, free of shingle. Had we taken that route, we wouldn't have had to climb the steep mountain sides. But our lives had been invaded by misfortune, and this meant that we now had to take the toughest route. We knew that the further away we could keep from other human beings, the greater was our chance of staying alive.

As we grew near Kahraman Bey's village the wind and cold weather seemed to be saying to us, 'Welcome to your new fate.' But at least the shingle paths and biting mountain wind were behind us. Now, our path took us frequently under thick oak trees. These lands were the lands of my mother's birth and she seemed to know every tree and the forest's every hiding place. As she walked along, she touched each tree, each hidden nook. Even her voice took on a new tone that was more confident and cheerful. I was now walking, and sometimes running, along beside her. We were looking for a pear tree known to be hidden in this part of the forest. When we found the tree with its small red fruits, we saw that bears had broken most of the branches. My mother still climbed up and was able to throw down one or two pears to me.

At the sound of a slight rustle in the forest, my mother threw herself down from the tree and onto the forest floor. We hid underneath a thicker part of oak scrub and saw two or three shadows passing between the trees. We stayed hidden like that for quite some time. I still had the sweet taste of the little red fruits in my mouth. As the weather drew in, we descended further to a place where a stream flowed out of the forest. Along the river bank the glow of faint gas lamps could be seen burning here and there. One of those lights had to be the house of my uncle, Kahraman Bey. My mother described it to me but still I could not work out which was his house.

We walked down to a dark meadow. The lights were now visible, now invisible. We heard the thundering sound of the Munzur river as it flowed along. We began walking along in a drainage channel and my mother put me on her back again so that I wouldn't be afraid of the barking dogs. Those dogs belonged to my Uncle Kahraman, she told me. This field belonged to him too. He had bought it from Koçar, the Armenian. And as for this great walnut tree, my mother told me, it had been planted by Süleyman Bey's father, Salih Bey. Apparently, as Salih Bey was travelling back from the town of Yildizeli in the province of Sivasö he caught sight of a walnut seedling at the side of the road and said to his men, 'This will surely be a great tree. We must dig it up and take it to Zeranik.' And it was indeed a great tree. Even though half the tree had been destroyed in a storm, it still provided enough walnuts to feed the entire village. I couldn't understand why my mother was telling me all this. What did it mean that my great grandfather Salih Bey had been part of the Kızılbaş uprising? When they were taken to Erzurum and hung? But my mother carried on telling stories about her family, without stopping, and we never seemed to get any closer to Uncle Kahraman Bey's house where the delicious food was awaiting us.

If I cried, the soldiers would hear. My mother was going to take me along such a way that Uncle Kahraman's two great Anatolia shepherd dogs from whom even birds couldn't escape, would not hear us. She said we mustn't walk out under the moonlight, but instead must keep to the shade of the secluded walnut trees. Even though we did so, a terrifying black shape jumped at us from behind a walnut tree. My mother clasped her hands around me, as a pack of dogs began running towards us, barking loudly together. In the black of the night, we heard the whistling and explosion of bullets.

Then, those who had fallen upon us in a flash, themselves suddenly went quiet. They began speaking in a language that I couldn't understand and were showing great respect to my mother. It turned out that they were the same people we'd seen walking in the forest whilst my mother was in the pear tree. They said they'd seen a woman there but had been unable to find her.

We reached my Uncle Kahraman Bey's house in the company of these three men as the dogs kept up their barking. I was clinging to my mother's neck in fear, and she was speaking to these three men in a language I didn't know, as if she was arguing with them.

These men were three Armenians that my uncle Kahraman Bey was hiding. Whilst staying in his house I was to come across another two women and five children living secretly in a hidden shelter underneath the mansion. The three Armenian men lived permanently in the forest and protected Uncle Kahraman's village.

There was great hunger everywhere. It had been two years since the burning of the crop fields. The soldiers had not only rounded up those who had run off into the forest and marched them into exile, they'd also seized every herd of cattle, sheep and goats that they could find. The people who had escaped to the mountains resorted to stealing as their only means of survival. Any men among them they would go into those villages that had not been burned by the soldiers, and take whatever they could find there.

My Uncle, Kahraman Bey, was a lawyer based in Erzincan. He'd managed to come out unscathed from the soldiers' destruction of Ovacık and the surrounding villages. In order to protect his village from theft he had the three Armenian men patrol the forests by day and the village by night. Despite this however, they were unable to prevent thieves from breaking into my uncle's house just a few days after our arrival and looting the entire village.

It was a dark night when suddenly the villagers saw the hay barn, where the animals' winter feed was stored, blazing away. Whilst the villagers were rushing in a panic, trying to put out the fire, the looters took advantage of the distraction and made off with the animals and sacks of wheat from the barn.

My uncle had quite a large house. If you included the two women and five children who came out from their hiding place at night, there was also Kahraman Bey's wife, their two children, my grandmother, (that is to say my grandfather, Süleyman Bey's, wife), myself and my mother. After the thieves targeted his house my uncle sent his wife and two children off to Erzincan in the care of his men. My grandmother was angry at him for leaving her behind at the house, but my mother said nothing at all.

My grandmother said he had one eye on his land, but that he really should have taken his sister and niece to Erzincan too. He didn't take us, and then it began to snow. The wonderful food my mother had described to me on our journey never appeared. We boiled up and ate the wheat left over from the looting. Our only food then was the snake-like curling root of a bitter spiny plant known as wild licquorice. The wild licquorice plants, which were found by foraging in the snow, were thrown in a heap next to the hearth. A mucus-like sap, yellowish in colour, seeped out of their veins.

My grandmother soon became malnourished and took to her bed. My mother pulled the bed I used to play on, twisting and turning the golden-yellow brass bed-knobs, from the corner of the room and brought it to the fireside. My grandmother was never to get up again. She lay there grumbling at us and giving her orders from this bed with its shining brass bed-knobs.

My grandmother remained angry with her son Kahraman Bey. According to her, my uncle was responsible for everything that had happened to us. She said that the reason for the deaths of Ali Rıza and Baki was down to the fact that they'd done as my uncle had told them and had not given land to my mother.

As soon as night fell the two Armenian women and their five children would appear. What's more one of the women's bellies was steadily growing in size. My grandmother would moan at them as well. She was not happy that her son was sheltering Armenians in his house, and that he was considering buying a considerable amount of land on the Erzincan plains.

The uncle that my grandmother had described and the one that my mother had told me about on our journey seemed to be two different people. I began to see him not as our saviour but as someone who had rejected us and who was like a soldier fraternizing with the other soldiers who had come and burned our house.

Our survival was again assured by the three Armenian men who had brought us in on that first night. The men went out at nights and came back once or twice with fish. Eating the fish that had been roasted in the embers of the fire was far preferable to the wild licquorice plant. Then, one day, they brought two enormous pigs to the house and the women and children came out of their hiding place and were suddenly so happy. My grandmother had never eaten pork and didn't want to eat unclean meat and be sent to hell at her time of life. Having said this, once the pigs were skinned and their meat was cooked on the embers of the fire, my grandmother soon forgot what she'd said and began to swallow the meat without even chewing. The left-overs of the meat were boiled and then braised in an enormous black cauldron.

These two pigs brought all of us, living under the roof that Kahraman Bey had deserted, into a new family. A family of eleven.

A short time later, my grandmother died. One morning I woke up and saw my mother sitting on my grandmother's bed, hugging her and crying. The Armenians were nowhere to be seen. My mother kept tucking the quilt in at the edges of the bed, over and over, as if to prevent my grandmother from feeling a draught.

She picked me up and we went outside. It was then that I realised that we hadn't been outside for months. Everywhere was white and the snow was flurrying around, being blow by a terrifyingly strong wind. The bed, with its brass knobs belonging to Kahraman Bey that my mother had prepared for my grandmother, stayed right in its place all winter. Once the pork meat was finished, the wild licquorice plants with their snake-like intertwining roots again began to pile up by the hearth. We'd found a new source of food. My mother brought an armful of clover from the barn, sorted out all the seeds and boiled them up with the wild licquorice roots. But before long all the clover was finished and the wild licquorice went back to tasting like bitter poison. We were helpless, and I couldn't stop my nose from running any more.

Once again, in the evenings, my mother began to tell me the Alik and Fatik stories. Whilst she was telling me a story, we saw a skylark fly underneath my grandmother's bed. It couldn't have flown in at the window. I think it must have flown in at the door when my mother went out to fetch wood for the fire during the day. My mother took the black goat-hair kilim and began to chase the bird around the room. The skylark, as if surrendering to its fate, came and fell by the hearth. Its breast was pumping up and down like tiny bellows. My mother caught the bird and broke its neck, before plucking it and tossing it onto the embers of the fire.

Birds became our new source of food. We'd open the back door and sprinkle chaff on the floor, to look like food. Once a bird came in at the door we'd slam it shut and begin the chase. As if sensing we'd set a trap the birds eventually stopped coming in; but even so, they'd kept us going for a few weeks. My mother would make a stew of these birds, or boil them up with the wild licquorice and make gruel.

One night, as my mother was telling me an Alik and Fatik story, the two Armenians, who'd disappeared the night my grandmother died, turned up with half a sack of flour. My mother hid this sack in the barn and made a soup with it every day.

As the snow melted, we started boiling up fresh plants and herbs. Then my uncle arrived with a cart loaded with wheat. He was a tall man and wore a hat, suit and tie. As soon as he came the villagers, who I hadn't seen once all winter long, suddenly appeared and gathered outside the house. As soon as her brother arrived, my mother moved into the back room of the house. The Armenian lady who lived in the hiding place under the house picked me up in her arms and took me, too. When I saw Kahraman Bey I went quiet. He took four sweets out of his pocket and gave them to me. The sweets were blue, yellow and white with spots on. When the Armenian woman set me back down on the floor I ran to my mother's side. I gave the sweets to her but she didn't take them. Just a couple of sweets like this was equal to two days' food for us, but my mother couldn't take them.

The oxcarts were unloaded and the wheat was carried into the mansion. Then it was shared out among the villagers. But my uncle went back to Erzincan as suddenly as he had appeared. We had wheat; even if we had no oil. The Armenians moved back into the house and were no longer hiding. My mother and I took the front room and they moved into the back. My mother and the two Armenian women milled flour with the handmill and made bread. Uncle Aret became the new father figure of our family. He made all the decisions. Kirkor, whose jaw bones were deformed due to poverty, spoke in a mixture of Armenian and Zazaki. His eldest daughter Meri, who was a few years older than me was the head of all the children. We'd follow her around and she'd make us collect plants to eat, once they'd begun to appear here and there, pushing through the snow. She knew exactly which plants were not poisonous, which ones were edible after cooking and which ones could be eaten as soon as they were picked.

The snow was melting fast and yet still the days dragged on. Finally, the first rain clouds arrived and a great excitement broke out, first in my Uncle Kahraman Bey's house and then all over the village of Zeranik. Early one morning the villagers all gathered in the village cemetery. Everyone was carrying something. Some had metal lids to bang together, some a drum, and some carried a long leather bag full of a buttermilk drink made of yoghurt, salt and water. It was hard to understand why people were rushing around making a fuss so early in the morning. The first thing that came to my mind was that we were running away again. Who knew to where we'd be going? The only thing was, this rushing about wasn't like the other times my mother and I had had to leave. The whole village then set off in single file on the road to the mountain. They walked, one man and then one woman, all the way down the line. Off we set in this long formation like a snake winding along the mountain road. The ones in front were beating drums and the men and women following behind, chanting. We arrived at the place we were supposed to reach. A great big fire was lit at the top of the mountain. Pans and drums were beaten in a joyful musical union and the noise began to resound and fill the valley below. We went round and round the fire as more wood was thrown onto the flaming pile.

This lighting of fires coincided with the beginning of April and was a welcoming ceremony, or festival, in honour of spring. A sack full of chaff was placed into the burning pile and if it exploded as it burned it meant that the following summer would be a bountiful one, the wheat ears would be heavily loaded, the leather bottles would be full of creamy buttermilk and the pots would never be off the fire. However, despite all of our comings and goings around the fire, the sack of chaff sitting in the pile of burning wood went out, as if it had failed to hear the banging of the drums and leather bottles. The rain began to fall and the flames too began to smoulder and die out.

We came back down the mountain with our drums and pipes in a state of great disappointment. Back in the village wheat was cooked with plants that had newly sprouted under the snow. The dish was handed out to everyone and the spring celebrations were over. According to Uncle Kirkor's daughter, Meri, the fire had not burned well enough, had not driven off Winter and so the coming of Spring could not be fully celebrated. All the same, at least the snow was melting and plants were bursting forth from the soil. There was no more hunger, no more dying now. The wheat would be sown and one single ear of grain would come back to our stores fifty-fold increased. The one sack of wheat set aside in a corner of my uncle's house would go out and, in its place, would eventually appear forty bags of wheat. Our sacks of wheat were sown in the fields, Then the traders from Erzincan appeared, driving their flocks of sheep, goats and cows before them. Everyone sold whatever valuable items they possessed and bought an animal for themselves. Uncle Aret bought a cow and Uncle Kirkor bought an old goat with a broken horn. My mother in turn opened her hidden purse. With the few gold pieces, she counted out into the trader's hand she was only able to buy two sheep. According to the trader both of the sheep were pregnant. However, only one of them actually gave birth.

Those who were able to buy animals for themselves were happy, as this meant new life. The animals would give birth, give milk, and before too long they would turn into a new flock.

IV

The wheat from the sacks had been sown in the fields, but just as the fields were beginning to turn green the snow fell again and draped a pale white cloth of death over the verdant landscape. One of our ewes gave birth to a lamb that was white with black spots on its belly and had a white blaze on its forehead. The other ewe proved barren. The trader had tricked my mother and had sold her a barren ewe.

Before long, the heads of wheat began to turn milky. In a few weeks we would be able to harvest them and make bread. But then one day, towards afternoon, a great panic broke out in the village. A black cloud that filled the whole sky was approaching from the valley to the south and was heading for the village. This great cloud from the sky was a swarm of locusts, and just as the soldiers had burned all the crop fields the year before, now these green monsters gnawed everything before them and left arid soil behind them.

Everyone closed their doors and a great war began against our foe, the locusts. Even so, they would somehow manage to find a tiny hold and get into the house. There were grasshoppers everywhere. With two great antennae on their heads and the tips of their green wings the same yellow as our heads of wheat, these locusts took and made off with all our hope.

The villagers then set out on the road to Erzincan to go in search of wheat seeds, but came back utterly despondent. The locusts had wreaked havoc there too. Whatever we could get our hands on we sowed in the fields.

Despite the havoc caused by the locusts, we were still relatively happy. At least we were not on the run and having to sleep in the forest. It also felt as if the threat of being marched into exile had lifted. No-one seemed to be looking for my mother either. Everyone began trying to make preparations for Winter. Every day, people were appearing from nowhere, all bedraggled, with their cheeks sunken from hunger and their jaw bones sticking out. All of them were begging for bread.

    With each passing day the women began to protest more and more. It was as if the ground had opened up and swallowed man after man. Late in the evenings or early in the mornings soldiers would appear at the doors of the houses in the village and each time they came they would take one of the men off to the army. No-one had done their military service and there was no age-limit to exempt them. Even men as old as sixty were marched off to complete four years in the army. The fate awaiting them was a crueller death than being marched into exile. This military service was the reason why the soil in the fields dried up and cracked open and why the little crop that we had, following the swarms of locusts, yellowed and grew pale in the ground.

    I felt quite happy in my Uncle Kahraman Bey's house. I still had my doll that my mother made for me when we were hiding in the willow grove. Uncle Kirkor's daughter, Meri, made a beautiful dress for my doll and also used to teach me a few words in Armenian. Meri had black eyes, large breasts and wore her hair in two long, thick plaits that lay on either side of her neck. Despite the fact that there were plenty of girls of her age around, she spent all of her time with me. I think she must have thought that we were running from something like the Armenians. She used to tell me about the house that they'd been forced to leave behind. From what she said, they had come from very far away. Their houses were not made of earth like ours. Theirs was a village where rain water poured off the red roofs and carriages passed by in the street. It made me really want to take my mother and go to that village that Meri had come from. Meri would take out her large breasts and put the tips that were the orange of birds' beaks into the mouth of my doll, Butterfly of the Night. My doll's Zazaki name was Perperik-a Soe. Meri became my little doll's milk mother. She would repeat the name of my doll, in that language so unfamiliar to her and be seized with laughter that never seemed to end.

I spent the whole of the summer with my doll, unaware of the plague of locusts or the men who had been tracked down by the soldiers. Perperik meant 'wing' in Zazaki. When I said Per-perik it brought to mind a pair of colourful wings taking flight. I think that's why Meri used to laugh. A butterfly with no body, made of nothing but a pair of wings...

The next thing was that, somehow, Uncle Aret and his two friends were caught in the forest by the soldiers. I'll never forget that day. I'd been playing dolls with Meri in the back room of my Uncle Kahraman Bey's house when Meri screamed and ran out. Suddenly there were lots and lots of women at the front of the house. Meri included, these Armenian women were throwing themselves down on the floor. One lady, was holding her baby of only a few months' old. She was rolling about on the floor like a ball, tearing at her hair and clothing. The women were crying out in Armenian or Zazaki and were striking themselves. My mother took me on her knee. I could hear a man's voice, his words unintelligible, coming from the forest on the opposite side of the valley.

We'd left a year full of hardship behind us. Despite the fact that an amnesty had been declared, people who had been in hiding continued to turn up, appearing from who knows where. They gathered walnuts from the forests and gave them to the villagers in exchange for flour and oil. From time to time, we'd see that a new shack had sprung up next to the houses. No-one would say anything. The old men and women would work together to build a house for the newcomers. Building a house was a difficult job, so they sufficed by digging out the soil at the foot of the southward facing slope and leaning small trees together upon it from the right and the left. Then they would cover the whole thing with oak leaves and soil. I remember five or six shacks being put up in Zeranik that summer. As well as these arrivals, women with children in tow and no husband would show up on a daily basis and take refuge in the barns of the houses. There were plenty of vacant fields, but because there were no seeds left, half the village was empty. Everything we could lay our hands on became precious.

A woman from Demenan and her two children moved into my uncle Kahraman Bey's barn. The woman's daughter was eight or nine years old. She was blonde with blue eyes. Her name was Melek. The little boy was three years old. His neck was long and slim like a lilac stalk and his huge eyes looked to be popping out of his head. His name was Mehmet Ali. They had not a stitch of clothing upon them. As soon as I entered the barn Melek took herself away into a darkened corner and sat with her knees drawn up to her chin. Mehmet Ali looked to me like two huge eyes crawling along the floor. Even though he could walk. he dragged himself along the floor. And whenever he found some wet soil, he would begin to eat it. As for their mother, she'd get up early and head out to the nearby Valonia oak grove.

I think my strongest memory that summed up the kind of Autumn we had in 1939 was fixed in my mind when I saw mother and daughter grinding up the acorns using a handmill. These black acorns of the Valonia oak that had been drying in a pile by the fire were more bitter than salted olives.

One day, we woke up to see that the snows had wrapped the mountain tops in shrouds of white. The acorn grove that the woman in the barn used to visit was now buried in snow. Winter had formed a ring around us and yet it still hadn't snowed in the village. People continued to come down from the mountains. My mother and the others would shout at the top of their voices at these people, telling them to hand themselves in. The death penalty and punishment for hiding from the authorities had been done away with and the state was now giving an identity card to every person who turned themselves in; taking those who were eligible into the army. But people stubbornly continued to hide with their entire families in dens they dug for themselves in the forest.

On the day the snow fell in the village a huge chestnut horse with a burnished copper coat began to trot in and out of town. It reared up at the barking dogs and filled the entire village with its whinnying. No-one was able to capture the horse. It appeared so full of rage as to want to tear down all the houses and to crush the baying dogs beneath its feet. Before long we found out why the horse had come into the village in such a state. This enormous ruddy-copper horse belonged to the lady who lived in Kahraman Bey's barn. The woman's husband had been on this horse when he had been shot. The horse had wandered over all the mountains until eventually it picked up and followed the scent of its owner. My mother said that dogs, cats and horses could find their owners by following their scent. This chestnut horse had come all the way from the province of Demenan in order to find its owner.

The appearance of a riding horse can mean lots of things. On the evening of the arrival of that beautiful horse half of the back room of Kahraman Bey's house came crashing down. The earthquake struck at night. All the wheat we had was buried under the fallen wall. The hastily-made shacks nearly all fell down or ended up skewed to one side following the tremor. There was a great panic in the village. God would not leave us alone. A couple of days later, we found out that the earthquake had devastated Erzincan. My Uncle, Kahraman Bey, lost his brother, sister-in-law and their two children in the earthquake. He managed to make it out alive and arrived with his wife and child amidst a thick bank of fog. They moved into the large room where my mother and I stayed. They decorated my grandmother's brass-knobbed bed, which still stood in its place, with throws and patterned cushions. Great big wall carpets were hung up on the walls. On the wall opposite the decorated bed, they hung a photograph of a man with eyebrows that bushed upwards and who held a cigarette in a holder in his hand. The man in this photo, surveying the entire room, was Mustafa Kemal Atatürk.

    The Erzincan that had turned a deaf ear to the events in Dersim, of 1938, had been destroyed. The people of Dersim, who had fled to the abandoned Armenian villages in Erzincan and the surrounding province, now began to flow in a steady stream back to the villages they had previously left behind. Every day someone appeared with their provisions loaded in a cart; the rest of their worldly goods upon their backs. We watched them pass through our village. Those who had escaped the worst of 1938 by fleeing to Erzincan now returned, having lost most of their families in the earthquake. When they first left, their Dersim homes probably still stood but now they had all been burned and the fallen walls lay under snow.

    When my Uncle Kahraman Bey arrived, everyone was anxious to hear what he would say. With his huge fedora on his head and his moustaches that reached to just below his ears he gave out an air of unnerving confidence to everyone he met. My uncle took the horse that had arrived only a few days earlier, gave a portion of the clothes he'd brought with him to the women and set off for Erzincan once again, accompanied by a few of his men.

    Uncle Kahraman Bey had now seen first-hand the poverty in the village. He realised that surviving the winter would be an ordeal. Two days later he returned on the horse who had come to us like a cry for help. He brought me a yellow dress and some black rubber shoes with thick serrated soles. He dressed me in the yellow dress himself and handed me the shoes to put on by myself. 'Come on, put them on! What are you waiting for?' he said, towering over me. I was wearing a pair of rawhide sandals made from calf leather that my mother had sewn for me; the fur of which had only just worn off. I tried to put the new shoes on over these sandals and my uncle laughed so hard that it echoed off the walls. Here was the first person I'd seen who was not trying to run away from the soldiers. Whenever the soldiers arrived my uncle would receive them and answer any questions they might have. The soldiers always respected my uncle, due to his having been a barrister in Erzincan. The soldiers no longer searched the barns as they used to. Every time they came, they would sit with my uncle and after writing a few things in their registers, they would leave. They were looking for army deserters and those without Identity cards.

 I think it was Uncle Kahraman Bey who officially registered my mother and I. In honour of my father, my mother named me Gülizar. That had been the name of his mother. She made them write down my father's name and everything so that I could inherit lands from him when the time came. I remember the day the Registrars arrived. It was a long time after the earthquake. My Uncle, Kahraman Bey, brought two registrars to Zeranik by cart. The two men were taken into the big room we used to live in but which was now solely used by my uncle. They called us into that room one by one and we were recorded in the registers in front of them.

 My mother and I went into the room together. My mother had wrapped her head up in a quilt that she'd found from somewhere. A great row broke out in the room on account of my mother being hidden from view in the folds of the quilt. Despite all the insistence of my uncle, my mother would not remove it. Uncle Kahraman Bey got up in a fury and started tugging at the quilt, but my mother just huddled deeper within it, letting out a piercing scream. The two civil servants who'd come to register us tried to calm my uncle down. Eventually, my uncle's wife came in, took my mother to one side and showed her face to the official.

 During this registration process some women ran off to the forest, which meant that the officials were forced to leave without registering everyone. My uncle fumed for days on end. But there was nothing he could do, the husbands of these women had died, been sent into exile or been taken into the army and it made no sense to these women that they should stand in front of two strange men with a register and allow them to write down their names and allow them to look at their faces to verify whether they were women or men.

This registration of our identities benefitted the Armenians hiding in the village more than anyone else. They told us that my uncle registered them and saved their lives by entering 'Islam' as their religion. Another strong memory I have of the winter that Uncle Kahraman Bey spent in the village with us is when Hem-e Albeg of Laçinuşağıgiller, his wife and four children froze to death in the shelter they'd built in the Valonia oak grove. Only the oldest child, Idare, survived. In the wake of 1938, Hem-e Albeg was the state's most wanted man after Çöyder Hüseyin. In 1938 when the soldiers came into Laçinan, Hem-e Albeg took five privates hostage. He took them up into the mountains and wanted to send one of them to General Abdullah Alpdoğan in Hozat in exchange for the release of his two brothers who were in a convoy being marched into exile. When Albeg received no reply, he killed the three of the soldiers in his custody, cut off one ear of each and gave the ears to another soldier who he packed off to Hozat.

And Albeg didn't stop there. He crept into an army tent at night in Lower Torunoba with his son Idare and cut the throat of a private. The state began hunting everywhere for Albeg and his family so he took his wife and children and came to Higher Ovacık, where no-one knew his face. He built himself a shack in the dwarf oak groves that proliferated on the Orta Mountain side of the Munzur Mountains.

At the time of the New Year ritual of *Gağand*, in the second week of January, there was over a metre of snow on the ground. The entire village was making its way to the cemetery in single file behind Hüseyin Ali, who had moved to the village following the earthquake and who was wearing special snow boots that we called *lakan*. I was on my mother's back on account of it being so hard to walk in the snow. Suddenly we heard a person's voice coming from one of the deep valleys; it was a wailing that sounded more like the baying of a wolf. The sound was coming from very far away and was now and then trailing off in the snow that was swirling in a thin powdery cloud. We stopped in our tracks and some of our party got down and put their ear to the snowy ground to try to determine from which direction the sound was coming. We always used this old method as the sound would echo through the snow and we'd shout back when we heard a noise. This time it was difficult to tell where the sound was coming from. Hüseyin Ali and another man climbed a hill to get a better sense of the direction of the voice, leaving us standing in a line, waiting for them in the snow.

As Hüseyin Ali and the other man reached the top of the hill, silence fell again on our little group. Two or three more people walked off and found that the sound was coming from oak grove across the way.

And so, our little entourage never made it to the cemetery. We formed a circle where we stood and everyone took out the candles dipped in oil that we'd each brought along, put them in the centre and made wishes as we lit them. We tore up and shared out the doughnuts we'd brought for the occasion. The offerings of the doughnuts for the guardians of nature unknowable to us were placed in the centre too, next to the burning votives and we all traipsed back to the village.

I spent the rest of the day glued to the window of that room that had first been ours and my grandmothers, then ours and the Armenian women's and was now, since the return of Uncle Kahraman Bey, his room decorated with wall carpets and the huge picture of Atatürk. I was waiting for the return of Hüseyin Ali and the other men because I knew that whoever's voice we'd heard wailing, would be brought to this room.

The snow continued to fall, without stopping, until evening. In fact, it had been snowing like that for days and weeks in a continuous flurry. Eventually Hüseyin Ali and another man arrived so covered in snow that they looked like big white monsters. They were pulling a sled on which lay a young man.

They left the sled in the outer hall because the big room was too hot. The barren sheep that had been sold to my mother by the dishonest trader was slaughtered, as she looked on and cried, and the fleece was laid on top of the young man on the sled. They then buried the young man with the fleece in the heap of manure in Uncle Kahraman Bey's barn. The young man was seventeen, or thereabouts. His hair and beard had grown long and were matted with one another and his eyes looked enormous, set as they were in this mass of hair. His frozen tongue had broken off and his nose had swollen up like a red balloon. The only things belying the fact that he was still alive were his eyes. I seem to think that this young man spent more than two days in the sheep's fleece, buried in the manure. This was Albeg's oldest son, Idare.

They shaved Idare's beard with the shears we used for the sheep. After two days he was taken out of the manure heap and fleece and was sluiced down with buckets of cold water. During the two days he had been in the barn I never once left his side, instead I played games with the two children that still lived in Uncle Kahraman Bey's barn. My uncle had brought this woman and her children some clothes from Erzincan but they still had nothing to eat apart from the acorn flour they had ground up with the handmill. This flour was mixed with a little wheat but was still as bitter as poison and would turn most people's stomachs. Even so the woman and children would eat the bread made from it, ripped up and soaked in water with great appetite.

Idare wandered round the village that winter like a half-dead man. The soldiers came and went but no-one told them that he was Hem-e Albeg's son. As for the family that had frozen in the acorn grove, they stayed in that grave all winter. Later, according to my mother, Idare took his mother, father and four siblings out of there and buried them in a grave in the woods.

The snows were now melting quickly and the sound of the meltwaters flowing and crashing down from the mountains filled the air. This rumbling torrent heralded spring. People and animals were bustling around. Everyone needed to find a piece of ground to cultivate so as to avoid the mercilessness of the next winter. Our sheep gave birth to a spotted lamb with a blaze on its nose. I used to pick up this lamb and carry it around with me everywhere.

The relatives of my uncle who had either escaped from exile or deserted the army continued to turn up. Dersim had been pounded in 1938 and now Erzincan was in the grip of the earthquake and a World War. The effect of the war being fought on European soil had penetrated as far as these mountains. Those who had gone were returning and those who were weak were being hit most by the war.

My Uncle, Kahraman Bey, was charged with protecting the reputation of his father, Süleyman Salih Bey and to ensure, as had been done in his day, that no disputes broke out within the tribe. The entire responsibility for protecting the family reputation lay on my uncle's shoulders. His sister, that is to say my mother became a concern. My mother's husband had owned a lot of land and we would now have to return there as it was impossible to leave such large tracts of land to lie with no apparent owner. What's more it was still not a custom to leave a share of the land to a daughter.

As for my mother, she wasn't asking them for any land. All she wanted was a place for her and her daughter to lay their heads. But there was nothing else for it, those fields could not be left for someone else to take over and my mother would have to go and claim ownership of her husband's property. You could call it a type of exile, less of an exile enforced by the army and more of an exile enforced by tradition. My mother was really depressed by all these problems for now we would have to take our sheep and little lamb and travel great distances again. Currently, we would take our sheep and its lamb out to graze and gather up plants which we would boil up and eat of an evening.

Eventually the lands were divided up and no fields whatsoever were given to my mother. She wanted us to go and stay with some relatives and so one day when my uncle was not at home my mother readied our travelling bundles and we set off. She dressed me in the rubber shoes and sunshine yellow dress with white frills that my uncle had brought from Erzincan. She didn't speak at all and I couldn't understand why she was making me wear these clothes that she had never dressed me in before. As she got me ready the only words that came out of her mouth were 'Come on!' And so we began the journey to our new fate.

She took me by the hand and as we walked out of the door she took one last look back at the room. All of our belongings were piled up together in a corner of the room. Apart from a small haircloth sack with a bit of barley flour in the bottom, we owned nothing. We went outside to find Hüseyin Ali standing at the bottom of the steps holding our sheep by a tether. Next to him was a bag full of clothes. Some of the women accompanied us to the edge of the village and gave us bread they'd made for us to eat on the journey. My uncle's wife walked with us for a long time.

When she turned back and left us it was just me, my mother, Hüseyin Ali and our sheep. Hüseyin Ali had lost all his family in the earthquake. He told us he had fought in the War of Independence in Çanakkale. All the way along the road Hüseyin Ali told my mother about Çanakkale in great detail; how he had been injured and how some soldiers played dead in among the corpses of their comrades. Our journey was nothing, he told us, they had walked for two months to Çanakkale.

With Hüseyin Ali we crossed raging streams and made it to the Hozat side. The leaves were newly sprouting and the hoofprints of wild boar were clearly visible in the soil. Every village we passed was a picture of destruction. Apart from the broken down, burnt wall there was no sign of human inhabitation. In some villages that had escaped the deportations only women and children could be seen. We passed the night in one village where the haircloth sacks filled with oak leaves pricked our skin. All the inhabitants of the village lived under one roof. Some of these were unable to get up from their beds. They were not as lucky as the villagers of Zeranik. There was nothing at all to eat apart from a white rooted plant that grew in the fields and forests, had five outgrowths and was known as 'glung' weed. Instead of keeping them alive, eating this plant was killing them.

They had found their own special way to prepare it. After boiling it they left it out to cool and then scraped the paste off the cooling plant to make soup. My mother gave them the bread that had been given to us by the women when we started off. These people, who had been eating nothing but the roots of plants and probably hadn't seen bread all winter were enormously grateful to her. They tore up the bread and boiled it up in the glung paste.

The next day we set off with no Hüseyin Ali beside us. We had nothing and no-one by our side to protect us. I think it was because of this that every time we came to dense coppices of oak my mother would speak in a loud voice and sometimes shout out loud. She would inspect the tracks of wild animals and look worried. Our sheep didn't seem to want to keep going either. The roads were unfamiliar to it and it kept on digging its heels in and stopping. At times like this my mother would put the lamb in my arms and make me walk in front and that would ensure that the sheep followed after us too.

Once, when we were crossing a stream, we came across a brown bear and her cub. The bear saw us, stopped in her tracks and then stood up on her hind legs and stared right at us. As soon as her cub had reached her side she rushed off into the forest. According to my mother, if you met a brown bear on the path you should greet it and pass on by, as they usually didn't interfere with people.

But the bear and her cub had frightened me and I started to cry. We climbed up a small hill and stopped. My mother started cursing Hüseyin Ali, calling on God to punish him.

'Mind you, without him, how would we have crossed those rivers… He fought at Çanakkale, but would any man who fought at Çanakkale leave his fellow travellers and go home? Then again, what should he do, poor man? He lost all his family in that earthquake. But he could have come along with us, I would even have given him two fields that he could have sown and reaped for himself.'

My mother kept on talking like this all the way along the road. One minute she was cursing Hüseyin Ali and the next she was showering his name with praise. Suddenly our road took a turn towards Elkaji where we might be able to find someone who'd accompany us on our way. We came to a village of three or four houses which, even though they still stood, were completely empty. My mother pointed at one of the houses with its half-burned window frames and told me that this had been the home of my uncle Sahan's fiercest fighter. We went and sat by the waterpump, that was running of its own accord. My mother took out the bread she'd been keeping in her bundle and broke off a piece for me, before fishing out the dish that served as our only drinking vessel. She milked the sheep a small amount and we ate our bread with milk. By now it was nearly evening – what were we going to do?

V

We walked towards Garipuşağı, the last village in the foothills of Sıncık Mountain that looked towards Ovacık. As we approached the lower end of the village two dogs came barking towards us. A young, slim woman called the dogs off and, as soon as she grew close to us, she recognised my mother. This woman had come here as a bride from Weroz before 1938. She took us to her home where she lived with her two small children. She said she thought her husband had been taken into the army. The soldiers had burned the village and all the crops. Despite this, the villagers had managed to find the wheat granary that Seyit Riza's son, Shah Hasan's men had secreted in the forest. There was only one cow left in the whole village as all other animals had fallen into the hands of the soldiers. This cow had somehow turned up two days later. According to the woman, had it not been for this cow the children in the village would not have survived winter. They'd also planted crops in a few fields. They brought us some white mushrooms boiled in milk that they'd collected on the mountain. There was no salt but still it was wonderful to find such good food after all these days.

The woman put us and our sheep in the same room where it chewed away at its cud all night right next to my ear. In the morning the woman and my mother went onto the mountain slopes behind the houses to collect some kind of spiky plant which the woman then went on to boil and squeeze out. She added sheep's milk to it instead of oil. The mountain villages were always more fortunate as nearly every plant there was edible and they all had their own distinct taste. As the sun began to rise over the village my mother, our sheep and I took to the road with the woman who had shown us so much hospitality. Our path took us through rocky terrain heading always towards the southerly foothills. There was still snow in some of the valleys that the sun's rays did not directly reach. Eventually, towards evening we began to see the lands that we had left behind us the previous autumn.

Below, in the bottom of the valley we could see the village of Malmes. The woman and my mother sat down on a sunny rock, the woman was holding our sheep's tether and she was full of advice for my mother, telling her what she needed to do. We were to go on from here on our own. The woman and my mother took a long time saying goodbye to each other. They were crying and embraced each other a few times.

'Come here, let me kiss you too.', the woman said to me, 'Your dress is just like the wings of a butterfly'. I looked at the white frills on the bottom of my yellow dress. I'd lost my doll Perperik-a Soe whilst we'd still been at Uncle Kahraman Bey's house. Maybe Meri had taken it for herself and kept it. My mother told me she would make me a new one when we reached the village. I said my goodbyes to the woman and we began to pick our way down between the rocky outcrops. She stood for some time gazing after us from the hill on which we'd parted. My mother and I didn't speak for a long time. We passed into dense oakwoods and took up the road to Hozat. 'This road will pass right by the front door of our house, my butterfly', said my mother.

'Where does it come from, mummy?'

'Who knows, my girl, who knows?'

Without realising it my mother had increased her pace. The sheep began to dig its heels in, snatching at its tether. The little stone I'd been nursing as my baby fell to the floor. I picked it up and ran to catch up with my mother.

'Mummy?'

'Yes, my girl,'

'What if there's no-one at the village?'

'I heard that your aunt's there.' She wouldn't look me in the face as she answered. Instead, she hurried up even more, pulling rhythmically on the sheep's tether as if she was fishing for the answers in its mind. 'Come on now, will you?

And don't be picking up and carrying every stone you see either.'

My mother was worried about meeting my aunt and I couldn't understand why. She was my father's sister, but who was she? And where had she been until now? Did she have any children? And if so, how many? As we walked along, I thought about all these things and tried to conjure up what kind of woman my aunt was in my head.

As we came up to Weroz it was beginning to get dark. As soon as I saw the houses the memories came back to me. I thought of that Autumn evening when my mother and I had walked out of the scrub of willow trees and had sat at the base of our favourite rock and taken our last look at the houses - with woodsmoke winding upwards from chimneys here and there.

Now my mother's pace slowed to a crawl and she looked stunned with sorrow as she stared at the demolished, barely recognisable village. She came to a standstill and appeared not to be able to take another step. She held out her hand for me to hold, and shuffled about as if looking for a place to sit at the side of the path. Eventually she said, 'Come on my girl, come on.' We had arrived. We had come face to face with the house that we had left behind and that now stood before us in ruins.

My father's sister had moved into our house and had piled oak branches onto the broken-down walls to serve as a roof. From the look of the branches and leaves she had come back here only a few weeks before. Several women had noticed our presence and they came out of their houses and looked at us. Apart from our old neighbour they were all strangers. After we had all left, families from the surrounding area who had been made homeless had moved into our village. In front of our door three scruffy little children huddled together and stared at us. One of them, smaller than the others, was sucking his left thumb. These children, who were not far off my age, stood looking us up and down and not saying a word.

My mother kissed each of them in turn and asked their names.

Just at this moment my aunt turned up with her arms full of firewood. She immediately leapt at my mother and began chattering at her like a machine gun and hopping from one leg to another, unable to keep still. She turned and started scolding the children and pushing them in front of her into the house like a mother hen. She soon bustled back out of the house, planted herself in front of my mother and began screaming and shouting without taking a breath in between. My aunt then made a dive for me and seemed to want to take me from my mother and push me into the dark leafy den along with her own children. She was saying that my mother should never have left her husband's house and should have stayed on the land. She carried on and on, telling us that if it were not for her having come here before us, strangers would have taken the whole village. My father's sister would not let my mother get a word in edgeways.

She went on to say that my mother should leave me here, take our sheep and go. It was getting quite dark by now. There was nothing else we could do but to leave and go back along the road by which we had come.

We set off walking and then headed down the road towards the neighbouring village of Dervişler. As we rounded the hilltop my mother called out and we heard a young girl's voice calling back. My mother called again, announcing herself, and two women came and accompanied us to the village.

The women told us that all their difficulties were caused because the men had all gone. If the men were here, none of this would have happened. But the men were not here, there were only women and children. And to have a husband is better than having a whole village to your name they said.

We went into one of the houses where a weak fire was burning in the grate. What were we going to do now? Should we go back to Kahraman Salih Bey's house? If only my mother could speak a little Turkish, then we would not have this problem. All we had to do was to go to Deşt to see Governor Fevzi, the area administrator, and he would sort out all our problems. What's more, my mother had identity papers and therefore had nothing to fear from officials like him. But she was not just afraid of going to Deşt, she was even afraid of hearing the governor's name. The next day I said to my mother, 'Let's go to see Governor Fevzi.'

But there was no-one to take us there. We needed someone who could speak Turkish. Someone who could explain our situation. We stayed on in the village for about a week. My mother went to Weroz two or three times to speak to my aunt. Finally, we found out that there was a Turkish-speaking man who was a refugee living in Torut. My mother and I set out for Torut.

The village of Torut was built on a promontory of rock jutting out from the side of a steep mountain. My mother told me that my grandfather, Olbeg Bey, was a fair man who was always promoted justice and she pointed to a place some way outside the village where overgrown walls could be seen, 'Here it is, that's where Olbeg Bey's house was.' Olbeg Bey's greatness could be seen by the setting of his house. The hill on which his house was set looked out like a great eagle spreading its wings over the valley that ran all the way to Deşt.

I remember that the refugee who could speak Turkish was aged in his forties and had a large red nose. He spoke a mixture of Zazaki and Turkish and his eye twitched constantly as he talked. He agreed to take us but was insisting that my mother pay him. When my mother told him that we had no money and that we would pay him later he started blinking his eye and said no, he would not take us to Governor Fevzi. The man started to walk away, so my mother rushed after him, grabbed him by the arm and began to beg him not to go.

He stood there with his eye twitching, 'Everyone says that, they all say "Trust me, I'll pay you later." But I have to get by as well, you know.'

'I'll give you two fields', my mother said, 'take them, plant them and harvest them.'

The man began to laugh. 'Fields, eh? Ha ha, fields, they're ten a penny here. Do you have seeds? Tell me about seeds and I'll listen.'

He was right. Fields were all we had, so many fields.

'I'll give you a sheep,' my mother said.

As soon as he heard this the man, who had been trying to get away from her, stopped dead in his tracks. He narrowed his eyes suspiciously, firstly at my mother and then at me.

'A sheep, you say?'

'Yes, a sheep. I have a sheep and if you take us to the governor, I will give it to you. I brought it with us from Ovacık and it's now in Dervişler village.'

The man blinked rapidly as if he were trying to count in his head. 'Look here, you said a sheep...'

'First, you take us to Governor Fevzi.'

The man could not believe his ears and the surprise was still in his voice as he said, 'Well if that's the case, you can consider it done.'

He told us to wait there for him. When he came back, he was wearing a hat. He set off immediately, hurrying down the slope in front of us. As we walked, he would turn to my mother every now and then and say, 'Governor Fevzi knows me well, and, if I tell him to, he'll put his stamp on the paper in front of him and even God himself could not undo that stamp.' He suddenly turned to my mother looking panicked and asked, 'But you do have identity papers, don't you?'

'Yes, yes. My brother is a civil servant in Erzincan. He got us the full-sized identity papers for both my daughter and myself,' my mother reached inside her clothing between her breasts, searching for the papers. 'Wait, aha here, see. My brother went and waited for them to be written up himself.'

Our interpreter was walking very fast and glanced sideways under his brows at the papers my mother had brought out. All he really wanted to see was our sheep. For this reason, he wanted to get to the town of Deşt as quickly as possible and to return home even faster.

'Alright, it seems that you have them, in that case the job is as good as done. Every day a hundred people come to me saying "take me to Governor Fevzi." You ask them and they say "yes, I have everything with me", you get there and they don't. I mean, that's ridiculous. After all, there's a law now. From now on, everyone has to have a name and a family name too. It seems that you do have all the necessaries so your job is as good as done. No matter if you wanted the stamp of Habeshistan, not Weroz, Governor Fevzi will see to it all. He's responsible for everything. And the Military Police is attached to him as well. I even took the great Seyit Ağa of Seypertek to Governor Fevzi. Everyone comes to me. They come from Hozat; from Orta Dağ. Everyone has a tale to tell and I know what each of them is praying for.'

At one point during the journey, he slowed down and turned to my mother as if he was about to tell her something dangerous. 'So, you're Hıdır's wife, are you?'

My mother quickened her pace to catch up with the man. 'Hıdır died, my friend. And I...'

'No, no', the man quickly said, 'I was only asking because that's who they said you were. Hıdır Efendi came to our village with his men. He could read and write as well, that man. Then again, his leaving Ankara and coming back here...'

'Well, he came, anyway,' said my mother, 'He was in favour of that law, but who on this earth would ever go and leave his brother...'

'Oh, I know... My father never left his brother. They were bandits in Bulgaria at the time. What's more he was an Ottoman Resistance fighter, just like Çöyder Hüseyin, and he was hung all over with gun cartridges.'

My mother hurried her pace.

'You've seen Çöyder Hüseyin, haven't you?' he asked.

'Listen brother, I don't know any Çöyder or whatever he's called, that was years ago...'

'Oh, don't get me wrong, sister, I don't mean any harm. I've seen him too. He came to our village last winter. He was so tall. It was like someone had uprooted a pine tree and set it walking about...'

'Huh! May God punish him as he deserves.'

'The government have put such a high price on his head. Never mind a village, Abdullah Paşa would give half of Eleziz in the blink of an eye, to whoever turns him in.'

'He would indeed, my brother, he would indeed. He gave plenty to Xide Pirço who cut off and gave him my brother-in-law Sahan's head!'

'Pirço! The Paşa himself couldn't save that one. His grandfather even attacked the soldiers of Hunh. He even went to Erzurum and took the Ottoman Paşa hostage.'

My mother tried to put an end to the conversation, 'Oh those are all things are all in the past; and now what's happened? Everyone's on their own these days – and the poorest have suffered the most. Women are left without husbands and children are left without fathers. Now the most beautiful women are fighting over blind and bald men at whom no-one would have looked twice before.'

'Can you do without men? No, of course not. Who will sow the crops, who will be in charge? The people have been left high and dry. We're refugees, by rights we're Ottoman; but Abdullah Paşa even sent we refugees into exile. And it's all because of that Çöyder or Chavdar or whatever you want to call him.'

We were nearing the village of Deşt which was set on the northern slope of a plain that stretched seemingly forever into the distance. The man didn't stop talking until we reached the village. As we entered my mother pulled out a large piece of cloth she'd taken from an old pair of shalvar. and covered her head with it. We stopped at the watering station of the village and washed our hands and face. My mother wet her hand and tried to remove some of the mud from my yellow skirt. She held my hand. We walked along a path which came out onto a tarmac road.

To our right were the Officers' billets. Each building had grapevines climbing prettily over the walls and the gardens were full of acacia trees. The lead roofs of the billets were shining in the sunlight and in front of them I saw something I had never seen before – the Officers' children were playing on bicycles. They stopped and looked at us as we went past. When I saw them, I imagined that this was the kind of village that Meri, my Armenian friend, had told me about. I thought of Meri, leaning out of the window of her red tiled house, listening to the tap-tap of horses' shod feet on the streets and watching them as they trotted by pulling their carriages.

Soldiers were everywhere. They ran about the plain in columns of twos, lying down on the floor and jumping back up again and now and then giving orders that sounded like an exploding cannon ball. At the same time, however, the place seemed to be so silent that we could hear nothing but the sound of our feet. We arrived at the front of a huge building where soldiers stood, row upon row.

'Wait here,' said the refugee who'd brought us this far.

My mother pulled me between her legs and crouched down, her legs were shaking.

I suddenly needed to go to the toilet. 'Mummy, I need to go!'

My mother didn't speak. We heard the sound of the soldiers' boots all around us. Time had stopped and seemed to be stuck. The refugee said, 'Come on, they've said Governor Fevzi will see you now.'

My mother said nothing.

The man tried again, 'God, God! Sister, wasn't it your idea to come here? We've come all this way and Governor Fevzi is asking me to bring you in to see him and you won't come! When we were back there you were saying, "Take me to Governor Fevzi" and now that we've arrived you've squatted down and won't move! Sister, didn't you say that to me? Didn't you say, "Take me to Governor Fevzi"? God, God!'

He then took my mother by the arm and started to pull her. But the more he said, 'Come on!' the further my mother's head sank down between her shoulders, disappearing from view.

'It's no good, sister. I will take my sheep. It doesn't bother me. I've put myself out too, coming all this way from back there, and now that we have come here you won't even go up those steps. Good god! I'll take my sheep you know, I will.'

Then another man came, and the man who'd brought us there said a few things to him in Turkish. This man must be the one they called Governor Fevzi. He leaned over a couple of times as if he was trying to see my mother's face, which she just wrapped all the tighter.

He said a few words and the refugee translated them, 'He says "tell her not to be scared and to tell me whatever her problem is." If you're hungry, the soldiers can bring you some bread.'

A soldier went and fetched two enormous loaves of bread.

My mother said, 'Tell him, my husband's sister has thrown us out of the village, my daughter and I have nowhere to go, so we have come knocking at the gentleman's door; the seat of government.'

The man went on about something for a long time, and my father's name was mentioned again and again. My mother became agitated on hearing my father's name.

'My brother, send us to where you have sent our villagers, never mind mentioning my husband, he's...'

The refugee said, 'The gentleman says, don't be afraid, there is no exile any more, if you have identity papers...'

My mother was all of a fuss, fishing around between her breasts for the papers she hid there, she took them out and gave them to the refugee.

'We're going to go upstairs,' he said.

We stood up and followed the him into the building that smelled so heavily of concrete.

He said, 'I told you, Governor Fevzi is a very good man, when we get into his room you should kiss his hand'.

As soon as we entered the room my mother threw herself at the official's feet and began to cry. The two loaves of bread she had been carrying on her lap flew off across the room. My mother was made to sit on a chair whilst the man began looking at the paperwork on the table and getting files off the shelves and putting them back again. He called another clerk.

The refugee, who was standing with one eye closed, said, 'The governor wants to know who took out your identity papers for you.'

My mother said, 'Tell him, it was my brother, a lawyer at Erzincan.'

The governor replied and the refugee translated, 'What was his name?'

My mother said, 'Kahraman Salih Bey.'

As soon as he heard the name Kahraman Salih the governor got up and came over to us.

In Kurdish he said, 'Kahraman Bey was my schoolfriend. I'm now going to give you the deeds to your land. In any case the records show that the village is in the name of Yusuf Güzel.'

My mother, instead of replying to the governor, turned to the refugee and said, 'Tell him, Yusuf Ağa registered the village in his time, but my husband's sister has driven us out of the village'

Governor Fevzi signed and stamped a piece of paper and gave it to my mother. He asked the soldiers for two more loaves of bread. My mother took the papers that had been signed and sealed with a huge red seal. We descended the stairs with this letter, the contents of which we could not understand and set off again down the road where the barracks were. I really needed a wee by now.

The man said, 'Take her behind that willow tree over there.'

My mother said to me, 'You see, he was your uncle's friend, may saints bless his path.'

And the refugee, of course, kept talking either about the sheep or how nice Governor Fevzi was, all the way back to the village. He took two of the loaves we'd been given and put them under his jacket.

'I said that there was no-one quite like Governor Fevzi didn't I? And now you can take these papers and even go to Erzurum and claim a village if you like.'

At the end of the day, our spotted lamb with a pretty blaze on its head was gone and, in its place, we had a white paper with a red seal that took its place in between my mother's breasts, under her clothes, with her other important papers.

VI

The man who'd been acting as our interpreter had come as far as Dervişler village, had taken my pretty little lamb in his arms and had made off with it. As he went off, he was smiling from ear to ear, every now and then turning around and saying to the other women, 'You know this woman's brother, he was Governor Fevzi's school friend. As God is my witness, if that woman doesn't give her lands to her, Governor Fevzi will send the troops into that village.'

As he spoke the women began to chatter amongst themselves. 'Hey, you bloodsucker, this Munzur Baba has made refugees of us just like you. Leave the woman's lamb alone.' The man kept winking his eye as he spoke. As for the sheep, she didn't want to be parted from her lamb and kept walking around it in circles.

'Don't say I didn't tell you,' went on the refugee, 'You persuade that woman to leave the village. Otherwise, by God, the army will rise up and it won't just be her who's affected, everyone will be. Nothing will grow where the army's boots have trodden it down. It's no good going over the earth with a mattock, because even if you were to harness the Prophet's own oxen to a plough not a single measure of wheat will come forth from soil that's been trampled by soldiers' boots.'

One of the women said, 'Hey, loudmouth. Why don't you leave the woman her lamb?'

The refugee carried on talking as if he hadn't heard the women, 'Now the Cihan War has broken out and the soldiers have been withdrawn from Dersim. Çöyder Hüseyin reckons that the army won't be coming back. The army have gone to Greece's Bulgarian border. Fevzi Governor told me so when I took Seypertekli Seyit Ağa to him.'

He was sitting opposite us on a rock, cradling our lamb and talking non-stop until Perhan, the lady who was putting us up in her house, picked up a stone from in front of her and threw it at him, saying 'What more do you want? You've got the woman's lamb, now take it and get out of here!'

'Alright sister-in-law. Calm down. If it weren't for me, in this big old Dersim, what would she do? I take everyone who asks me to Governor Fevzi asking for nothing in return. The soldiers insult me and push me around. But me, I do it anyway, so that these poor people can take their troubles and lay them at the feet of the state and be heard.'

Perhan picked up another stone and shouted at the man, 'Go on, get out of here, you son of a dog; saying that you're doing us a favour!' she shouted.

The man disappeared along the path that ran parallel with the foot of the mountain, our sheep in his arms. As for my mother, she kept on crying over her sheep as if she's hadn't been the one who'd made the deal.

The next morning my mother and I set off for Weroz, taking Perhan along with us. As soon as my aunt saw my mother, she turned into a fireball again and began attacking her. She took the deeds from my mother's hands and without giving a thought to the official seal she ripped them up and threw them away before stamping on the pieces on the ground. She looked just like a hedgehog with her thin, pointy nose and her hair all sticking out like a bush.

Perhan said, 'Alright then, you are Yusuf Ağa's daughter too. There's more than enough land for everyone, you take the land on the other side of the river. Move into Veli Ağa's villa, the walls are still standing. Without men and animals who's going to farm this land anyway?'

My aunt replied, 'Why should I move in there? This is my father's land, her place is in her father's house, let them give her two fields in Zeranik. Why should I give them to her...?'

Perhan pointed at me, 'What will happen to this girl? If it's her daughter, that makes her your niece too. We all know how you hid her so that she wouldn't be taken away in '38', she said.

My aunt grabbed me by the arm and pulled me towards her, 'Give her to me, I'll look after my niece.'

Another big fight broke out. Afterwards we turned and went back. I'd been frightened by what had happened and was crying.

On the way Perhan, tried to console my mother by saying, 'The village of Bend is empty, there's no-one left alive there. As a last resort you could live there. It has a nice cold-water spring too.'

'And what will I do there as a woman all on my own?' replied my mother, 'Everywhere is empty, Banemik village is empty too and the houses there haven't even been burned. Perhan, do you really think there's life where no-one lives? The wild wolves will come and tear us to pieces. And quite apart from there being nobody living there, how can someone be expected to go and live there with all those dead bodies?'

We arrived at the village of Dervişler. The red-stamped document that we'd swapped for our little spotted lamb with a blaze on his head had been torn up under my aunt's feet.

The next day my mother and I set off for Bend village with Perhan and her two daughters. Bend village was set on a conical-shaped mountain between the villages of Kirgan and Abasan on the rear face of Sıncık Mountain. Walnut trees surrounded the entire village; wild pears and one or two apple trees were also in flower. What's more, there was no birdsong. Directly below the houses a cold spring flowed out from deep under the oak forest. We sat by the spring. I didn't feel very much like moving to these high mountains. Perhan's daughters began running in and out of the houses, some of which were half-demolished. Then, Perhan took me by the arm and in a state of panic and fear we hurried out of the desolate village. We left behind us the flowering wild pear trees, apple and walnut trees and demolished houses. For a long time, nobody spoke and we made our way back to Dervişler. We made some thick soup by tearing up what we had left of the bread Governor Fevzi had given us and adding it to the cold wild beetroot pulp. Then I asked my mother what had happened at Bend village. In one of the houses the girls had seen two corpses of people who had died of starvation. Wild animals had eaten the remains.

Our only hope now was to go once again to visit Governor Fevzi. But how were we going to do that? He wouldn't want anything from us but we had to find someone who spoke Turkish. We set off to find the refugee man again. Even though more than a week had passed he was still carrying our little lamb around in his arms. He'd even pluck grass from the ground and feed the lamb by hand.

So then we set off to walk from Dervişler village to Kızılmezra. My father had very good friends there. We were sure we would find someone there who spoke Turkish and who would interpret for us with the state. Kızılmezra was a hilltop village surrounded by forests and crags. We were walking along a path that wound like a serpent along the hillside. Suddenly my mother said, 'Keep up, my girl, don't let me have to deal with you as well. And throw away that stone that you're holding on to.'

The stone she was referring to was my new dolly. I hurried my steps to catch up. Suddenly, from nowhere, a huge black dog leapt snarling at my mother, grabbed her by the lower leg and dragged her down the hill. My mother grabbed onto every plant and stone she could reach and shouted to me, 'Run, my girl!' The black dog pulled her into a stream and then retreated a few steps. My mother got up and swayed on her feet as the dog started snarling and baring his rows of deadly teeth, waiting for the moment to pounce. In a panic my mother grabbed a stone and threw it at the dog. She tried to keep him away from me and started fighting him off with a branch until he finally retreated.

She climbed up the slope and came to me. I was stood in the same spot and was still screaming. My mother pulled me to her and hugged me tight. We were standing in the middle of the road in the place where the dog had attacked. The black dog had ripped off nearly half of my mother's lower leg. A piece of flesh above her ankle was left swaying. My mother was crying and cursing god for allowing this to happen. And then she'd start swearing about the refugee man who had refused to help us.

After a while, a woman from the village came along. She took my mother under the arm and helped us to her house. She said they would have to find the black dog or my mother would get ill and die. They did find the dog and cut off a clump of its black fur to bind to my mother's torn leg. A few days later my mother's leg swelled up like a balloon. She lay all day long on a straw sack on the floor. And I sat by her side.

'Don't worry my girl,' she said to me, 'It will be gone in a couple of days and I'll be well again and we'll go and find our little sheep. Who knows how much she'll have missed us. You will take it grazing and I will sit and watch...'

I didn't know what to do. Sometimes my mother broke out in a fever. The sweat would stand out in little beads along her brow as it creased in pain.

My mother wanted the lady who had brought us to her house to take us to Dervişler village. Our sheep was there. The woman felt sorry for my mother and said, 'If only I had a mule, you wouldn't even have to ask, I'd put you on it and take you there. But how can we go there with your leg like this?'

'Get news to Perhan,' my mother said, 'she'll find a way, she'll take me there.'

'Sister, don't worry yourself with things like this, in a few days' time the swelling will go down and you'll be able to get up and go off with your daughter.'

'Just climb up that hill and shout for Perhan,' said my mother, 'At least she can come and take the girl. We have a sheep over there...'

Day by day my mother grew thinner, lying there on the sack of straw. The woman changed her bandages regularly, placing more of the dog hair in the poultice. I didn't know how to help her. I went to the pump to get her water. 'Drink, mother, drink.' I'd say. I would get angry with myself for not knowing any stories to tell her. In the story she used to tell me of Alik and Fatik there came a point when they were locked in a barn. They were helped by a friendly cow in the barn, who said, 'Lift up my horn and drink the liquid you find there.' Where was this helper now? Where was Duzgun Baba who we called 'god' and 'saviour Hızır'? He was supposed to come in your time of need. Why didn't he come down to us - this saviour up on Sultan Baba Mountain?

When I look back now, I have no memory of what I was going to do had my mother died. There were so many other children in Dersim who, like me, had lost both mother and father. And what did they do? Did I think about any of this as I sat next to my mother on her bed on the floor? I can't remember. But I am sure that at least if I did not, then my mother did think about all these things. She would lie all day on the sack and look at me. As well as the pain in her eyes I could see something that looked like worry and a longing, as if she was missing me.

Apart from going to the pump to fetch water I did not leave her side. The woman whose house we were staying in, and who had given us the stuffed sack for my mother to lie on, would bring us wild beetroot mash. After it had cooled, I would put some on the end of the spoon and lift it to my mother's dried lips. I would beg her to eat. But she was so weak that at times she did not have the strength to even open her lips.

'Come on, mummy, eat, please eat mummy', I would say. If only I could get news to Perhan, I thought, if only my mother could drink some of our sheep's milk she would get better. But who would fetch Perhan? Why had this whole village refused to listen to us and why were they all waiting in silence for her to die? What had we ever done to them? Why wouldn't this woman go and tell Perhan what had happened? Perhan was a very kind woman and so were her daughters. They knew which plant was medicinal and which ones would make people better. If Perhan knew what was happening she would come straight away with her daughters and they would gather healing plants along the way and as soon as they put them in my mother's mouth she would start to speak and say, 'Up we get Perhan, let's get up and leave this damned Kızılmezra. They can't even cope with an attack by a black dog. Come on, we're leaving this place!' And Perhan, would not say that she had no mule, she would take my mother and carry her on her back. She would make up the most beautiful bed for my mother, wait on her day and night and help her to drink fresh sheep's milk.

Once the woman realised that my mother was going to die, she said, 'Go to that hill and shout down to Dervişler village. Seeing that you have a sheep your mother should drink some of its milk and she'll be better in a day or two.'

My mother heard these words and opened and closed her eyes with a look of great gratitude on her face.

The woman continued, 'Seeing as you have a sheep, she should be drinking the milk. Anyway, they should bring the sheep here. You know sister, I have no milk at all here. The old miller Kare has two goats, but he's as stubborn as the day is long. Would all hell break loose if he gave out a jar of milk? If you saw his goats, as well, their teats trail along the floor. But no, he says, if I give out milk what will the children drink in the winter?'

Whilst the woman was chatting away she was plumping up the straw-filled sack under my mother and trying to make a pillow for her head.

'What has happened to us? We used to send a hundred goats per house out to pasture in the old days in Kızılmezra. Now there's not a cow left or a man. And that Abdullah

Paşa didn't even send us into exile, like the men. Exile would be better than this. The government sent you the orders, saying "Come and give yourselves up", and you didn't go sister... If only you'd have gone, you'd be eating the government's bread now...'

The woman would not keep quiet, one minute she was swearing at the government and another minute at the bandits. When was she going to go? When was she going to go and tell Perhan?

'May god damn that Abdullah Paşa... god, we've had so much death in this place, and as for exile... Sister, I'd have been happy with it, at least my children would have been with their father. We'd have gone into exile. As it was, they took us to Hozat and made us wait for two months before sending us back here. If you're going to do that, I say, then give us back our goats too. Did the state do all this to get their hands on my goats? They didn't tell us what these four children are supposed to eat, when you've taken their father away, what have these young ones done to deserve that...?'

The woman carried on and on, constantly wandering around the house with the pile of rags she was wearing, in place of a dress, dragging in the dirt. Anyone would think that she had a million and one chores to do in this darkened hovel.

'That's it, I'm off. Mine aren't many and I'm not going to look after yours', she said. By 'yours' she meant me. The woman went out and was gone. Once she had gone, I was filled with enormous joy.

'Mummy, Perhan's coming, you'll see, she'll come now with her daughters. We'll leave here. You're going to be drinking milk...'

I could hardly sit still and kept getting up and sitting down again. It was as if the joy at the prospect of my mother's recovery was so big that I couldn't fit it inside. I dabbed her sweating forehead and, every time she opened her eyes, I tried to feed her wild beetroot mash. After the woman had left my mother's eyes, too, seemed to come alive. Any time now she would get up and say, 'Come on my girl, we're getting out of this forsaken Kızılmezra, the state has hit them, don't let Hızır the saviour blight them as well... come on my girl, up you get.' She hadn't spoken for two days. Another two days later she opened her cracked lips and gasped, 'Au-ter.' She wanted water. I got up, grabbed the copper pot and went to the water pump. I reached the pot out to catch the water that ran from between the stones into a wooden trough. I couldn't take the water to her. My fate was waiting there for me. Like a sparrowhawk she fell on me, took me under her arm and began running down the hillside. My legs were wriggling helplessly and I tried to get free from the fingers that had closed over my mouth.

My aunt had kidnapped me, and she took me away. I was not there to hear my mother's last breath or to see Perhan come, at last, from her village.

We passed through dense forest and over rivers. We climbed over hill-top paths and arrived at Weroz. Now a new life and new fate began for me. What was I to do? I spent all day crying and calling out 'mummy, mummy', my wailing filled the whole village. When my aunt saw that I was crying over what had happened to me she would bustle over, grab me by the hair and drag me along the floor.

'May God punish you, she's dead, dead... from the very day that she entered his house, Yusuf Ağa didn't show his face. She made enemies of those two brothers. Yusuf Ağa had a house on every hill-top and his name was on the lips of every community round here, he was Süleyman Salih Bey's grandson, and there was Salih Ağa too, if only they'd given me just two cows for myself. If only she'd given that perfect little lamb to me instead of to that blind refugee. One of my kids is dead from hunger. If only she'd have given me one dish of milk, I would have lain down in gratitude at her feet...So I go and take my brother's child so that she can die with us too...'

She wasn't an aunt to me but instead an oak scrub with her hair all matted and tangled. Just as she never kept still, so did she never stop talking. Her cursing started with God and went all round Dersim before ending up with the Paşa. 'How did that idiot every become a Paşa? If I'm to call someone Paşa I'd rather it was Alişer Efendi; Paşas come from fine stock. If you offend them, they won't strike back, if you swear at them, they'll ask you to come and sit down. He was a true Paşa. You can't call someone a Paşa if they come and rain bombs down on your head, can you? So why don't you come and bomb us? Have you ever heard of such a thing? A Paşa burning crops, requisitioning property and leaving poor people to suffering, starving in the snow.'

'If she had just gone and turned herself in, and her husband too. If she'd have turned herself in, they wouldn't have burned all these villages. Her brother's a lawyer with connections in Ankara. If she'd only have given us two cows, then I would have been the first one to say that she was a grandchild of Süleyman Salih Bey...you can shut up too, it's been nothing but whinge, whinge, whinge since you got here. She's dead, she got what she deserved from a black dog.'

My aunt never stopped going on. Sometimes she would leave the arguments that had broken out between her children and come over to attack me instead. I would go over and hide between the piles of dried plants in the corner and cry to myself. What had happened to my mother? Had she really died or had Perhan eventually come? The same questions went round and round in my head all day. I imagined that I could hear the very last 'ow' sound that my mother made to me.

The first two days or so of my captivity passed in the house. There was nothing whatsoever to eat besides the plants that my aunt had picked in the fields. A whitish sticky liquid was flowing from the nose of one of her daughters. This pale mucus was the illness brought on by eating wild beetroot and the only way to stop it flowing was to eat bread.

I used to go out of the house, look towards the foothills of Sıncık Mountain and try to figure out behind which peak lay the village of Dervişler. It had to be behind one of those peaks. One day, when my aunt was foraging for plants in the fields, I thought about setting off on the path that led off into the forest.

The first time I ran away a woman called Bese said to my aunt, 'The child's running away Bale, don't you think God's made us suffer enough, that now you have to steal a child away from her mother and bring her here...The floods will take that child.'

When I saw my aunt come bustling out of the fields, I stood rooted to the spot and began screaming. I was sure she was going to beat me but for the first time, kind words came out of her mouth...

'Come my little Gülem, I'm your mother too, come now. Your mother is dead...Look, the rains will come soon and wash you away.'

An ominous black cloud was approaching from where the woods stretched off to the south. Thunder and lightning began and it started raining drops the size of hazelnuts. At one point it looked as if it would clear up but then it broke into steady rain. It rained for nearly three days without ceasing. It would stop and the sun would look as though it would peep out from behind the clouds but then it would start raining again. I couldn't cry. I would sit in the doorway and stare at the water as it wound its little paths. Of course, there wasn't much difference between the inside and the outside of the house. The thin earth roof couldn't hold off much rain water and so large puddles started forming on the floor. The girl who had the thick sticky stuff running from her nose began to sit closer and closer to the hearth where oak logs burned. The pale water dripped at regular intervals from her nose and into the hot ashes of the fire just like the dripping of the earthen roof. Sometimes I would go in and sit on a stone placed next to the fire and stare into the burning logs just like her. The sacks for storing dried plants that we slept on were more or less swimming about in a large puddle in the centre of the room.

Three days later it stopped raining, the clouds moved off from the high peaks and were replaced by hot summer sunshine. The rosehip bloomed immediately and bees that seemed to come out of nowhere began to buzz about while butterflies with spotted wings began to flutter in the air.

I started sitting once more at the base of the rock where my mother and I had sat before the exile. I just sat and looked into the distance. It was as if an instinct I couldn't understand was telling me to sit here. Sometimes my aunt would look over to see if I was there, before going into her house and starting up her ranting again. How did she find so many things to say and why did she never grow tired? You could always hear her voice coming out of the house.

'That bloody Paşa, you've gone and done it so why not just hack up whole root of Dersim?'

Sometimes she would shout loud enough for the whole village to hear, cursing the state and the soldiers who had not sent her, too, off into exile. My aunt lost her husband and her oldest son in '38. Soldiers had killed her husband, his brothers and her oldest daughter in the Emirhan River. Then they poured petrol on the corpses and lit them. My aunt was as strong as a man though, and would put enormous oak logs on her shoulders and carry them into the house.

'Seeing as you've burnt so many of us why didn't you finish the job and burn us all? Then I'd call you a big man, I would. In what law does it say that you should leave the snake injured without finishing him off?'

Who was the snake and who was the big man? My aunt would wake up with these words on her tongue. As for me, as soon as day broke, I'd come out and sit at this rock where my mother and I used to sit. It was as if everything was back to normal, as if people were running around and Gülendar would poke her head out of her door to see if we were sitting there. Where had Gülendar gone? Maybe she'd died. What a strange and massive thing death was. Why did the past seem so beautiful to me now? It almost seemed to me like Uncle Veysel was there too and that the house had never been demolished and burned down. His black spotted cat still hunted, weaving in and out of the stones that were now all cast about at ground level... Where were they all?

One evening, just after the sun had hidden itself behind Balıkan Mountain I spotted someone's head in the willow scrub below me. They were signalling to me saying, 'Come, come quietly.' Then I realised that these willow branches had been moving for quite some time as if saying over and over, 'Come on, see me at long last!' As soon as I saw the hand beckoning me, I looked over to the house. My aunt was still ranting.

'And he was supposed to be a Paşa, from our Armenians too.'

Immediately I set off, full of fear, for the willow grove below. The person waiting there for me was a woman with her head tightly covered, with only her eyes showing. It wasn't Perhan. She came forward a step or two out of the willows and, as she turned her back to me, I jumped on and held tightly round her neck. She started running downhill, through the river.

'Whatever you do, don't make a sound. Perhan is waiting for us further down.'

We ran through the river, the woman running in and out of the water as she went. She was running along with no thought for the branches that smacked us and tore at our faces. As we approached the spot in the river where my father had been shot, I heard my aunt's voice.

'She's coming. My aunt's coming',' I said.

'Don't worry, it's alright, you just hold on tight to me, that's all.'

When we turned away from the river and off towards one of the hills, I could hear my aunt's angry voice wailing all over the village.

'They've abducted her, they've run off with the girl, they've taken my brother's only little mite.'

As we got over the hill, I saw Perhan waiting for us, an enormous rifle in her hands. It was the first time I'd seen someone with a gun since 1938. Perhan took me on her back and we set off, going back below Kızılmezra on our way back to Dervişler.

VII

The swelling on my mother's leg had almost gone and she now walked with the aid of a stick made from a poplar tree. Our only protectors were Perhan and her two daughters. The girls foraged for every type of edible plant and then dried them in preparation for Winter. My mother took some of the barley seeds from the half bucket or so that she'd brought with us from Zeranik and sewed them in the furrow in front of the house. At night time they'd run out at any sound just in case wild boar had come to spoil the furrow.

As for my mother, she was bursting with happiness at being reunited with me. We'd take our little sheep off to graze and she made me a doll that was even nicer than the old one. She also started telling me Alik and Fatik stories again.

'Let me tell my little girl... Alik was both little and also very good. The jay bird said to her once, "If you give me a crumb of your bread and dripping, I'll tell you a piece of news." Alik didn't want the jay to fly about her or to share in her bread and dripping. She got cross and stood up to shoo the bird away. But Fatik said, "Wait Alik, let's give him a little piece of it and see what news he tells you." They tore off a piece and gave it to the jay. The jay bobbed his tail up and down with a 'chuckrr, chuckrr' noise. Then he flew down from the chimney...'

I always interrupted her at this point. It was as if I could see the jay with my own eyes and I'd finish the line by saying, 'And then he landed on the juniper tree in front of the house.'

My mother would continue, 'He'd fly down from his perch on the chimney and would land in the juniper tree squawking, "I've got some news for you, I've got some news for you."

Fatik would shout, "Tell us jaybird, tell us!"

"Your step mother is going to take you away and abandon you somewhere. She's waiting for you to finish your bread and dripping."

Then Fatik realised why their step mother had suddenly been looking at them so strangely.

"Come on Alik, let's run away", said Fatik.

Alik answered, "The jay thinks he is really clever, he's trying to get us to give him the last bit of our bread and dripping."

When the jay saw that Alik didn't want to go he began to wiggle his tail up and down again saying, "I know how Alik will come, I know how to make Alik come."

"Please tell me, jaybird, please tell me!" begged Fatik.

"If you give me another piece of your bread, I'll tell you", said the jay and he took off from the juniper tree and landed on a branch of a walnut tree.'

It was as if we'd gone back to our old days, our sheep, my mother and I. Our sheep was the only thing we had. Its milk was all that was keeping us alive. Each day we'd take it off to graze and the tether we'd put on it had stayed on at all times since we'd come from Zeranik. My mother would attach the other end of the tether to her wrist and didn't even take it off at night when she went to sleep.

The weather was warming up and edible plants were flourishing. The furrow of barley outside the house had shot up to the height of a boy. The barley had sprouted early and we knew we should cut it as soon as possible and replant the crop. The wound where the dog had bitten my mother had healed to such a degree that it had shrunk, until it was a small dark walnut shape on her leg. Every day when we were grazing our sheep my mother would squeeze this small black lump so that the pus ran out mixed with blood that was dirty and black. Before long she was able to walk without the aid of her white poplar stick. Unless you observed her closely, you'd hardly notice that she had any trouble with her leg.

As soon as her leg got better my mother began thinking about going back to see Governor Fevzi. There was someone living in the villages of the White Mountain who spoke Turkish and she wanted to go there to find him and then set off to see Governor Fevzi.

Perhan offered to come with us. I couldn't understand my mother. That big piece of paper with the red seal that he'd given us had been ripped up and trampled in the mud by my auntie.

One day, as we were grazing our sheep in the field by our house twenty or so soldiers appeared. Everyone ran back inside. The soldiers, however, didn't come into the village but instead went up a hill towards Sıncık Mountain. 'Don't worry,' said my mother, 'they're looking for Hüseyin-e Çöyder. He cut the throats of two soldiers.'

Since we'd been living at Dervişler, I'd heard the name of Hüseyin-e Çöyder again and again. And suddenly, one evening before sunset we saw Hüseyin-e Çöyder in the village. He was carrying two enormous English rifles. One of the guns was hanging across his back and he held the other like a staff in his hand. On his head he wore a helmet taken from one of the soldiers he had killed. There was a hole in the side of the steel helmet near the right ear. His clothes too were taken from soldiers he had shot. On his feet he wore soldier's boots, ripped at the side. But in those days when most of us didn't even have a pair of sandals on our feet, army boots were a luxury item. He was extremely tall and his whole body was hung in ammunition belts among which shone pieces of tins left from the food supplies he had stolen.

The women, who normally cursed him every time they opened their mouths, gathered around him when he appeared sitting on top of the earthen roof of one of the houses. I was surprised when Perhan of all people brought him a dish of milk from our sheep.

I sat with the women and children and couldn't take my eyes off him. I was transfixed by his tiny eyes that seemed lost in two crevices either side of the arch of his long and pointed nose. I thought it was strange that someone so very tall had surprisingly small eyes, moving like two small marbles in their sockets. He was thrusting his hands into the pockets of his army parka and showing those gathered around him the spoils he'd taken off the soldiers. At one point he pulled out from the ripped pocket of his parka a large tin of conserved food, about one kilo in weight. The river beds were full of rations tins empty of their conserved food. But this was the first time I'd seen one that hadn't been opened. The women who saw it shouted, 'What's that Çöyder? Çöyder open it!'

Hüseyin-e Çöyder laughed derisively at the women's ignorance.

'Ha ha... your husbands went and gave themselves up for food from these tins. Ha ha... of course they didn't get to eat them, they rounded them up, tied them to each other in the Emirhan River and shot them... Ha ha.'

He began to slowly open the conserve tin with a knife he took from his belt. Those who were witnessing it imagined that he was turning the key to the door of the palace's treasure chamber. Everyone had stopped breathing and was waiting for what was coming out of the sealed tin. Eventually the lid came off the tin and sitting inside the tin in a dark oil were purple cabbage wraps as thick as a man's forefinger. I noticed that, as Çöyder opened the tin, no-one, not even Perhan, made a sound. He sniffed at the oil on the tops of the cabbage wraps and let out a sigh of pleasure from deep within. He cut up the rice-filled cabbage wraps into small pieces with the knife he still held in his hand and he held out the food to us, 'Here, help yourselves. You are more men that those husbands of yours!'

But Perhan said, 'Çöyder, Çöyder! Giving us the provisions of the soldier you killed is a sin...'

Hüseyin-e Çöyder gave Perhan a hearty laugh in reply and kept offering the cabbage parcels to the women.

'Well, this is the food ration of the soldier who killed your husband...'

All the women laughed out loud together when he spoke like this.

Perhan spoke up. 'Çöyder, is it true that you went right into the soldiers' tents and cut their throats?'

On hearing Perhan's question, Çöyder laughed even more. Even though his eyes rolled in his sockets in a way that didn't inspire trust, it was obvious from everything about him that he enjoyed such questions. He pushed himself back on his wooden seat with the air of a great hero and struck the ground a few times with the butt of his English rifle. He pushed his hand under the layers of clothing he wore, saying, 'Ah yes, this flannel vest is one I took off the back of an infidel I'd killed in his tent. It's pure wool. You could sleep in the snow in it and not feel the cold.'

Then he showed off a watch with a broken strap that he'd taken out of his inside pocket, 'And this is an infidel's watch.'

He began taking all kinds of objects out of his pockets that had belonged to dead soldiers. This time he was showing them another knife he'd pulled from a pocket, 'This knife belonged to an infidel who killed my father on Pakire Mountain...'

Perhan interjected, 'Stop it, Çöyder, that's enough. How do you know which soldier killed him?'

'Ha ha, sister-in-law speaks. If that soldier had fled as far as Ethiopia I would have gone after him and taken revenge for my father's death. And if I didn't, then my name's not Çöyder.'

My mother spoke up, 'Eh! My brother, may God make your death a good one! I would have told Hıdır Efendi not to do that. What happened?'

Hüseyin-e Çöyder let out another huge laugh. 'Fecire Hatun, Hıdır Efendi was a learned man but he did wrong too. He kept quiet about the deeds of his father. If this lot in Dersim hadn't got one eye on each other's property then not just the Paşa but even if his whole army had turned up, they never could have entered Dersim. Why didn't I do it? I didn't even take one poor soul's goat. Everything down to my underpants is off a soldier's back. But the Dersim lot, they kept attacking each other and leaving their enemies in peace.'

Then Perhan spoke, 'So, Çöyder, now all the women of Dersim are left to you. If you looked around for a fly that was male you wouldn't find one anywhere.'

When he heard Perhan talking like this Çöyder once again burst out laughing, 'I saved a lot of women and children from starvation this winter.'

Pointing to one of the women he went on, 'Isn't it Milte? If it weren't for me, you would have died underneath your roof with your children.'

'Praise be to God, my Hüseyin, if Albeg were to come back from exile I would sacrifice a ram to. You are Munzur Baba's envoy to us.'

VIII

Once my mother's leg was completely healed, we set off on the roads again. We'd left our sheep in the care of Perhan. We passed the village of Torut and were heading for the village of Bornek on the slopes of the White Mountain. At Torut we came across a group of soldiers. 'Don't be afraid', said my mother, 'they're searching for Hüseyin-e Çöyder.'

'Mummy! Did he really sneak into a tent at night and behead the soldiers?'

'How should I know my girl? Is he telling the truth or lies? Who knows? Shame on him anyway.'

We stayed overnight at a village that had huge, two-storey buildings with carts parked in front of them. Even though most of the men had been taken into the army there were still quite a few young men around who were capable of carrying out hard work. My mother was known everywhere we went and we were put up as guests at one of the houses. A big pot of bulgar wheat soup was boiling on the hearth. An old man with a grey beard that reached right down his chest was throwing wood chips onto the fire below the pot that was bubbling on top of the flames. He held forward a chair for my mother, 'Sit Fecire Hatun, we're all family. You brought our people to this place.'

The old man stoked the coals underneath the pot with an oak twig he was using as a poker and asked my mother questions about who had died and who had been taken into exile.

Then he said, 'If you'd have turned yourselves in they would have issued a pardon.'

'Oh Hıdır! Where was I supposed to go, a woman on my own like this? There's not even anyone who speaks the language who can take me to this Governor Fevzi...'

The old man continued, 'So, they killed them there, did they? What men they were too, what men.'

'Who knows where the corpses were burned? No-one knows who is dead and who's alive.'

The old man kept mentioning names to my mother as he tried to work out who had been killed, and where. The man's daughters and daughters-in-law and his grandchildren were sitting all around us in a circle. As they were talking my mind was fixed on the pot of bulgar wheat soup that was boiling away. One of the women took the black pot and put it down in the ashes of the fireplace but still there was no sign of our food.

Eventually the bulgar wheat soup was poured out into a wide dish and very soon our wooden spoons were dashing in and out of the dish. Everyone was eating so quickly that by the time I had raised my wooden spoon to my lips some people were on their second spoon already. The old man said that I should have what was left in the bottom of the dish. This was the first time I'd been in such a generous household.

The next day the old man arranged for a youth called Sayder, of fifteen years old or so, to join us and sent us on our way to Governor Fevzi

On the way, my mother asked him, 'Where did you learn their language, Sayder?'

The pride was audible in Sayder's voice as he replied, 'Ma'am, I worked at Eleziz, I did.'

'Good. Praise be to God.'

'The state has brought out a new law, now everyone has to be taught the language. They came to our village too and they're going to open a school in Deşt. When my father gets back from the army, I'll be going there, ma'am.'

'And when's your father getting back?'

'We don't know just yet, ma'am. If the war hadn't broken out, he might have been back by now. The Germans have attacked the Russian's homeland. And as for Dersim? There's not one stone left on top of another.'

'Oh dear, dear. What's happening is happening to everyone. What do they want?'

'Ma'am this is a world war. You saw how the airplanes bombed Dersim? Well, when I was in Eleziz I saw the airplanes that came to bomb Dersim from really up-close. What planes they were! One would take off and the other would land.'

'Were you in Eleziz when they brought Seyit Riza from Erzincan?' asked my mother.

Sayder looked at my mother in askance, 'Of course I was there, ma'am. Oh, if you'd have seen it that day, if you'd have thrown a needle into their midst, it wouldn't have hit the floor. There were people from as far away at Bingöl and Muş, who'd come to ask the Rayber for a pardon. I saw the Paşa, too.'

'May God punish that blind fool, he's starved all these women and children, made them beholden to a spoonful of hot water.'

'Don't talk like that ma'am. You can curse God but not the Paşa. They'll throw you right into jail by God. It's not you but your poor little girl here I'd feel sorry for.'

'I didn't swear my friend, I just said may God give him his just desserts.'

'That's what I'm saying, ma'am. They told the Rayber they were taking him to Eleziz, to the Paşa. How was he to know they were taking him to be hung? Had the Rayber's men known that was going to happen they would have taken the whole of Erzincan from the control of the army.'

'Why didn't they do that then? If they had, if they'd only done that, then this earthquake would not have struck them.'

The young man began telling my mother all sorts of thing, hardly pausing for breath in between. 'You know what too ma'am? I worked in a vineyard. If you'd only seen them, all the grapes were this big! And you could eat as many as you wanted.'

'If you'd only brought some of those for me, your poor old elder.'

'I brought the raisins, ma'am, the fresh whole grapes get mouldy very quickly. As for the dried raisins though, you can store them and eat them in winter, stew them up into a compote. And the moment they hit hot water they swell up like this...!'

'Did locusts attack your fields too, my dear Sayder?"

'Of course, they did, why wouldn't they? They left not one leaf on the trees. Those locusts ate up half of Eleziz. That's why everyone had to get by on one shared sack of flour this winter. Our little field down by the river once again bore a crop but Seydesen Ağa commandeered it. He did give our lot a handful or two of wheat. And you, ma'am – all of Hıdır Efendi's lands were left to you, weren't they?'

'What do you mean left to me? There were three villages, two of which haven't got one of God'' souls living in them and his sister's there in Weroz.'

'My mother says it's good to have land. She says that even if a person dies you can't eat grief. When my father gets back, I'm going off to Eleziz to work again. So, ma'am, if I save up enough money, will you sell me one of your good crop fields?'

'Yes, I'd sell you one dear Sayder, but each field is already allotted to a crop-sharer. So let's see who comes back from the exile march and who doesn't.'

My mother and Sayder chatted on and off all the way until we reached the plain of Deşt. The plain once again seemed quiet at first, then there were the soldiers once more, running in pairs, jumping up and crouching down. We once again passed by the billets and found ourselves standing in front of the big building. Our interpreter explained the situation to the soldier standing guard at the door. But he then came back over to us.

'What's happening, my dear?' my mother asked.

'He says you should wait.'

We waited once again, my mother with her head covered and me sitting between her legs, peeking my head out over her folded arms and looking around like a little bird looking out of a nest. I was wondering if these were the soldiers that had killed my father. Even considering this, I still had no feelings towards them. We were here in the midst of those soldiers from whom everyone would run when they came to our village and yet I felt nothing. It was as if the soldiers were only dangerous when they came to the village and that, when they went home, they were no longer dangerous. Or it might have been something else, but the fear that they gave me when they came to our village had disappeared once I was among them like this.

Sayder, the lad who had brought us here, was still in his original position, standing and waiting. At one point he leaned over and tucked his trouser leg into his sock, and a little while later he leaned over and took it back out of his sock again. He stuffed his hands into his pockets, and then took them out again. The world had come to a halt. The sounds of soldiers' boots could be heard, the leaves of the plane tree were rustling but it felt as if everything was outside of ourselves was making sounds and noises. As if we were dreaming, or we were observing a dream.

Sayder tucked his trouser legs back into his socks, and took them out again. He sighed, as if in protest at time's refusal to move along.

'Ma'am?' he said.

'Say it, say, "that woman ripped up the document that was given to you." Say it, my dear Sayder.'

Time passed.

'Ma'am, I was going to say, 'Shall we go?'

'Go?' my mother asked.

'It's not working, ma'am, we should come another time.'

My mother stirred where she was sitting. For a moment, she didn't know what to say. I think she was trying to decide whether to leave or to stay. The soldiers passing by were staring at us too.

'But my dear, what shall I do with this daughter of mine?'

'We'll come back tomorrow ma'am.'

I was looking at Sayder's face and then back at my mother's. My mother's face looked so unsure. Sayder looked as though he wanted to get out of this hell as quickly as possible and yet my mother knew that if Sayder went, there would be no way on earth she would ever get him back here. I was surprised that he'd even come this far with us.

My mother called out to Sayder with pain and pleading in her voice, 'My Sayder, this poor woman has fallen at your door, let's wait a bit longer and if nobody comes then we'll go.

'It's alright, ma'am, I'll wait if we have to. I just didn't want anything bad to happen to you with all this waiting, I don't know...'

'I'll tell them that I made you come along, that nothing's your fault,' said my mother.

'No, it's alright ma'am. I have an ID card.'

He took it out of his pocket and showed it to my mother. 'Governor Fevzi came in person and gave them to us in the village. He told me my name from now on was Serdar, and that my father would have wanted it so. When I was working at Eleziz I'd say my name was Sayder and no-one would understand. I had to learn to say Serdar.'

'My dear Sayder, I have an enormous village and once the exile period is over people will start to return in ones and twos. Those who were in jail will be released, those who've been doing military service will come home, so just wait a little longer and tell Governor Fevzi that my husband's sister ripped up the state seal and that she trampled the state's deed title under her feet. That's all you have to say, then we can go. The rest is up to him.'

'No, ma'am, I... alright then, all I said was we could go to the village of Sin, stay the night and come back in the morning...'

'Sayder, just say what I've told you, tell him that my sister-in-law stamped her feet on the seal of the state. And afterwards, this woman will give you a whole village. Look, you'll be getting married any day now and you haven't even got one field. If you say to the governor what I've asked you to then I'll give you Mahmut Ağa's crop field. Mahmut Ağa used to feed ten people from that one field, there are springs bubbling on it in two places, and the water there is so cold that, if you threw in a watermelon and waited five minutes, you'd hear it split right open.'

My mother continued mumbling to herself. The sun passed over Şakak village and returned to Pakire Mountain. Sayder paced about, tucked his trouser leg into his sock, then pulled it up to the top of the black rubber shoes he was wearing. Finally, a soldier came and took Sayder away. Once Sayder was gone my mother began to panic.

'It's my fault', she began to say, 'Oh dear, oh no... such a young boy, oh no, and he'd said, "come on ma'am let's go, there's something not right here." That's what he said, oh, oh.'

As time went by my mother grew increasingly panic-stricken until she was extremely nervous. Finally, Sayder appeared, coming out of the building with a soldier.

'Ma'am, Governor Fevzi is asking about Çöyder Hüscyin. He's asking if he comes to the village.'

'My brother I don't know of any Çöyder or Moyder or anybody, may God mete out his punishment to him too.'

Sayder turned and began speaking to the soldier at his side.

'Come on ma'am. Let's go. I did say she wouldn't know Çöyder.'

'How am I supposed to see the face of that devil when a whole army is out searching for him and can't find him?'

My mother kept on talking as we crossed the plain. We'd come to the place where we'd washed my hands and face with the refugee man and so we drank a few handfuls of water.'

'What did he say Sayder?'

'He didn't say anything ma'am. Just, "Alright, take the woman and go." A very important person from Ankara had come, if you'd only seen the man ma'am! He asked me if I could read and said, "Do you love Atatürk?"'

'If only you'd told him how my sister-in-law ripped up Atatürk's seal and trampled it under her feet...'

The plain was behind us and now the forest began.

'Sayder, my lad, may God make all you touch turn to gold. Can you take us as far as the Anafatma road?'

'Ma'am I'm sorry but I did what you wanted me to. The man said, "Alright, Take the woman and go."'

'Sayder, come with me. There's no-one left in Bend village and I have a sheep. Bring your sister and your mother. The houses in Bend are all still standing. You should see them. You'd die for those beautiful straight walls. You'd think they'd come fresh out of a soap mould... We've got a bit of barley seed we could sow on the fields, if you could just see those fields... you'll get a return on the crop of forty or fifty to one.'

'Ma'am who'll give us that land over there? The tribes would burn us out of there.'

'Tell your mother that the crop fields are good and the houses are in fine shape, with their deeds available. Go and get your thing and come back, I'll be coming too once I've collected my sheep from Dervişler Village. Perhan will come with us too. She's got two daughters. You can marry one of them. And if you could see how beautiful they are. And I'm Yusuf Ağa's granddaughter, all of the deeds of the villages are in my name.'

Now I knew my mother's latest fantasy. It seems that Sayder was keen on the idea too. In fact, Sayder was so taken up with this new dream that instead of leaving us to make our own way, he walked with us all the way to the peak below Torut.

'Ma'am, we haven't got a single crop field. The only one we sowed got taken from us by Seydesen Ağa. And as you know, the locusts hit us last year, we didn't get as much as one portion. If only my father had come back from military service.'

'He'll come back, Sayder, your father will come back and he'll see that his son has prepared for him a huge village, with two-storey houses. And if you could only see the view. You've got the whole of Dersim at your feet including the Haydaran Mountains. There aren't even any tribal people or anything like that left.'

For a while they walked side by side in silence.

'Ma'am, you said that the houses were all intact, didn't you?' asked Sayder.

'Perfectly intact, Sayder my lad, and oh what houses they are. Two storeys high with doors wreathed in beautiful trellises. Armenian-built houses, and what fine houses. No matter how many times this Dersim of ours has been burned to the ground, no matter how many times the Armenians have rebuilt it, once an Armenian stone mason gets that hammer and chisel in his hands the stone turns into a cheese block, smooth from a mould in his hands. If you only saw the work Sayder, if you tried to fit a needle between the blocks of stone it wouldn't find a place. And you'd say to yourself, "It's not made of stone. They've piled up blocks of soap one atop another."

'You tell your mother, go and get her too, it's an empty village, you just have to see it. It's got a fountain that a person just can't get enough of listening to. The waters boil up and flow out between the stones and it's a heavenly sound. If you sit down at the fountain, you don't ever want to get up again and you'd think that a herd of winged mountain goats was flying in and out of the waters. If you only saw them, such exquisite goats.'

My mother stopped for a while, and then she'd begin describing Bend village all over again.

'We went there with Perhan and we could hardly bring ourselves to leave. But Sayder, you know, when there's no man amongst you...'

'That's what it's like there, ma'am. If it weren't so good, I wouldn't have come back from Eleziz. Now I have quite a bit of money too. Ma'am I picked cotton on Eleziz plain. They say that the plain's great, don't they? Well, that's a lie. A person can't even find one tree under which to find shade. And the heat, it's so hot that if you do find a spot to lie down and stretch out, then the flies find you right away and don't stop biting. And the water of the plain, well, ma'am, urine is colder than the water of that plain, and even that water's alive with flies too.'

'Sayder, my boy, people die on the plain, there's no wood there to make a fire. If you saw it, you'd think no human had ever been there. And those great high trees that have grown so big you could fit a house inside? And what mighty trees they are, they're not trees, each one is a monument, you wouldn't cut trees like that down now would you?'

'No, you'd never cut them down ma'am. You'd never chop down a mighty tree like that. When I visited the plain, lightning had struck one of the great trees but, even then, no-one would go and collect the wood to burn. One winter was really cold, but still no-one could bring themselves to burning any of the wood from the great tree that had been struck by lightning.'

'Well said my lad Sayder, no-one should burn a great tree like that. Every creature and being in nature is indebted to those great trees. In the shade of those mighty trees even wolves and lambs are like brother and sister...'

We walked on for some time again in silence. The oak trees had lost most of their leaves and little field birds were landing on branches ahead of us, taking off from one and landing again on another. We passed by a small river just as the afternoon shadows were lengthening and headed up a path towards a bare peak.

We parted ways.

My mother said to Sayder, 'I must go and see my little sheep, and then I'll come and see your mother.'

'I don't know, ma'am, I don't know.'

When we were alone again, I asked my mother, 'Mummy, will we actually go there?'

'Oh, my girl, it would be good to have a man at our head. And what a nice boy he is, he set off with us and went all that way, and what's more he didn't even ask for anything.'

IX

After we parted ways with Sayder we walked in silence for a very long time. We came to Torut village and we sat for a while on the field where my great grandfather Olbeg Bey's house had been built. We stared out at Torut village. My mother told me that long ago Armenians and Alevis lived side by side here until the state moved refugees into the houses that were left empty after the Armenian incident. The time she was talking about must have been a very long time ago. My great grandfather Olbeg had apparently not wanted the refugees to be settled permanently in the village. In those days the Ottoman army was still in existence. They came with the mounted Hamidiye Corps and burned Olbeg Bey's residence to the ground. The Hamidiye cavalry stayed in the area for a long time. But the refugees were really good people and they helped everyone as much as they could.

'But that refugee took our lamb,' I said.

'Everything's different now my girl. Humanism is dead. In the old days in Dersim if a woman went to someone's door and intervened in a dispute, no matter what the row had been about it would be resolved. The tribes got rid of all that. They didn't understand the nature of Dersim.'

My mother spoke in Kurdish to a man who'd called out to us. Then, we got up and proceeded to Dervişler.

Our hopes of living in Weroz again were completely dashed, we now realised that Weroz belonged to my aunt. My aunt, who had gone as far as trampling a state document with its seal had now acquired a huge village and she was waiting for people to return from exile and to be ready to work for her there. Perhan was of the opinion that we should go back to my uncle Kahraman Salih Bey but my mother didn't look kindly at all on this idea of Perhan's.

I wanted to go back to my uncle's house, too. His wife would surely ask us to stay. Later on, I was to learn why we didn't go back to my uncle's house. The pain my mother was feeling was even more intense. She had drawn a curtain over the pain of losing her children in 1938 and yet she still suffered the fact that her brother had not stood up and protected her children. All she could think about now was moving to Bend village, even though she didn't quite have the courage to do this on her own.

As for Perhan, her motto was, 'we didn't die last year, so we'll probably survive this one as well.' She and her daughters were gathering up every single plant that was edible and were drying them for winter.

After returning to Dervişler village all my mother's hopes disappeared. We'd take our sheep and go quite far off to graze it. While the sheep was busy grazing, we would forage for all the edible material in between the meadows and when we returned home in the evening, we'd spread it all out on Perhan's roof to dry. My mother took out her tiny store of barley seeds that she had so carefully saved up and sowed them in the earth. My mother, Perhan and her daughters raked and hoed the soil, sowing the seeds in the ground.

Perhan began, 'Fecire Hatun, we're late in sowing these, I did tell you. Look, the other seed we sowed will begin to ear soon. Just wait until you see the barley that'll grow here! Every head that develops will be as big as a child's head, and once it has eared, just you see how the heads of the barley will lean over. You are always going on about Weroz. Well, isn't this the same soil here? Does the wind that blows from there not come here too?'

And of our foraging for plants she'd say, 'Fecire Hatun, my girls collect a sackful of plants every day. Once that barley has headed, we'll have enough food all winter long, we'll mix together the barley and the dried forage and it'll be enough for us and for you...'

The days were passing quickly and my mother's discontent was growing. We had no home and we needed at least a roof under which to shelter during the coming winter.

'You can stay here,' said Perhan, 'we'll throw a few more branches on top of these walls. You of all people shouldn't be left out in the cold.'

'Perhan,' my mother replied, 'this exile will end some day and people will attack the land like hungry wolves. If a person hasn't got any land, what will they eat and drink? Everyone has had a bit of land registered in their name, it's been a real opportunity and everyone has had deeds made up and registered, they've got no fear at all, by God, may he never give anyone an opportunity.'

'That beautiful village of mine is standing empty Perhan, not one person left to live there. The youngsters will come too, the houses there are so lovely, and when the military police come around, we'll register all the deeds too.'

'No sister,' said Perhan, 'What good is a place like that to anyone? If you cried out for help in winter no-one would hear you. Don't you remember seeing those dead bodies, dried out in the houses? We'd be food for worms and birds there.'

Life did not desist each day in showing us a new aspect of itself and throwing yet another difficulty in our way. Then, a man who had heard that we were in difficulty showed up one day as a suitor for my mother. He'd heard of my mother from when we went to the White Mountains. From then on, I would often see this suitor of my mother, who was a man well into his fifties with white moustaches that he had fashioned with almond oil into points to resemble ram's horns. Who knows where he got it from but he also had an old mule that he rode about on. When people saw this old mule beneath him, they'd go into raptures thinking it was the great horse of Zaloğlu Rüştem. When he'd lead the mule up the slope by the barn or towards a stone to use as a mounting block he'd say to it, 'C'mon my little one, come on! That's it, my blessed one, that's the way,' then he'd jump on his poor old mule and strike its sides with his heels, saying, 'Giddup, giddup, hup, hup,' and off he'd ride.

He was always telling people that he was rich. He knew all of the military police commanders and many of those people who had not been marched off into exile were totally indebted to him for their good fortune. Every time he visited, he'd sit on the same chair outside Perhan's house crossing and re-crossing his legs, always in the middle of telling Perhan about something.

'And so, you know, I can tell you, Perhan Hatun, I couldn't get there in time to prevent the killing of Çemşit Ağa up on the summer pastures. On the one day when I wasn't there, Abdullah Paşa actually asked, 'Where is Alişan Efendi?' In other words, had I got there in time I would have said, 'Paşa! Oh, my Paşa! Çemşit is an important man, the one and only son of Diyap Ağa. And were it not for Diyap Ağa, Paşa, where would even Paşa himself be?'

Then he would wait a while, for Perhan to agree with what he was saying, all the while pushing his chair back and forth and crossing his right foot over his left.

'What I mean, Perhan Hatun, is that would never do, never. If Diyap Ağa were present, these events of 1938 wouldn't have come to pass. Off I went, and I could see that the soldiers had taken the road up to Çemşit Ağa's summer pastures and I said to myself, Well, will they really kill Çemşit Ağa and all of his kith and kin? Would they kill him and leave his wife standing? And the wily state official what did he do? He bombed the summer pasture with cannon fire and still didn't leave Çemşit's wife alive. I mean, you'd say, "why don't you just kill Çemşit Ağa," wouldn't you?'

My mother's suitor would then look at the women's faces, as if reading them, for a while. He'd shuffle his chair forwards a bit, then backwards again and sit up a little straighter. 'What I mean is,' he said, 'Perhan Hatun, I mean, wouldn't you agree that in such a case you'd want the wife to go down to Hozat and set the entire army on fire?'

Perhan replied, 'Hello? Hello? Who do you think you are? That Abdullah Paşa should listen to you?'

Whenever Perhan made remarks ridiculing my mother's suitor, he took no notice whatever. He'd recross legs again and continue to talk at them using long words that were usually used to address an audience. He told them that he held counsel with the most prominent people in the state and at every opportunity he tried to impress on the women that he was a man of great esteem. My mother wasn't paying attention. Her mind seemed to be elsewhere. It was as if the man hadn't actually come all this way to see her. Every time he started off again with another, 'Perhan Hatun', my mother would show no sign of a response, either negative or positive, that might give her away. It was as if she didn't hear most of what Alişan Efendi was recounting to Perhan.

'Yours is just empty talk, Perhan Hatun. If Alover was here now you could ask him too.'

Perhan, in a voice that contained a mixture of anger and ridicule, would say, 'Hello? Hello? And show us one living witness to this?'

'Perhan Hatun', he would go on, 'Alover was a great man. These Bactrian peoples have accused him of such sins, as they have done to me also, but God knows that I did not report one of God's servants to the military police. If that were the case, I surely wouldn't have lost those two giants of brothers of mine? They still haven't returned their dead bodies to me.'

He paused, recrossed his legs and took a long breath, as if he were bone tired. Then he took on a slightly tense air. 'Now then, Perhan Hatun, I was brought up almost at the knee of the Honourable Diyap Ağa. Çemşit Ağa would have put me in charge of his entire people. Now then, Perhan Hatun, the state's airplanes have bombed every inch of Dersim ten times over, and so do you really think that in order to escape with my own life from the summer pastures, I went to Abdullah Paşa and informed on Çemşit Ağa, that treasure of the world, possessor of great humanity and son of the Honourable Diyap Ağa?'

Perhan replied, 'Hello? This Dersim of ours has been razed to the ground, will it ever recover? God alone knows. God saved those who died. But those who are in prison, those middle-aged men that were taken into the army and those who were marched off to exile, if they return, healthy, then I'll be sorry. Because then the real fire will begin raging in Dersim and tell me, who will put out that fire?'

'Well, it won't go out, Perhan Hatun. But then, those who went off into exile won't come back again, I can tell you that. The state has given the vine-laden Greek houses on the Aegean coast to those forced into exile. Who would come back to this hell, a place where, in winter, the mountains close in upon you like the ramparts of a castle and even a crane that flies into those mountains can't find its way out of there? That bird the crane that carries the seal on its wing of this earth's most holy Excellency Ali Efendi, even that bird would end up as captive between these mountains in winter. I've seen it with my own two eyes, a great big crane was stranded in Dersim all winter long and Çemşit Ağa fed it by hand every day with special barley bread.'

He paused, recrossed his legs once more, cleared his throat and looked at my mother.

'What I'm saying, Perhan Hatun, is this. Has anyone who has been to heaven ever gone back to hell? Can't you see, Perhan Hatun, a person won't look a gift horse in the mouth; this Dersim of ours is teeming with women, women get in touch with me all the time, but Perhan Hatun, I was raised at the door of Dersim's most select residence, I ate food at the same table as the Raybers... I mean, who else possesses a mule like this one, that's as good as a horse?'

'You see, Perhan Hatun,' he went on, 'those who've been marched into exile won't be coming back. Have you ever known the state to forgive a rebellion? You think that a pardon will be passed and that suddenly every man will leave those vineyards of paradise growing figs and grapes and return to this hellish spot? If only you saw how the Greeks make their houses, from cement, and you could mistake every house for the palace of Seyit Riza at Ağadat. So why would they up and leave such a place? Have the refugees gone back from here? No, they haven't. In other words, one doesn't go back in such circumstances. In other words, Perhan Hatun, I am a gift from God, what women in these times wouldn't want a man at her head?'

My mother, who until then hadn't spoken, and had sat with her back against the well with me tucked between her legs, suddenly leapt from her place saying, 'Get out of here! You dog of Abdullah Paşa! If you were a man, you wouldn't have informed on Çemşit Ağa and told them where to find him!'

Perhan grabbed hold of my mother who had a stone in her hand and was trying to bring it down on Alishan Efendi's head.

'No let her speak, sister,' said the suitor, 'She's obviously troubled, let her speak a little...'

'Let him go off and speak somewhere else', my mother went on, 'The place is full of women. He's taken three already so what would he do with a fourth? He should feed the ones he's got first.'

My mother had sat in silence and listened to this man for days and her sudden outburst of anger frightened him so much that it sent him reaching immediately for the halter of his mount.

'So I'm to blame am I?' he started, 'And I said to myself there's an Ağa's daughter, who's seen better days and she's stuck in a difficult position with her little girl. So, I'm to blame am I, Perhan Hatun? After I said to myself, it's Yusuf Ağa's daughter-in-law'. I could have ten virgins from Dersim if I wanted them. I only came all the way here because I felt sorry for you.'

My mother replied, 'Get out of here. I know only too well why you came here.'

As he was struggling onto his mount, the would-be suitor, Alishan Efendi, fired off a remark at my mother, 'Yes well that was yesterday. If I wanted to, I could go now and register all of Yusuf Ağa's lands in my name. I can even get the deeds to this here Sıncık Mountain. Well, I am disappointed, Perhan Hatun. I only came all this way because I heard that the daughter-in-law of the great Yusuf Ağa was in trouble...'

My mother couldn't listen to the man any longer, and lunged forwards to attack him. After these events, my mother's suitor showed up once or twice more and eventually took away with him a young woman who had lost all of her family in 1938.

X

Once my mother got over this annoying situation, she seemed to relax considerably. New people were showing up every day. Everyone seemed to be searching for a place, a piece of land on which they might start a new life. Those who spoke a little Turkish, or who could find someone who did, were allowed to register any village they liked in their name. They may never have set foot on the soil of that village before and yet with the aid of one Turkish speaker and two witnesses it could become theirs.

During those spring months we spent in Dervişler Village we witnessed something new every day. One such event was the arrival of a one-armed man in his thirties, with his wife and five children. The man had lost his arm after falling into the conduit of a water mill, as a young man, and trapping his arm in the water wheel. He wore layers of clothing, the arms of which would flap on the side where his arm was missing. And because he was unable to tie them up properly using just his good arm, these pieces of fabric flapped about on their own like the wings of a dead bird. This one-armed man's name was Musa and he was the only man living among we fifteen-to-twenty women and children.

As soon as they arrived, the armless man, his wife and their five children set up home in one of the demolished houses. Even though he only had one arm the man was incredibly strong and could lift up the rocks that had toppled from the walls and put them back in place. He cut huge trees down with just one arm and dragged them behind him to lay on top of the newly-erected walls of the house. The man and his wife set to work so quickly that their five little children would trail like chicks, chirruping behind them. In the blink of an eye, they had sowed an enormous field with the corn-seed they'd brought with them. They then patrolled the edge of the field to scare away any foraging birds that might try to eat the seeds that had not yet sprouted.

Now that he had found a village in which to settle, the one-armed man went and brought his animals to Dervişler village; one cow and three black barbel goats. He began to give out milk to sick children, and not only to those who lived in Dervişler Village.

He'd get cross with the women and give them a piece of his mind. 'Are we supposed to wait around in this place we find ourselves in? What will the children eat when winter is here? Sow corn. One handful of seed will sow a whole field and yield one hundred in return. Is barley as good as that?'

The man was crazy about corn and according to him it everyone should plant it. You could sow a field with a handful of it and from a handful you'd get a sackful in return. What's more corn could grow in a month and in six weeks you could have done it all start to finish. And he was right. His corn grew and headed faster than that barley crop of ours.

However, the joy of this man who thought he had found himself a piece of land of his own was short-lived. It ended when the owners of the house into which he'd moved came forth. The owner of the house had died with his whole family in the massacre at Emirhan River. However, relatives of the dead came forward from another village and declared that the crop fields in Dervişler should not be sowed.

The one-armed man pleaded with the family members who had come to discuss the fields. However, life was so merciless that they demanded two thirds of the crop from him.

The man and his wife found their greatest ally and sharer of woes in my mother.

'If I'd have known, Fecire Hatun, would I have sown my corn, the corn I scrimped by holding back from feeding it to my starving family over winter, in this barren soil? There are empty fields everywhere, why should I cast my golden yellow corn seeds on a field that turns out to have an owner? Tell me, Fecire Hatun, why would I sow seed there? Didn't you say to me, "Let's go to Bend village. It's a huge village with well-watered fields and will yield fifty or one hundred in return for one seed." And I didn't go, and why? Because I said to myself, "Let's be somewhere where there are a few faces around, let these poor mites grow up around other children. In other words, I gave up sharecropping and came over here. I came all this way, sowed all those seeds with this one arm of mine, and now I'm supposed to give my produce to someone else?'

But there was nothing to be done. The man had sown his corn on the field and it was already transforming into a future harvest.

The deceased owner's relatives had shown up and Musa and his family were now only partners in the crop.

My mother's new partners in her fantasy of moving to Bend village were now Musa and his frail children who ran after him, squabbling and crying, and his wife Hece with whom he constantly bickered. Hece had somehow managed to fashion a large sack made from black goat's wool into a dress. She had huge black eyes and a slim, small nose. Her woman's figure could not be made out at all in the hair sack she wore. Sometimes her two smallest boys would disappear under this black sack and giggle as if they were playing hide and seek between their mother's legs. The three girls and two boys all had their mother's nose and eyes. Their faces were as pale as lilies and their eyebrows and noses were as diminutive as their mother's. She would fashion them clothes out of rags, taking cotton thread from any white cloth she could find.

Before 1938 they had lived near Demenan. They complained to us about the lot of sharecroppers saying they'd been treated cruelly by the local Ağas. This was the reason why they'd come to Dervişler, ignoring the spring rains and crossing rivers overflowing with meltwater just to get here.

This pale-faced lady, in her black sack, would bring her cow and goats along with us to graze. She had an eye on the tether made of woven animal hair that my mother had put around the sheep's neck. Every day, without fail, she would try to persuade my mother to hand this woven leash to her.

'Fecire Hatun, look, we graze our animals together every day, my goats and your sheep. Such a tiny group of animals can hardly be lost, can it? If you love God, then you'll give me that woollen woven tether so that I can make a pair of socks for my child out of it! Once the goat's hair has grown, I'll weave you a thicker leash.'

My mother got angry with Hece who was constantly coming and going from her side. 'Sister, listen, I don't even take this leash off my arm at night. The sheep's used to it now too. Believe it, by God, I took it off just once and the sheep kept on bleating until the morning. She's got used to it, poor thing, and I have too. If this tether weren't attached to my wrist, I'd feel as though I'd lost an arm and I'd start shaking as if my daughter Gülizar was suddenly no longer by my side.'

'Fecire Hatun, look at these pathetic little ones, doesn't it cut a person up inside just to see their state? Give me that wool tether and I'll make it into a pair of socks. I've knitted one of them, it's at home, so even if you only give me half of the tether, it'll be enough. A person wouldn't need such a long tether to tie up the horse of Kamber Ağa, himself. It's such a shame.'

'My dear Hece,' my mother replied, 'whether I gave it to you on not, is not the point. If this tether weren't around my wrist, I would feel as though the army had come and utterly destroyed Dersim, destroyed it and left me all on my own, here behind the mountains.'

This little squabble over the tether continued between Hece and my mother for days on end. The woman would get cross with my mother, then she'd start begging with her. In the end she took a piece of the tether and began knitting.

'Everywhere's empty, ma'am,' Hece would say, 'not even birds fly over any more, but wherever you go and step someone pops out of the woodwork saying, "I'm so-and-so and I want such-and-such." There are no people left in this Dersim, but even so they still consider a fistful of earth too much for us. We've been to the Mameki villages of Huneli, the villages of Orta Mountain, there's nowhere we haven't been, and no-one's given us a hand-span's worth of land.'

Our situation was not so different from theirs. Whatever we got our hands on, whoever we turned to in hope, we profited from none of it. God hadn't seen fit to give us so much as a single-windowed earth hovel under which to stick our heads. Sometimes my mother would name, one by one, the places we'd been and I'd wonder how each place could have proven so unlucky. And how could my mother almost not blink an eye in the face of such hardship? What kind of God must he be that he could allow our lives to resemble a nightmare and our bad dreams to resemble our lives? Didn't he see how so much disappointment could turn a person into a spectre in a mist? Couldn't he see the spectres of people as they passed before even his exalted form?

'Hece, tell your husband. Let's go to Bend village. You haven't even seen it. If you did, you'd think nothing of Dervish village or the Pertek plains. If you just saw them, you'd die for those houses, with two storeys and beautiful trellises climbing the outside, the oaks of Bend village are renowned, black oaks, each one reaching so far up to the skies that you'd think their topmost branches would reach Buyer Baba. Those houses were built by Armenians. Having built them, they walked to the other side of the valley to look across and admire their own work.

'When you talk about master stonemasons, you won't find better than the Armenians anywhere in the world. Kopo Rayber went all the way to Erzurum to bring master stonemasons when he was building his house, that great Kopo Rayber pulled down his house three times and rebuilt it. He'd rebuild it, and then be dissatisfied with the result. In the end he went and brought some Armenian master stonemasons from Halvoru. He'd say, "I've never known anyone like the Armenians to cut that stone just like blocks of cheese. In the hands of an Armenian the stone comes to life and talks."

'My grandfather Süleyman Salih Ağa's first residence was built by Armenian master stonemasons. The Ottomans demolished it in the World War, but the walls are still standing. The Armenians didn't even use mortar on those stones, Hece. It was as if they weren't even hitting the stones with hammers, but stroking a veritable Yemeni handwoven rug with their fingertips. When I was a child, I listened to the hammerblows made by those Armenians and you would really think you were listening to nightingales warbling. And those master stonemasons would strike up a folk song so poignant that you'd think the stone in their hands was going to come to life and begin to cry.'

Hece was listening to my mother as if she were hearing a fairy tale. 'Yes, that place may be like that, Fecire Hatun, but I don't know, I do keep saying to Murte Areyici (32) 'Come on, let's go to Bend village, the woman has gone on and on about it until her jaw is aching. And she has the deeds and everything.'

My mother excitedly piped up, 'Yes, my sister, there are deeds. My husband, Hıdır Efendi, used to tell me before he died that his father Yusuf Ağa had taken out the deeds to all of these Bactrian villages. He registered them way before the Republic when Dersim was still a district attached to Erzurum. That refugee from Torut heard it from Governor Fevzi with his own ears, "All the land belongs to this woman, she is the sole heir", he said. And when he said it, the refugee smiled so widely his mouth nearly touched his ears. Oh yes, and he sat on this very rock and said the same thing to Perhan. He said it and everyone in Dervişler heard it.

32Her husband, Musa, son of Miller Murtaz

'I don't know, Fecire Hatun, I too say we should go. It's empty of people, and has walnut trees. With such trees, a person could eat nothing but walnuts quite happily. Two walnuts are enough to power a person for a whole day. And you should drink water. How can a person ever die if they've drunk water on a winter's day?'

'No, you're right, my Hece. With our girls we got by all winter on clover seeds we picked out of the hayloft. With clover seeds, unless you boil them and boil them you stomach will react. And when it accepts them, then you get ill and foam bright green from your mouth. Is it the same with walnuts?

'There's nothing like a walnut tree. One tree got these poor mites and I through a winter.

'These trees, Hece. If you just saw them! Each one's like a mountain with one branch on the ground and one in the sky. And how they hold those branches! They come curving down like trailing vines. And it has a fountain, springing up foaming between the cold oak trees. A person would be moved looking into the water and seeing a herd of winged gazelles flying inside the babbling waters. I said to Perhan several times, come on let's go and she'd say that the place was full of curled-up dead bodies. My Hece, has humanity died? Have those bones seen one shovelful of earth? O God, may you be bequeathed all the beneficent prayers of Saint Aleyselam. Seyit Riza went and made a grave in the forest for every single member of his family and relatives after combing all of their bones out of Laçinan Gully. Didn't he, Hece?'

'Yes, he did.'

'Hece, the dead bodies stank under that summer sun and the smell got all of Dersim on its feet, it got them up. The Rayber sorted out every single corpse in the middle of that smell. He identified who was who and had a grave made for each of them. Do we have to do as much as that aged man? If you saw it, they were nothing but bleached white bones the poor things, we could at least put them onto a sledge and bury them in a hole. And we could plant a plane tree on top of them. We could come with you, bury them and then come back to collect the children and take them there.'

Whilst my mother was chattering on about moving to Bend village, Musa was coming and going around the edge of the cornfield. The first barley furrow we'd planted had sprouted verdant green ears. It would only be a day or two now and we'd be able to pick the first ears and make a yoghurt soup with them. Our only fear was that someone might come in the night and steal the ears of barley. And we were worried that wild pigs and bears would eat them too. If only we'd had a dog, it would have made things a lot easier.

As the ears of barley grew, we'd rush outside at every creak we heard. Perhan's two girls would patrol the little furrows of barley.

My mother would say, 'Sister, didn't we tell you that the barley round here was really good, this is nothing yet, just wait until they start to go golden. Once the ears turn gold, each one will grow as big as a child's head. Once they're mature, the ears we'll collect every one and dry them in the house. We'll make buttermilk yoghurt soup with some of it and we'll plant the rest in the soil again. We'll get three harvests and be able to line up four sacks of barley along here.'

However, one night the soldiers who'd come to Dervişler trampled our furrows of barley with their boots until it looked as if it had been threshed. Hundreds, thousands of soldiers passed by, crushing our two barley furrows and half of the cornfield with their combat boots. Everyone was crying. My mother, Perhan and her two girls, everyone. It was only when the soldiers had gone that I understood the situation. The refugee who had escorted us to Governor Fevzi was accompanying them and no-one had had the courage to tell the soldiers that they were trampling a barley field.

All of our hopes and dreams had been crushed beneath their boots. We had no new barley seed to sow either. Musa's cornfield had come off better than our barley. The soldiers had still passed through the field but to see our barley rows you'd think they'd been trampled by horses.

But the barley in those furrows proved similar to us and our lives; just when you thought they were dead, they picked themselves up again. The barley in the furrows began to straighten up and stand tall, raising their weak, once bowed heads and beginning to turn golden again. The girls, Perhan, my mother and I filled a sack with the golden ears. It wasn't the harvest we'd been waiting for, but even so we used the seeds from the part that the soldiers had trampled and sowed them again. Towards the middle of summer, we could now expect this barley to grow again and, if winter was late, we might be able to harvest another crop in late autumn. We were already comforted by the fact that there were now several sacks of barley stored at home. It was less that we expected but it was still something. However, we still had no house.

Perhan would say, 'Fecire Hatun, why don't you give up on this stubborn idea of yours? Let me get this empty house ready for you, the uprights are still standing. We'll just chop down some oak foliage for a roof, cover that over with earth and it will be fine.'

My mother would then reply, 'No, Perhan, I'm very grateful to you, for putting us up like this but I am Hıdır Efendi's wife and I will not leave that village to that woman. In the old days I was quite merciful, and thought that I'd give her a piece of farmland to work too. But she drove me to that refugee's door...'

'Don't, sister. Look, winter's nearly here and it's not just you, it's this little girl I'm worried about. There's no place like home now, is there?'

'Perhan, what's the point of fixing up a ramshackle house when there are houses ready in Bend village? And what houses? With glass windows, each pane as tall as a woman, so that you'd think the sun was rising from inside the house in the morning. How can a person live without eating and without having their own arable field? Look at Musa, he had to take to the roads, everywhere people are having to share land and no-one will even take us on as share croppers. And who would award the share cropping to a woman? Surely the man whose land it is will ask, "Who's going to sow and reap this field and have you got an animal to help you with the work?"'

'Yes, they'd ask you that.'

'Yes, they would ask, Perhan. This Dersim has turned into a living hell. They set fire to these mountains and then left whilst they were still burning. Perhan, that man didn't raze the root of this place, as he threatened. That godforsaken man left the snake lying injured, and then he went away.'

My mother would stop for a moment and then on she'd carry on, 'Perhan, if we don't find ourselves a scrap of earth before the men come back from exile... if we can't find something by then we'll be disgraced in front of that woman. And this is a daughter I have, not a son. If it were a boy, I'd take him off to live in Bend village. You've seen how beautiful the houses are... Didn't your two girls start crying when they saw those houses that stand like neat little boxes? You'd think they'd designed those fields by taking out a plumbline and drawing them, they're so straight, with each furrow neatly set apart from the one beside it. If you won't come, then don't. That Musa needn't come either; let him go off and live inside a hair sack like his wife. I'll take my due from this hoard of barley, I'll take my sheep and my daughter and I will be off.'

XI

As my mother carried on talking this way the idea of going to Bend village became more and more frightening with each passing day. Even if the place was billed as heaven, who would want to go and live there knowing that people had died of hunger there? And that their corpses had dried out where they lay. And even though mother knew this too, she still kept the idea of moving there alive. As for me, I was at a place where dreams had run out. Even my new dolly now shared in my fears and no longer my dreams. And what could a child dream of anyway. Toys? How could I dream of toys that I had never seen in my life? It was enough for me to be there with my mother. So that whenever she went, I wanted nothing but to be beside her, wandering along and clutching onto the material of her *shalvar*. I'd nearly forgotten how to daydream about bread, let alone anything else. And to think how much I'd cried at being hungry when we were running away to Ovacık, to Uncle Kahraman Bey's village. A person got used to things so that accepting the fact of having nothing was a little bit like accepting the fact of death. I'd got used to having nothing by now. There was no meaning to the words 'I'm hungry.' It was better to forage edible plants from the fields and eat them, just like the animals did, rather than say 'I'm hungry.' But then again, the one thing I did miss was salt. If you had a little salt, the plant itself tasted so much better. How could we find salt here when we weren't even able to find any at Zeranik? When my mother was foraging for all edible plants in the lower meadow, she'd always say, 'My beautiful girl, my Butterfly of the Night, if we had some salt as well, we could boil this up like spinach, squeeze it out and eat it with salt sprinkled on it.'

    I couldn't get into my head what kind of thing this salt must be. 'Mother, why don't we have salt?'

'My Butterfly of the Night, there's no salt. Salt is a blessing from God. There's nothing quite like salt. In the old days your father's men would go to Kemah to bring back salt. Pure virgin rock salt. You'd only need to add a tiny pinch between two fingers to the soup to ruin it and make it taste of salt alone. And this pale fluid coming out of the children's noses, that's due to lack of salt. They say that it wouldn't happen if bread was available, but don't you believe them, my Butterfly of the Night. A person's insides will rot for lack of salt.'

'But mummy, remember when you gave me that rock to lick? Can't we find some rocks like that and boil one up with the wild beetroot?'

'There's no reason not to,' said my mother, 'but barbel goats are the only ones that can find them. Goats are very intelligent animals and they're very well behaved. Goats have got better manners than horses. Just like people, they select the plants they want to eat and then they go and lick a salty rock. And goats' tongues are rough and prickly too.'

'Are the tongues of the goats belonging to Musa and family spiky too?'

'Yes, they are. And if you open your hand like this and let the goats lick your palm with their prickly tongues, it makes you feel all tickly inside.'

Then we sat on a hilltop on some pebbly ground near where we would gather and eat the plants that grew there. My mother told me a story about salt in the Zazaki language. From where we sat on the stony outcrop the village of Dervişler looked so beautiful. It was all laid out like a mirror below us and you could see exactly what people were doing and who was working in whichever field. Perhan was busying herself with a task in the barley furrows. She was lifting up the branches of something we called *mamugh*, the cranberry bush, and supporting them within another tree so that wild animals in the night would not eat them. The reddish bush would flower even more than the rosehip. If it didn't fruit and go off and if a bear didn't come along and eat it all we were going to make cranberry jelly. Milte was in a field at the mouth of the stream with a hoe in her hands, rooting out the tuberous plants. Musa and his wife Hece with their squawking children were come and going along the edge of the cornfield.

Sitting on that hill I somehow felt sorry for Milte below, rooting out the plants. As she was digging out the edible roots with a single-bladed tool tied to a dried oak shaft, her children were crouched down on the earth watching the soil rising and falling with the movement of the hoe. She was silent, and her children were at least as quiet as her. Maybe she was saying something to herself but no-one would hear. Whenever she sat down the children would nestle at her side like chicks and would lay their heads down to the left and right on her knees. Perhaps she, too, was telling them a story. I always imagined that she was crying. Çöyder Hüseyin had taken her and brought her to the village.

I don't remember all of the story about the importance of salt. Mother would say, 'I'll tell the story to my little Butterfly of the Night, and she'd begin.

'Once there was a Sultan who was incredibly rich and whose name was known by all the world's great powers. He had three sons, each of which he loved very much indeed. However, the Sultan could never work out which of his three sons he loved the most and so, one day, he had an idea. He said to himself, "I will call them to me one at a time and tell them that I have a problem that is worrying me. I will see how they respond so that I can decide which one I love the most. I will then nominate him to take over my place that he may then govern my people."

He told his Vizier about his idea. The Vizier said, "You are right to do this, my Sovereign, I will call each of your sons in turn into your presence so that you may ask them."

The Sultan said, "In that case call my eldest son that he may come."

The eldest son could not understand why his father had called him into his presence. The oldest son thought to himself, "My father and I dine together every evening, if he has heard something then why wouldn't he talk about it over our evening meal?" However, he kept silent and went to appear before his father. "Yes, my father. You called me."

After sitting opposite his son for some time, the Sultan told him of his quandary and of how he wondered which of his sons loved him the most.

The oldest son thought to himself, "I must first say something that will please my father." Then he remembered that his father was fond of sweet things. He smiled and said, "Oh father, look at what you've been worrying about! You are the most merciful Sultan in the world and the sweetest father. Of course, I love you as much as sugar candy."

The Sultan was relieved to hear his eldest son's answer. "'That is to say he loves me very much", he said to himself, and heaved a sigh of relief.

He called his Vizier and told him the answer that the eldest son had given.

"My Sovereign, I told you the same, all of your sons love you very much."

However, the Sultan still kept on wondering how much each one loved him. "Call the middle one," he said.

The middle son also began worrying, just like his eldest brother. "I wonder what my father has to tell me," he wondered. He was summoned into his father's presence. The Sultan said the same things to him as he had to his brother.

The middle son said to himself, "I wonder what I can say to please my father.'" and he thought for a while. He too remembered that his father liked the sweetest of food and drink and he smiled to himself at having remembered this. "Oh, look at what my dear father is saying," he said, "I love you more than the sweetest dessert on earth. Whatever honey may be, I love you even more than that."

On hearing the middle son's reply, his father puffed himself up even further upon his throne and smiled from ear to ear.

"Seeing as these two have answered in this way, who knows what my youngest son, the one who loves me the most will say," he said to himself. And even though he knew full well how much his youngest son loved him, still he ordered the Vizier to summon him.

The youngest son came. His father recounted the same things to him as he had to his brothers. The youngest son, knowing how much he loved his father had no hesitation, "I love you as much as salt," he said.

At this part of the story the father became enraged and called for his youngest son to be executed. However, the executioner did not carry out his duty and, instead, he helped the youngest son to escape. The youngest son crossed mountains and villages until he came to a land, the king of which had recently died. Here he became king and then sent out an invitation to his father, the king, to visit him in this new land that he now administered.

The Sultan did not know that the one who had invited him was the very son he had condemned to death. Great preparations were made and the Sultan set off, accompanied by all of his best men and his two sons. He liked very much the country now administered by his son.'

The thing I remember about this story is that the people of that country were very happy and that they all lived in peace. And the thing I liked better, even, than the salt on the table were all of the foods. But the Sultan, seeing all the fine food, would eat none of it as it was all without salt.

Each time he tasted a dish the Sultan's face would sour in distaste.

His youngest son said, "Your Highness, why don't you try this one too?"

The Sultan tried the next dish but he once again winced in distaste.

"Why don't you try this dish?"

The Sultan did so, but no matter which dishes he tried, each time his face crumpled in displeasure. "Each of the dishes looks beautiful", he said, "but the cooks have forgotten to put salt in all of them."

I don't remember how my mother's story continued, but somehow the Sultan knew that the king who ruled this small country was his own son and that it was he who loved his father most of all.

As for us, everything we ate was tasteless and without salt. It was with this story that my mother explained to me what salt was like. If there had only been some salt, we could even have dipped a fresh oak leaf in it and eaten it.

'If we had salt, my beautiful girl, these children's bellies would not blow up so much and the worms would not be creeping out of their bellies as they crawl out of the earth.'

But there was no salt to be found in our lives. All of the plants and weeds that we gathered from around the edges of the crop fields such as wild spring goatsbeard, knotweed, *gruz* weed, wild beetroot and common purslane – we ate them all without salt.

Some days my mother would not speak so much as a word to me. There were many times when we went for weeks, walking side by side, without talking to one-another. She would talk to herself and repeat the names of people I'd never heard of, having rows with them in turn. At times like this I would hold onto her *shalvar* and tag along wherever she went, clutching the new dolly she had made for me. Now I had learned how to speak silently to this new doll. No-one could hear the games that we played together. Nobody knew. As my mother continued talking to herself, my dolly and I would go off into another world. If you ask me, that doll actually spoke to me all the time during those years. She even had her own voice. I knew all of the things that she did; how she winked her eyes at me, how she would open and close her tiny fingers as she spoke to me, how her heart beat as she slept at night. For me she was not just a lifeless doll. I imagined the clothes she wore were not just made of weeds and Perhan's daughters were not the ones who had dressed her. She had a real mother who had given birth to her, someone who brought her up, who loved her and someone who cried for her and worried about her when she was alone.

    I would play the best games in the world with her, and we faced the same fears. The idea that my aunt might appear and steal us away was enough to freeze us both to the spot. We were afraid to go outside on our own.

XII

After Musa had been made to harvest the corn and give over two-thirds of his crop to the relatives of the field's owner he decided that he would go off to Bend village with my mother. The day that he gave away his corn, Musa was even angrier than usual. For almost a week we heard nothing but his angry voice.

'I mean, this sort of thing just shouldn't happen. They were relatives. Didn't your relationship to them occur to you when I was sowing the corn? Seeing as you were relatives, where were you when Veli's dead body and all of his children were left at Emirhan River for the birds and beasts to eat?'

Musa was so angry that you'd think he'd forgotten to breathe as he spoke. The loose arms of the layered jumpers on his amputated side would swing around angrily, mimicking him. The place near his shoulder where his arm had been amputated was like a small fist and it bobbed around like a nestful of skylark chicks under the cloth. When Musa was in a rage like this it was my mother who best understood him.

'You know, Fecire Hatun, you were brought up in the house of noblemen. You're the granddaughter of Süleyman Salih Bey, the bride Yusuf Ağa gave away and bound to Hıdır Efendi like bindweed. So, you tell me, was not poor Veli's dead body left out in the open with no-one to claim it? His body was left there and the stench from it filled the surrounding area, didn't it? It did, and the soldiers had to douse the body of the man they'd killed with petrol? Had they not burned those corpses, wouldn't disease have utterly wiped out this young Republic? What I'm saying, Fecire Hatun, is, didn't the General swear at those who had left his body out in the open like that? He did, you know.'

Musa stopped and started, stopped and started talking to himself. He'd ask a question and answer it himself. 'What I mean, Fecire Hatun, is that the people who left that corpse in the open should had come to me and said, "We're the inheritors of poor Veli's field." You wouldn't have left the bodies of those kith and kin of poor Veli under the red-hot sun, just left there to stink out the rocks and mountains all around...'

'You know, Fecire Hatun, if only he hadn't died, that great Paşa, if only he'd have rooted out these dishonourable wretches. The Paşa came here and saw for himself, and he too couldn't find a solution for the suffering imposed by the Ağas, "Burn it," he said to the esteemed Fevzi Çakmak, "If we don't lance the boil caused by the Ağas of Dersim they will cause suffering upon suffering for us."'

'You see, Fecire Hatun, you are a woman of experience. The suffering caused by the Ağas, it wasn't a little thing by any means, was it? What I mean is, have you ever seen such a thing? People coming forward and claiming land after the crop has been sown there?'

'You know, Fecire Hatun, whatever you say is right, and you're right from the soil to the sky. You told me. You said, "Come there, it's an Armenian village and its crop fields were drawn up with a plumbline and string." That's what you said, and I said, "May poor Veli's soul be happy. May poor Veli find peace beneath the ground. Let him see that his fields are filled with fresh life." How was I to know that seven tribes of his family would show up from nowhere? That they'd come and plant a fig tree right in my hearth - such bad luck!

'Well, Fecire Hatun, why shouldn't I go to that village that's like a high summer meadow? You told me it has magnificently tall trees, walnuts, pear trees... and didn't you say that there was a water pump, a fountain that bubbled up, foaming between the pebbles, frothing so much it looks as though mountain deer are leaping in it? That's what you said. Yes, you said so. And I just stuffed up my ears with cotton wool. I mean, who would come here to this Dervişler village, drowned as it is by the forest, buried in potholes in the ground? I only came here for poor Veli's sake, that his soul may find peace. They even told me, as far away as the villages of the White Mountain, "Go! Veli has no family left alive, get on with it quickly. Whoever first sets foot there can claim everything." That's what they said. But it turns out you were related. So why did you let the worms feast on Veli's dead body. Because, that's what you did and the Military Police in their mercy had to come and pour petrol all over him and light it.'

At this my mother said, 'Musa, that is what I said to you. I said it and still your ears wouldn't hear at all.'

'You're right, Fecire Hatun, whatever you say is right, I didn't hear it, and even if the Prophet Muhammed had risen up from his place in heaven and come to tell me, still I wouldn't have heard it.'

This is how we ended up leaving for Bend village. Perhan and her daughters and all of the women of Dervişler village begged and begged us not to go. But nobody, now, could stop my mother and Musa. We took our sheep, the cow and goats and off we set.

Perhan and her daughters came with us as far as a hilltop. Perhan said, 'Don't go, Fecire Hatun, if you call for help way behind those mountains, nobody will hear you. And there's winter to think of. People flourish and grow by looking at other people. What is there to look at on top of a mountain? If you shouted out for help there'd be no-one to hear you. And, most of all, what will happen in winter?'

But my mother couldn't imagine living without owning a little piece of land. To her, sharecropping was a terrible thing. After walking for half a day, we arrived at Bend village, where we had once been before with Perhan and her daughters. A few times along the way Hece had asked, 'Is it much further?' She was carrying her two crying children, one on her back and the other one in her arms. When, from a hilltop, we saw the little village nestled in the foothills of the mountain we stopped for a rest. Musa took the corn bread he was carrying on his back and gave us each a piece. Corn bread is not the kind of bread that you can eat without water. Even if you bite off a piece half the size of a normal mouthful of bread it will stick in your throat like a handful of sawdust and you'll cry dry tears.

Despite this, Musa declared, 'You know, Fecire Hatun, I've never seen a corn bread like this. You'd think it was pure wheat bread and not corn at all, look, see how sweet it tastes. And if only we had some water, well, you should try it then! I mean, if you tear it up into some warm water, you'd think you had torn up some wheat flour pastries and dunked them in yoghurt. It melts in the mouth in the same way as sugar. Blesséd it is. You know, they'd said so but I couldn't believe it. They said, Veli's field will give a return of fifty-to- one, the corn will be as sweet as the beetroot, that's what they said and I didn't believe it. You know, if it weren't for those Ağas and their oppressive ways, if they hadn't been oppressive then why would the Paşa send all the troops swarming over this poor people, going as far as to trample everything with their boots. Yes, Fecire Hatun, the Ottomans have gone, and now we've seen another state within the state…'

'Musa, you should see what the bread of Bend village is like, and the Armenians have gone and left this world. They left Muş, Eleziz and the great plain of Van, but they couldn't leave Bend village. They left villages like Vazoğlu and Halbori. There's nowhere like Bend, you can't see it so well from here, but do you see that walnut tree there, Musa?'

'No, Fecire Hatun. In the greenery in front of these houses?'

'They're all walnuts, they're all crammed in together, stretching as far as that stony outcrop over there. If we were to pick them all they'd feed everyone, kids and all, throughout the winter. If we gave them a handful a day, that would do the trick.'

After I'd eaten the corn bread, which had brought tears to my eyes, we started walking down the incline. Walking downhill was easy.

My mother said, 'And Musa, if we had a dog too...'

'Yes, we could, Fecire Hatun,' Musa said, 'I can go and fetch us a dog. The Hozat Regiment's rubbish dump is full of dogs, I could throw a rope around the neck of one and catch it and bring it here. If only you saw them, they're all pure bred Kangals, pure Anatolian shepherd dogs. All of the ownerless dogs have gathered together at the military's rubbish dump. I mean, I could go and get one, and it would be a pure bred Kangal too. The Kangal's bark is beautiful, you'd think a drum was playing, and they bark with such a rich sound.'

Whether it was from having to carry the weight of the children or what, but Musa's wife Hece sometimes made sharp remarks when he began speaking like this. 'Hey you, you ass, firstly fill the bellies of these poor babes. They came and took your corn out of your hands and you didn't say a word. How are you going to feed a giant Kangal?'

Musa replied, 'Well, Fecire Hatun, the woman's right, a Kangal feeds *you*. You can give it one dish of slop in three months and he won't bat an eyelid. They eat plants, they hunt mice and rats like a cat, they'll catch a wolf in two shakes of a tail. Come on now, you girls, come on. They're dragging their feet these two, Fecire Hatun, look how well your girl walks though...'

We were heading towards a new life, to restart the life that had been abandoned in the foothills of these steep mountains. We were going to breathe new life into a small Armenian village nestled behind the mountain with, in my mother's words, fields that had been 'laid out with a piece of string and a plumbline' they were so straight. Our final destination on the journey to escape this oppression called hunger. And really, how could the fields of these Armenians be so pretty? Their walnut and pear trees, and their apple trees aligned in rows as straight as an arrow? I remembered how my friend Meri, in Zeranik, had described that far-off village that they'd had to up and leave. If only we had gone there, if we'd gone that far away. If only we'd gone to that village where the wheels of the horses' carriages echoed on the stone roadways and the horses' shoes clattered after one another. But life had led us up into these highlands. Weroz was behind the mountains, Dervişler was even further away and now we were going to a place far behind the mountains where there was no sign of life. Off we were going to Bend.

There were lots of wolves. So what if there were? These forests were teeming with dens of brown bears, but what did that matter. Musa was going to go and get a Kangal. This year would pass, next year we'd sow the barley in our straight-sided fields and we'd bring an Anatolian Kangal shepherd dog; in fact, not one but ten of them. Our sheep would give birth to new lambs, and if we got two goats as well, as my mother said we would… Goats are very polite animals, and very clean. Their coats shine like human hair that's been washed with loam. Goats are not like sheep. They can rear up on two legs and bend the branches of the oak tree with their front legs to get at the leaves, just as a human does. Goats also have prickly tongues and they love to lick the tiny hands of children. One time I opened my hand and held it out to Musa's goat and how nicely he licked my palm, it felt like frothy, soapy water was tricking underneath your skin. My father used to have a lot of goats. The Military Police took every single one of them. According to my mother, the state brought out a law that meant that they could take away everybody's flocks. She also said that the soldiers didn't know about this village, hidden behind the mountains. Who on earth would imagine that a village existed here?

Now we were going to bring new life to that Armenian village where a little spring boiled and bubbled out among the oak trees, hidden behind this remote mountain. Six children, two women and Musa. Along with a cow, three goats and our sheep with its rope around its neck, we made a total of fourteen souls.

We descended a hill and began climbing up another. How many such hills we climbed up and down I can't even remember. But with each hill that we climbed the houses of Bend village looked ever closer. As we left each little hill behind the excitement in Musa's voice grew and grew.

"As you know Fecire Hatun, if we brought a Kangal here it's bark would resound along these rivers like a drum. The only thing a wolf fears is a pure bred Kangal. And it is cleverer than a human. It can look a bad person in the eye and just start howling. Who ever saw a Kangal howling at a good person? If seven tribes of strangers were to come and look the Kangal in the eye, and you took the bad ones out and hid them away in a barn you still wouldn't silence a Kangal. He'd whine like an injured gazelle and beg for his master. As I say, Fecire Hatun a Kangal is not a dog, it's a human in dog's clothing, it can see who's who in the wink of an eye. All you have to do is respect the Kangal. You should respect him as if he has a royal pedigree. If you say a bad word to him, he'll sulk like a child. When a Kangal gets offended he won't eat for days, and even if the world were to be washed away, he'd never bark. In other words, to get him to bark you must always respect him and if he sulks you should patiently talk him around as you would a child."

You know, Fecire Hatun, your little Gülizar, does she know why the soldiers came and burned down and devastated Dersim? No, she doesn't know, and if you told her, she wouldn't understand, I mean, what can a child know? As I was saying, Fecire Hatun, would a child know why one person can be afraid of another? No, they can't know... They can be afraid, but they won't know why..."

Whilst Musa was talking, we rounded a hill and there below us lay the village of Bend. Musa's last sentence was left hanging in the air. The goats he was leading sidled up either to side of the cow. My mother pulled the rope around our sheep's neck towards her. The children ceased their crying. Musa's cow began bellowing. She bellowed over and over, as if calling to her young. She lifted up her head and began scenting the air with her huge muzzle. She began lowing, over and over again, as if she were searching for a life once lost."

Directly beneath us was a field of clover that had grown as high as a man's head. Only a narrow stream separated us from Bend village. The banks of the stream were abundant with walnut trees and weeping willow. The fields stretched away from either side of the stream as far off as the forest. The empty crop fields were full of poppies and chamomile. The poppies of red, blue, black and pink gently nodded their heads in the light breeze towards the mountain slopes.

We stood rooted to the spot on the hill. It was as if we'd come all this way on the road we'd been travelling along for half a day just to be able to stand here and look upon the houses below. Nobody could move an inch. Everywhere was silent, our heart beats were accompanied by the sound of our breathing. Our feet did not want to go forward another step. I don't remember for how long we stood there in our places.

Then all at once our feet began pressing forward. We crossed the clover field and the little stream and came out in an empty field. We arrived at a single storey earthen house that was a hundred metres or so away from the rest. The door of the house was ajar and hung off its hinges. To the right of the door was a neatly stacked wood pile. The hearth brush lay on top of the pile as if tossed upon it yesterday. I had a feeling within me that at any moment a kind old aunt might pop her head out of the inwardly collapsed door and say, "Welcome, why don't you come in?"

We walked towards the fountain that we had visited last with Perhan and her daughters. There was an indescribable odour, as we got closer it got stronger. It was a smell that stuck to your throat like a viscous resin. We came to a little square where the doors of the surrounding houses were all facing inwards towards the central fountain. Musa's cow again put her nose up in the air and began lowing. As soon as the cow let out her bellow a nearby door was flung open almost off its hinges and a dark shadow in human shape threw itself upon us. We let out a volley of screams. The shadow, instead of screaming at us, was hissing and was attacking Musa, his wife Hece and my mother and making as if to snatch up one of we children. Suddenly in the middle of all this shouting and commotion the shadow tore away from our midst and was lost from sight in the nearby thicket of oak.

XIII

In all of this panic and fear we somehow found ourselves back on the road from which we had come. Everything had happened in the blink of an eye and we'd now left Bend village well and truly behind us. We climbed up a hill and set off again for the village of Dervişler. All I can remember is Hece's constant screaming. She was about two hundred metres ahead of us and quite literally dragging her children behind her. Musa was bringing up the rear, following halfway between his family and ourselves and herding his goats before him.

Hece was chattering like a machine gun. 'Four months, mother of mine, for four months this one-armed miller has been parading his family around. Tell me, who at a time like this will give a person some land? Go back, let's go back I tell him. The Deaf Sultan can hear me but oh, not him, he can't hear the screeching of these children. Come on then, you're a man, why didn't you stay, I'd have seen it all then. Oh, Bend village, where the Armenians staked out their fields with string so precisely. And their houses with their dressed stone cut as cleanly as with a cheese wire, oh mother of mine who can fill their belly on stone-built walls? I said to him, "Don't Musa, don't make these children suffer by following you around, don't believe a woman's word about a village and make us take to the roads like this." The Deaf Sultan heard, that there was someone in Bend village that lies down and embraces the desiccated corpses.

'Oh, my mother, who can I tell my troubles to? All of those people in Dervişler village begged us, "Don't do it, don't go and put that poor thing through all that suffering." That's what they said. And what did our one do? He went and followed behind this woman. Woman, you had the deeds to Weroz, you had them and what happened to them? Do you think you can do anything with deeds in these times? If you have deeds then why can't you even find a hole someplace that you can shelter in? Woman, there's plenty of people who'll kick you when you're down, so just don't fall down.'

Hece kept talking non-stop. As she chattered on, she hurried even faster along the road we'd come by. Anyone watching her as she dragged her children up the steep incline would have thought she was crawling quickly on all fours up the mountain slope. Every now and then she'd look behind her to see if her husband Musa was following her, and seeing that he was not rushing as quickly as she was, her angry voice would rise even further with rage.

'It's what I expect of you, you good for nothing, it's all I expect. Count your footsteps as we go back. You made all these kids come trailing after you along these roads and brought them here. Aren't you even afraid of God? Didn't you even say to yourself, "How will these children grow up stuck behind these mountains?" People grow by watching other people. Didn't you ask yourself how these kids will grow up without seeing a human face around here?'

Hece didn't want Musa to wait for us. We could tell he was embarrassed. He was upset for my mother and I, and seemed to be trying to hang back and wait for us to catch up. He didn't want to leave us behind those mountains. But he couldn't speak. The only words that came out of his mouth were, 'Fecire Hatun, pull your sheep along!'

But my mother seemed to be allowing the sheep to graze on each and every blade of grass. She wasn't speaking and even the sheep didn't let out a bleat. It was as if she wanted to spend the night behind those mountains and didn't want to go back to Dervişler. It was as if she couldn't even hear Hece's voice and there was no sign on her face that she was aware of Hece's fury.

A short while later we lost sight of Musa in the forest. The sounds of him and his wife arguing continued to drift over for some time.

'It's such a shame, Hece. How was she to know that there was someone over there who was sleeping with the corpses. Who's ever heard of such a thing?'

And Hece's angry voice sounded,

'Look at the level these poor children have fallen to. And if you were a real man, you wouldn't have given the corn you'd sowed to seven complete strangers. You didn't stand up for the corn that you'd planted. Oh, it was an Armenian village, with houses so smooth it's like they're made out of concrete. Mother of mine! I should have said, 'This is the smell of corpses. Who doesn't know the smell of a dead body?' "Don't do it", they said in Dervişler. They begged right in front of us, "Don't do it, there's someone there who sleeps with the corpses." They did tell us, but they couldn't discourage my one-armed husband who was following a woman wherever she went...'

Some time later there came a deep silence. The oak woods got thicker the further we went. We didn't want to go back to Dervişler. At one point, the path forked as it snaked through the thick oak trees. We left the path Musa had followed, and went away from the sunny slopes and towards the setting sun. After a little while the evening shadows descended on the forest. After walking for about an hour through the thick oak woodland we arrived at a bare peak. The mountaintop we'd come out onto was one of Sıncık Mountain's southern peaks. As we climbed up onto the bare peak, my mother's voice became calmer. It seems it was safer for us to be higher up. I remember when we ran away, last Autumn, that my mother became calmer as soon as she was near the bare mountains. Here the treeless mountain slopes were covered in meadow vegetation and a light mountain breeze was billowing. A field full of giant fennel was mixed in with clover and we came across a small herd of mountain goats. The goats raised their heads for a moment and looked at us.

'Come my girl,' said my mother, 'look, those are mountain goats. Do you see them?'

'I see them, mummy'

'Sultan Baba is the owner of the mountain goats and he protects them summer and winter. Sultan Baba takes them between his enormous wings and he will never kill them. Did you see how that man left the dead bodies in Bend and ran off? He'd been lying down and embracing them there. The Armenians are very loyal to their land, didn't you see my Night Butterfly? We weren't even allowed to open a single door to look inside.'

'Mummy, is Sultan Baba bigger than Duzgun Baba?'

'Yes, he is, my Butterfly, Sultan Baba is bigger than everything. The Prophet Ali was last seen on his blessed horse Duldul, setting off from Sultan Baba Mountain. If you could just see how big it is! Look! You can see its peak from here, all swathed in haze. See! Just behind those really dark clouds, his head is always covered in misty smoke like that. And if he gets angry, he drops bombs and rains down rocks.'

'Does he drop them on the soldier's heads too?'

'Yes, he does. But now he's silent because he's unhappy. Once he's gone quiet like that, he won't raise his voice again, Sultan Baba. It will snow all over this Dersim and the only place it won't snow is one the peak of Sultan Baba. And it's very hot. Some poor outsider folk made it to the top once and those who didn't die were able to take some of its hot ash to keep warm. Smoke comes out of its stones as if they were on fire. But he's gone silent in his anger, my beautiful girl.'

'If he hadn't become upset, would he have rained down rocks on the soldier's heads?'

She didn't reply for quite a while. She began looking around as if unsure of which way to go; and talking to herself, saying, 'He would have rained them down, rained them down, if he hadn't been cross and gone so quiet on us.'

We walked down a little bank and onto the road. There were piles of rocks one atop another at the side of the road and my mother bent down to kiss each one. I knew the meaning of this and I touched my lips down to a little red pebble tucked between the other stones. My mother bent down again. She put her head on the stones and began to cry and to pray. I too bent over the stones and began making wishes, over and over. I wanted to kiss these beautiful stones that thousands of devotees had passed, had bowed down in front of and had placed their heads against, time and time again. But I could not recount as many wonderful things and names as my mother.

As my mother leaned over to kiss one of these visitation points I quite liked waiting there by her side. It was as if she were talking to me in a different language which I had never before heard. Her voice was like a magical lullaby coming from deep within the ground. Those prayers in Zazaki always began like this, 'Ya Kerte Hızır, ya Koye Sultan Babay, ya Kemere Duzgin, to girsa...'

How many mountains and stones there were and how many guardians. Every mountain, every peak and every tree began to speak through that sound that my mother made. Everything would go quiet and listen to our whispering sound. The sound of our pleading spread out like a magical wind. On the peaks of the mountains at the junctions of pathways there were so many Kert stones piled one atop another that each one of them seemed to me to be the ears of the mountains. My mother whispered so well into these ears that I was convinced that I could actually see the tears of the soil.

And really, whoever said that the ground cannot speak and that the mountains cannot speak, whoever said that? Whoever said that prayers such as, "Oh mighty one, greatest of the great Sultan Baba Mountain, the towering rock upon Duzgun Baba Mountain, how great you are...", repeated over and over, cannot come to life and be heard? So many times,

I witnessed my mother leaning over the rocks and whispering to them and bringing their voices to life. So many times, I saw my mother become one with those rocks, enter their world and talk with the guardians of the earth, the mountains, rocks, trees and the winds. And how beautifully my mother cried to those solitary stones on those mountain tops. And how desolate were the mountains, ownerless and silent.

Those mountains were covered in mountain goats, partridges, pennyroyals and thousands of varieties of the brightest yellow Everlasting flower. And the wind would blow with a whistling sound among the mountains. And the mountains would whistle in the same way as a child does when she's learning, alternating between whistling and losing the note and going quiet. If you put your ear to the ground, you could hear a 'vvuuuuuu' sound come from very far away. As it was, I thought that the 'vvuuu sound was the sound of my mother pleading on the mountain. The golden-coloured partridges and mountain goats were grazing to the sound of the mountain whistling and I could smell the scent of pennyroyals and thyme being spread by the billowing mountain breeze as it whistled along. And this loneliness, this isolation up on top of the mountain, how strange it was. How it wrenched a person inside, how it took and did away with all words that belong to or relate to people.

My mother stayed in that position, prostrating herself over the rocks for a long time. She pleaded, without any sign of protest and with no sign of anger in her voice. She spoke to the gap in the Kert stones and, as she spoke, she became more at one with these stones, ceremonially placed to mark the place of worship. She went quiet. She waited for the sobbing in her throat to subside. Then she began to cry again and once again she called out the names of all the mountains and all of the places of visitation. She lay her head upon the Kert stone and went to sleep. She sobbed once or twice and wiped her nose. And just as she sometimes stroked my hair when I was sleeping on her lap, so now did she stroke the stones very, very gently. Then she covered them with tiny, gentle kisses in case they had become hurt. If she could have, it was as if she would have squeezed between the stones and disappeared. She pushed herself into the gap in the Kert stones again and again, as if she was trying to bequeath her soul to the wings of the whistling wind.

She broke off a piece of ribbon that was tying up my hair and tied it to a piece of fabric she'd torn from the sleeve of her dress. She placed them together between the stones. As she placed them there, she moved her lips again in tiny, tiny movements.

I knew all these so well by now that I knew this marked the last phase of our ritual. Firstly, we would speak to the visitation stones, then recite the names of the mountains and the great saviours. We would remember that they too had suffered and we'd cry to them, and finally we would leave something belonging to us there before departing. Some of these stones I imagined to resemble the ears of the earth, and thought that if they had heard and accepted our prayers then the blowing wind would take our prayers off and into eternity.

Somehow, I felt as though I could hear her saying inwardly, 'You know, if we lit a candle and put it here, if we put a candle just here then all of our wishes would come true. All of the mountains are visible from here, the sun leaves this spot the last of all, from here you can see everywhere, Sultan Baba, Kemere Duzgen, Silver Star, Gola Ostoro, everywhere is visible, if we were to light a candle.'

We stood up. Our sheep had settled down beside us and had been chewing the cud. My mother pulled at its leash once, twice and we began to walk off towards a new life. Hece's voice and Musa's pained and fateful-looking face as he kept turning back to look at us – all of these things had passed and gone as my mother lay prostrated over those stones.

'Come, my girl, look it's Weroz, did you see?'

'Is it there, mummy?'

'Come this way, you can see it better from this hilltop.'

At times like this it was as if she was talking to herself and not to me, or so I thought. She looked down from that southern peak of Sıncık Mountain, to where the evening sun lay on the mountain that sliced its way like a knife. That mountain was home to the Hozat road. No matter where she looked, my mother knew all of the people of those places. She knew who lived where and how they had been killed, each and every one. It seemed like a fairy tale to me, to know every single village and to be able to tell the story of every mountain. I would listen to these tales as if they were the tales of the very distant past and, what's more, as my mother described those times, I would even see the people who had lived then, each one of them, in my mind's eye. I saw my father, hiding out with his men on Sıncık Mountain. I saw and my uncle, his severed head being transformed into a burning ember by the evening sunlight on Balıkan Mountain.

My mother pointed to a spot where a tin roof was shining brightly in the sun like a tiny lake. 'That's Kerelan, look, the roof of the Military Police outpost is shining. Not there, no, that's the waters of Balıkan River. Look, the roof is all shiny over there, do you see it?'

'Is that where the Military Police that we saw are stationed?'

'No, that's another place. Your father and your uncle went and burned that guard post.'

'Didn't the Military Police fight back?'

'Of course, they did. But your father and uncle sneaked in there at night and killed all of the Military Police and Commanders and they bound the arms of two soldiers and paraded them around the Bactrian villages. You cried when you saw the soldiers, don't you remember?'

'I can't remember,' I said. I couldn't remember those times and I'd always ask the same questions. If my mother was having a good day, she'd answer my questions and would tell me the full story of everything that happened.

'My dad had a gun too, didn't he mummy?'

My mother would laugh at my childishness. 'Everyone had a gun, and the state fooled them all, "Come and surrender your guns, and we'll make peace", they said. Your father and your uncle said, "The state is tricking us, they'll gather up all our guns and then, just as with the Armenians, they'll murder us all," but nobody listened. Everyone went and handed in their guns. Had they not, no-one would have been killed.'

'In that case, they wouldn't even have been able to take our house?'

'No, they wouldn't, of course. The fields wouldn't have been burned, and the villages wouldn't be empty as they are.'

As my mother told that story, it was as if I could see Sıncık Mountain from the peak where we stood. I could see Çöyder Hüseyin and Pirço's son Hıdır entering the Military Police outpost, crawling along like tortoises with oak branches tied on their backs. I pictured Çöyder Hüseyin just as I had seen him in Dervişler, thinking of his little eyes, spinning like billiard balls in his head. If only my father had struck out on his own like Çöyder Hüseyin. If he'd only gone and brought us back tins of rations from the Military Police. Çöyder had so many knives on him too.

'Mummy?'

'Yes, my girl, what is it?'

'Did Çöyder Hüseyin get all of his knives from that Military Police outpost?'

'Who knows, my girl? He would wriggle into every hole. Who knows which parts are true? It's a sin he has to bear. He stripped the dead of their possessions, or so they say.'

I thought my mother didn't really like Çöyder. Whenever I asked about him, she would always cut the conversation short.

'Çöyder Hüseyin always lives in the mountains doesn't he, Mummy?'

She acted as if she hadn't heard me, and pointed to a village set upon the northern bank of a stream at the foot of the peak we were standing on. 'Look, that's Sövge. This road goes around all of the villages and off to Hozat. In the Armenian times lots of wagons and caravans would pass along these roads.'

The evening sun had turned purple and was like an ember on the very peak of Balıkan Mountain. We sat down.

My mother would do this. She would sit wherever the sun could be seen going down and she'd stare at the setting sun, moving her lips in tiny silent prayers. We'd sit there for a while, opposite the evening sun. The sun would go pale yellow, then turned reddish purple. It would stay there for a while as if it didn't want to leave us and then it would slowly, slowly go and hide behind Balıkan Mountain, leaving a sky wreathed in a reddish dust cloud.

I thought a lot about how my mother could sit, so completely ensconced in her loneliness, staring at the setting sun. To think of a person sitting, watching the setting sun and crying out of loneliness was always a great source of distress for me. I knew that the people in the tiny Dersim houses set down in the valley would also cry like my mother as the sun that left them every evening. It was the fire of the sun that reminded us of both loneliness and love. The sun went away every evening and the fear of losing it would only dissipate with the miracle of new life was announced by the dawn's rays. In reality, who here in this Dersim ever experienced harm at the hands of the sun? Who was it that protected us from the cold, from the snows that turned life to living hell in winter and from the raging floods? Was it not the sun, also, who gave life to nature, who opened the flowers in their multitudes of colours and shared out among them their many, varied scents? Who was it that lit the waters with shining beams and caused the spotted fishes' scales to sparkle?

I would sit on my mother's lap as she recited prayers, facing the setting sun, and lay my head upon her shoulder with an enormous sense of peace. I'd stare into the distance as if into a void. I imagined that, with every tiny movement of the sun, my mother would murmur a different prayer into my ear. Sometimes she would wail out a lament for the dead. These laments had no particular formal words, but were instead made up of words that came from deep within her. At moments like this, when she began a lament, there were many times I remember her recalling and talking about the lives of her dead children by her former husband. Baki had been poor, Baki's father had died of the plague, 'Baki, working as a slave in the salt mine, Military Police - are you not afraid? Baki, a poor soul like you with no-one. His mother is thinking of Baki, Baki, whose feet are bound with chains, being marched to exile, Baki, still a child, how can you bear the weight of the convoy chains?'

I always listened to these sad little lullabies with my eyes open, staring off into empty space. The murmuring sound made by my mother's voice was so in tune with the wind blowing on the mountain that I would stare at the way the wind bent the grasses, at the way that a clump of dry grasses would resemble an eddying whirlpool as it was tousled by the wind and, somehow, I would imagine that the crop of grasses being buffeted by the mountain wind was Baki. If we too had been a clump of dried grass, the lightest wind would have whisked us away.

Sometimes, without rising even to a whistle, the wind would whisk the grasses as if they were a whirling pool and tear them away, sending them flying through the surrounding pebbles. And why was it that swallows were the only birds found so high up? They would land on the stones, on clumps of giant fennel or Anatolian oregano before chirping once or twice to each other in preparation for flight, and then take to the air. For some reason the swallows always made me feel sad. Perhaps it was because they always lived their lives in pairs. But if you were to ask my mother, she would tell you that God made all things on earth in pairs. Humans are amongst death in life, and as for the swallows – if they were to have three chicks, they would not feed the first to hatch, but would leave it to die as it had not waited for the others. And this is why swallows are always in pair, because they have known suffering from day one, from the day when the parents fed the two chicks that waited for each other to hatch and left the early bird to starve to death.

But then again, I couldn't take in the fact that every single stone and every bird had a story of its own. I couldn't understand how Sultan Baba Mountain could throw out bombs just like the airplanes that bombed the villages, or how the mountain could, without warning, light up the night sky.

The sun left us and crept behind a peak above us. It was time to go. My mother pulled at the rope of our sheep who had been sitting chewing the cud, with its legs folded beneath it. She looked around her, one last time. We began to walk downhill, towards a small village settled on northern bank of a stream, right at the foot of Sıncık Mountain.

XIV

As we descended the hillside strewn with grey stones, we found eggs of red partridges hidden between the clumps of giant fennel. My mother placed the eggs along with the giant fennel in the embroidered shawl she used as a bag, and tied its neck.

We came across two women gathering firewood near the fork in the river. One was a few years younger than the other. The women told us that they had spotted us sitting up on the hill. The soles of the women's feet were so covered in callouses that they looked like bunches of broom shrubs. In between the callouses were cracks big enough to put your finger between. They had become so hardened to destitution that they had come to a state where they were genuinely surprised to meet someone with a handful of wheat upon them who was actually wearing full clothing.

All the way, as we walked to the entrance of the village, the women told my mother of all they had been through and how they had survived. The older one had lost every member of her family, apart from her sister's youngest son. And this little boy had only just died, when the wild beetroot illness got hold of him. As for the other woman, four of her six children had died and the other two lay at home, waiting to die. The woman's husband and oldest son had both escaped in different directions when the soldiers had come to the village. Then the husband and older son had taken the family's goat and headed off towards Balıkan Mountain. The wife herself, and her children had headed to the little den they had already prepared for themselves in the woods. They had saved their own lives, but had not heard again from either husband or son. They heard that they were among those killed at Ali Boğaz and then heard another story that they were imprisoned somewhere near Bingöl.

The two women took us to the house in which they were staying. To identify this place as a house would need a thousand witnesses. It was a smaller and darker little grave than the one we'd called a house back at Perhan's. They had covered over the hearth end of this demolished house with brushwood and scrub and had taken refuge underneath it. Wooden planks with burned edges that had lined the wall where the fireplace was, stood with their other ends touching the floor and in one corner, the burned roof formed a kind of first floor. There were a lot of children in the house and all of them had pale fluid running from their noses, just like my Auntie's daughter. They were all jostling for spaces close to the fire. The children were so thin that nothing but their huge, bug-like eyes were visible when the light leapt and flared out of the fire. Other women who had heard us coming now arrived and all began talking at the same time.

Among them was a woman called Haskar who had no clothes on at all. As the women were talking, I couldn't take my eyes off Haskar, no matter how I tried. This strange woman's face was changing colour with the flames flickering in the hearth and she stood there, hitting herself, hissing like scalding water in the darkness. She showed me her breasts that were covered in blood from her scratching and wanted me to suckle from them. When Haskar did this, it made me nestle in even closer to my mother. At one point, as she held out her hand towards me my mother said, 'Hey now, how is it you've found my child in amongst all of these children?'

When Haskar saw that my mother wanted to hide me for protection further between her squatted legs she hissed at her. Another woman said, 'Haskar, that's not your daughter. It's Hıdır Efendi's daughter, don't you remember? Sahan Ağa's brother Hıdır.'

Haskar stopped for a moment, as if she had remembered something. She nodded her head in a 'yes'. 'Are you Sahan's girl?', she asked me.

My mother replied, 'She's my girl, Haskar. Sahan had no children.'

Another woman spoke, 'Haskar, this is Fecire Hatun, Hıdır Efendi's wife. We went to Hıdır Efendi's funeral, do you remember?'

Haskar began to scream as though the death had only just happened now. As she wept her fingers tore at her skin and she cried out, 'Who didn't know Hıdır Efendi? My brother Gagim's son, Goyr, was by his side. Why didn't you tell me? Why do you always tell me when it's all over? If anyone rules on Sıncık Mountain they will have come from your family line. Why didn't you tell me Hıdır Efendi had died? What happened to Goyr? My brother Gagim's, son Goyr? Oh, may God blind me. I only went the other day, went off to the forest to call for him. There was no answer. "Come!", I shouted, "my one and only brother, the soldiers have gone." That's what I said, and he didn't reply.'

Haskar got up from her darkened corner and came closer to the fire. Even though the hairs between her legs were clearly visible she didn't seem to care at all. She scratched at her head with both hands at once as if it itched, and kept on doing so, swearing to herself.

Every now and then she would turn to my mother and say, 'So then you're from Pakire, you're Turabi's wife.'

'Haskar, Haskar', the women would say, 'You've got it mixed up again, this is Hıdır Efendi's wife, Fecire Hatun. Don't you recognise her?'

Haskar scratched her head as if remembering something. 'How could I not remember, Goke? Who hasn't heard of Hıdır Efendi? They were together, he and my brother Gagim's son, Goyr. My brother Gagim's son was one of a kind in this here Dersim. I wish he would come. If only he'd come, my baby lamb. I wish he would bring him to me.'

When Haskar fell quiet the other women began talking again, all at once, and even began to argue with one another too.

'Oh, mother of mine! *They* died on the Laçinan Plain. Thirty-five families, the whole of Seyit Riza's family was there.'

Another woman spoke up to disagree with the former, 'Mother, listen, the people of Malmensan saw with their own eyes those people having convoy chains slapped on their necks. Ali Kadir was the only one of them who got way, and that was at Haçeli. The others were tied up, two together and bayonetted right through.'

No-one seemed to know where their own relatives had been killed. As for Haskar, as the other women spoke, she had her eyes on my mother. She was looking my mother up and down from head to toe. She'd sidle up to her and stroke our little sheep before turning to my mother and saying, 'So, you're from Pakire and you're Turabi's wife. Aren't you?'

The other women heard, 'Haskar, only a minute earlier you remembered Hıdır Efendi. You said your brother Gagim's son was a comrade of his.'

'And who wouldn't know Hıdır?' Haskar went on, 'They slipped a rope around the neck of that Military Police from Gur, almost under our roof. And when the Military Police began to cry, Hıdır would give him some water.'

'Don't confuse her, poor thing has lost her mind,' my mother said.

We boiled up the partridge eggs we'd brought from the mountain, chopped them up with the fennel and ate them. We spent that night there with our little sheep. By morning we saw even more clearly the degree of poverty we were amongst.

There was desperation all around, which brought with it a need to hold on even tighter to life. Having said that, there seemed to be no visible effort anywhere in this village of an attempt to stay alive. Half of the children had died, and the rest appeared to be simply waiting for death. They had given away a female child in exchange for a tin drum of barley seeds. However, a herd of wild boar had broken into the field on which they'd scattered the barley seed and eaten it. Desperation was crushing them in its fist and when the soldiers had come and burned the village the desperation, naturally, increased. This helpless 'waiting for the inevitable' frightened my mother so much that we left the village the very next day.

As soon as the sun was showing his face we set off on the road. We began to follow the road that wound in among the crop fields, leading to Hozat. This road passed between thick oak forests and progressed by twisting around small hillocks that were themselves covered with tiny streams and oakwoods. Some of the river beds had already started drying out as a result of the steady increase in the strength of the sun and all that was left on their beds were their pebbles.

For a while we went along without speaking, walking among the heavy oak woodland along a path that traversed streams here and there. We stopped and washed our sheep at a stream that had almost dried out. We were going back to Dervişler. The skim-milk cheese and oily residue made from our sheep's milk were there, along with the plants that Perhan's daughters had gathered and dried. So was our share of barley. In short, everything was in Dervişler village. Even so, it still felt to me as though we didn't know where we were going. The loneliness that my mother drove onward before her seemed to be broken as we stood for a moment in a dried river bed and turned towards the north. We were now heading to Ovacık, to my uncle Kahraman Salih Bey's house. After all, last time we were there, hadn't he told us to stay?

My mother hurried her steps. 'Come on, my girl. May God mete out his punishment to these Bactrians. These two brothers – did they not just set about one another, and destroy each other? If they'd have been any good then they wouldn't have had such black fortune. They wouldn't have left the fertile lands of Tabriz to come all this way, to come here and be faced with so much trouble. Seriously, my girl, when do you ever see a brother deceiving a brother like that?'

Then she began to talk about the village in which we'd spent the previous night. 'May the sheep's milk that I gave them turn to poison and flow from their noses! They all had their eyes on our sheep's teats, really, you can't stay when it's like that, can you? The haysacks we slept on were boiling with fleas and we didn't get a wink of sleep all night long. That lot were nothing next to Perhan. Perhan didn't leave an edible plant standing in nature. She foraged the lot and dried them out. Have you ever heard of someone escaping death by just standing there and doing nothing? Honestly! There's no need for the state to kill those people, they're walking into their own graves all by themselves. Even if they don't feel like doing anything, they could at least gather the seeds of plants. But no, they want bread made from pure wheat-flour. If there were proper people, they wouldn't have lost the crop in the barley field for which they'd given away a girl child. Come on, my girl...'

My mother carried on talking. As she was chattering away like this, I was collecting shiny stones from the dried-out riverbed. I loved to gather up the stones that had been turned into all sorts of shapes by the water on the riverbeds.

When my mother saw that I was dawdling she called, 'Come on, my girl, throw them away, what are you going to do with them?'

The hill we were climbing by following the dry riverbed led us down over the other side towards Emirhan River. Here we entered the middle of a dry valley. My mother sat down on a flat spot that formed a circle where pitch had been burned and began to cry. In the centre of the circle, a mound rose up made of stones and earth, as if a pile of coaldust had been dumped there. Under this lay some of our neighbours.

How strange life was, how cruel and merciless. We were completely alone. My mother pulled at the sheep's rope in her hand and off we set again on the journey towards life with our only living companion, our sheep. We turned onto a forest road and headed back towards Dervişler along the path that wound through the foothills of Balıkan Mountain. My mother had given up on going to my uncle Salih's house.

XV

When Perhan, her daughters and Musa saw us coming they jumped up and came running. Perhan's daughters immediately took the rope of our sheep from my mother's hand and tied it to a hook in front of the door. They fed the sheep something to eat, by hand.

'So, you came back. Look, Goe, how the sheep's fleece has gone so white. Auntie Fecire, did you wash her?'

My mother sat on a little chair. She said absolutely nothing. She couldn't even hear the emotion in the voices of Perhan and Musa...

Musa spoke, 'You know, Fecire Hatun, may God make you believe me. As soon as I'd left my children here on this side of the mountain, I went back for you. I went back almost as far as Bend village. Look, Hece came too... Come, come Hece, you've bent my ear enough, look, Fecire Hatun's here.'

Hece leaned over and kissed my mother on the shoulder. 'Fecire Hatun', she said, 'I'm sorry. God struck me and my own ears couldn't hear what was coming out of my mouth.'

Musa went on, 'Sit down girl, I mean, how was Fecire Hatun to know that there was someone over there who had set themselves to living with the dead in those houses. I mean, if someone had told you – you wouldn't have believed them. If they'd have said that the mourning of the Armenians lasts a long time, I wouldn't have believed them. It's been two years, for goodness' sake, does a dead man still smell after two whole years? There was a smell of corpses as soon as we began to walk down that hill. There was, you know, and how was I to know? I mean, I know the smell of the dead from when it rose up from the Lach River. I even went to the Laçinan Hollow. No-one could approach the Laçinan Forest. – such a stink, you would have said that the ground was steaming as it does after rain. That was the first time and place I saw the reek of dead bodies seething out of the soil like steam. I mean, I know people get angry about it but the state was merciful – they came and poured petrol on them and burned the dead bodies. By God! If they hadn't have done so, the survivors would have died from the smell itself.'

'That's enough, Musa,' said Perhan, 'You've started again, you keep saying, "If they hadn't burned the bodies. Well, if they hadn't, I wish the stench would have travelled as far Eleziz or Erzincan, I would have liked to see that.'

'You see, Perhan Hatun, the stench of dead bodies is worse than hunger. I did come after you, Fecire Hatun, I shouted, I wept, Bend village was torn in two with my cries, but you weren't there. I came back, and Hece chewed my ear off.'

Whatever the women, Musa or his wife Hece did, not a word came out of my mother's mouth. She was silent, and sat staring off into the distance. At one point, Musa got up and laid himself down before her feet.

'Fecire Hatun, I have all these children, please don't curse me for this. I've never said boo to a goose, my entire life. I've never hurt anyone. If I do have a fault, it's in the way I talk to Hece. And this Sultan Baba Mountain knows well enough that I can't stop these things coming out of my mouth. I couldn't live without her. Whatever I do, I can't control my tongue. Her father used to turn his face away from me every time we met, because his daughter had married a man who was missing an arm. Oh, if only the Military Police hadn't killed him and if only he'd turned just once, to look at me. I'd even partake in his suffering. I said to Hece, "If the soldiers find out where they're hiding, I won't mind so much about your father, but I'd be so upset for your brothers." I mean, have you ever heard of such a thing? They hid in the silage mound, don't you know? And when soldiers come, they burn everything before them, and they burned it, Perhan Hatun.'

'Musa, Musa, don't make this woman cry,' Perhan said.

'Not cry? Everyone's children died. I mean, Fecire Hatun, I never said boo to a goose, and my children were all saved from death. I mean, when I was a little child, I too paid my pound of flesh to God. I'm half the man I used to be. What I'm saying, Fecire Hatun, is that if I didn't have Hece and the children, I'd grab a sack of provisions and be off to the mountains just like Çöyder Hüseyin. I mean, do we really deserve all this suffering? So, you soldiers have killed people, you've rained down bombs on people, why then would you want to burn the crop fields and the houses and take away all the animals? You know, Perhan Hatun, even a dog will eat its young when it's that hungry.'

Musa once again leapt up from where he'd sat down and threw himself at my mother's feet.

'Look, Fecire Hatun, here I am at your feet. On my children's lives! I lost my arm when I was just a seven-year-old boy. I can't even hold the pickaxe, and when I do it goes in my foot. Honestly, I went back for you, I went all the way back, the mountains gave no answer to my call, and that strange thing that was in those houses with the dried out, dead Armenians, that alien thing that didn't even bury the dead, even that found a tongue and talked.

'You turned into Jel Ana and disappeared. Just as Duzgun Baba searched for his sister, Jel Ana, for years and years, that's how I went looking for you. My heart broke. You are the daughter that Yusuf Ağa gave in marriage, the daughter of Süleyman Salih Ağa. I mean, your grandfather fought against the Atilla armies. And when Timur fled to Egypt he sent an embassy to your grandfather.

'Fine then, if you don't want to talk, don't speak to me. But you can at least talk to Perhan Hatun, you can at least look in her face. Look at her, so that I will know that you haven't cursed me, and that you've forgiven me. You are our elder, you're our maternal figure. I mean, who would go from mountain-to-mountain learning who has died and where, and light a candle for them? The whole of this

Dersim was covered by the smell of corpses and no-one would go into the woods out of fear, nobody buried the dead, because they were afraid. The corpses burned under the blazing sun. And yet you went and retrieved the headless body of Hıdır Ağa, that learned man, you brought it back and you buried it will full ceremony. I mean, who else did what you did? Who else went right as far as Hozat and tried to steal back the severed heads of Sahan and Hıdır from the poles they'd been displayed on? I am here at your feet, Fecire Hatun, if you won't speak, then cough, cough so that I can know you haven't cursed me.'

As Musa said this my mother made a slight movement or two on her chair. She turned her head in the other direction. But she didn't speak. Thinking that he had provoked a reaction in my mother, Musa leapt from his place like a child. He ran over to where the sheep was tied to a hook and sat down. Then he rushed over to Perhan's daughters, Goe and Sede, who had been looking at him in pity. He grabbed one and then the other girl and shook them excitedly.

'I told you, didn't I? I said, didn't I? Didn't I tell you?' running from one to the other. As he ran, his armless sleeve flapped about him so much that it made the girls laugh out loud.

'I said, you know, I said Fecire Hatun wasn't angry with us. I told you she'd come, ask Goe and Sede. I said so, didn't I, Hece my girl. Didn't I say that Fecire Hatun would come back one of these days. She'll come and show us what to do. She'll say, 'Do it like this, and like that.' She'll say, 'Never mind if it didn't work out at Bend village, let that strange creature live there with the dead. Water leaps from beneath every rock in this Dersim of ours. Come, let's set up a village over here. We'll set up a village and show this Dersim how it's done. We'll show those people who destroyed each other over a piece of land, those others who didn't leave one stone standing atop another." I did say it. I said, Fecire Hatun has suffered so many hardships, she carried that headless body here on her back. Who else has covered their dead with as much as a fistful of earth?'

When Musa realised my mother hadn't cursed him, he began circling around her in his delight.

But my mother said almost nothing in the days that followed. She was buried in a deep silence. She only spoke to tell me stories when we grazed our sheep outside the village.

The long yellow dress that my uncle Kahraman Salih Bey had bought me was by now in tatters. The Erzincan clogs, too, that my uncle had brought had worn down and come apart. My mother took some dry leather, the kind used to make rough sandals and bound it around the soles to make new shoes for me. In this way she made me shoes with uppers of dried leather. My dress had now become unwearable, so my mother and Perhan's daughters began to unpick a rough hair sack from which they were able to make a pair of trousers and a top for me. Now I had become like the other children in the village, I was dressed in sack cloth woven from goat hair. For the first few days I couldn't get used to these new clothes, my whole body erupted in a rash. In the hours around noon, when the sun was burning down, it was impossible to wear the rough, hairy clothes. When we went to graze our sheep outside the village my mother would pull off my clothing and sit me next to her, naked. However, no matter what we did, it was impossible to escape from this goat hair cloth that aggravated your skin like stinging nettles. As soon as I put the clothes back on again, I felt as if salt were being rubbed into my skin, which had broken out in lots of little spots.

There was, though, a solution to everything. One day my mother and I found a new solution. My mother would rub sandy soil all over my body before putting on my clothes. By experimenting we managed to find the best soil for the purpose. There was a red kind of soil next to the rocks above the village. We sat at the foot of these rocks almost every day and whenever my mother went to rub soil on my body, I always wanted that red earth. Whenever my mother didn't rub the soil on, I would be itching all day and I always said I was itching simply because she hadn't done so. Before too long my body got used to the goat-hair clothing. In this way, apart from the soles of my shoes, which were different, I became just like the other children in the village.

It was my mother who was most affected by the fact that we were now no different from any of the other villagers. My mother had been brought up in houses belonging to figures of respect, she had been an eligible young woman taken from house to respectable house in the hope of becoming a wife to a lord. All of these Bactrian villages had once depended upon my mother for a living. It wasn't easy to go as a bride to the house of those who led and administered all of the tribes of an area. What's more, if my mother cursed someone, no matter where that person went to pay homage on the mountain, even if they went to Sultan Baba Mountain itself, even if they slaughtered an animal in sacrifice, my mother's curse would still seek them out and work on them.

But there were some things of which my mother was afraid. She was scared of people who had lost their mind. According to her, cursing a mad person was one of the greatest sins. She would frequently warn me about this. You should be afraid of three things, she would tell me - very tall trees, mountain springs, as each one of which was one of Sultan Baba's tears and you should never get angry at a person who has not got all their faculties. Because the things they say are not a product of the mind, but rather a voice of the heart. The heart is clean, whereas the impurities of the mind are too numerous to count. God had washed clean the souls of people, but had failed to do this with their minds and so left them as they were. He left them like that so that people would suffer, would remember their suffering and be crushed under the weight of their bad deeds. But if a person not in possession of their mind were to call out to Sultan Baba Mountain, then his or her call would be heard by God right away.

    Haskar, the woman from the village, had gone mad and would have died of her troubles were it not for Sultan Baba. Sultan Baba Mountain had taken her mind and given it to God. In this way she wouldn't understand what had happened, and why she had strangled her own daughter. Like this she would forget and so would be kept far away from harm. All the terrible things that had happened to Dersim were a result of people not being able to forget the past. The people of this land had long ago been faithful servants, honouring all of the visiting stations on the mountain. But God had intervened and had not allowed them to forget. Had he let them forget then none of this would have happened. Seyit Riza was a great man, but he too could not forget and he burned down Sin village because they had killed his son, Baba. Baba's four children had been orphaned. Sultan Baba looked down and saw that the tribes were all fighting each other and trying to destroy one-another, so he set the soldiers upon them.

    'Is Sultan Baba the government?' I asked.

    'No, how could that be my girl? The government is in Ankara, why should Sultan Baba be the government, praise be to Sultan Baba or to the Duzgun Baba standing stone.'

    I'd often get confused about this, my mother said so herself.

    'But you said so, mummy.'

    'That's something else,' she said, 'They broke the laws of Dersim. No-one had ever heard of an argument continuing after a woman has been called to sit people down and sort it out. Neither had they ever heard of a woman being killed. Sultan Baba saw this, saw that the laws were being broken and he opened the way for Abdullah Paşa, and said "Go in and destroy these people. Otherwise, they will ruin the way things have always been done, ruin it from top to bottom."'

'And what about my father? What about him?'

'Your father was a learned man. Your uncle Sahan listened to his father, but your own father never got involved with any argument among the tribes themselves. God damn them too, they destroyed each other with infighting. Thirty graves were lined up in row as a result, and all over these oak leaves, these forests. First they killed one-another and then they all wept together.'

My mother had told me that people who were not in good health in their minds could not keep a secret and therefore didn't know right from wrong. And because they couldn't think of the consequences, they would always tell the truth. I thought of Haskar, the woman we'd met in Sovge village. Haskar had come to Dervişler a few times, as well.

'So, what about Haskar', I said to my mother, 'Does Haskar know no evil too?'

'Yes, she doesn't know what wrong is.'

Haskar wore no clothes at all. And because she always pulled at her hair there was almost no hair left near her forehead. Haskar had strangled her little girl in the place where they were hiding. They were hiding in a hollow in the rock. When she heard the sounds of the approaching Military Police, she thought that they had seen her and so she strangled her daughter with a cord that she had ready in her hand. This is why Haskar always came to my mind when my mother spoke of people who had gone mad.

'But why did she kill her daughter, mummy?'

'How was she to know, my girl. She thought the soldiers had seen them. And that's why Sultan Baba took away her mind.'

'Why did he take it?'

My mother thought that these questions of mine were nonsense. And she got angry when I didn't understand. 'He took it, my girl. He looked and saw that the mountain and all the stones were crying in pity for Haskar, so Sultan Baba came to her rescue and took her mind, he took it away so that she wouldn't remember.'

'But she still doesn't wear any clothes,' I said.

'Who, knows? Perhaps, if there were some, she'd wear them. May God not take anyone's mind like that, because when he does, they don't know what they're doing. Didn't you see how she always holds in her hand those little beads she'd put on her daughter as a bracelet. She goes from village to village showing people those beads.'

'And what about Çöyder Hüseyin?'

'That devil? Why should he go mad?'

'But didn't you say that he was crazy?'

'He might be crazy, he might not. If he wasn't mad then why would he tie those empty conserve tins to himself and call them his medals?'

XVI

My mother would also tell me a story about people who had lost their minds. It was as if these stories too were told according to where we were. For example, if we were behind the village, she would usually tell me the story of Alik and Fatik. If we were on the southern slopes of Dervişler village, there was a half-dried up juniper tree right at the bottom of the Torut road and here my mother would tell me the 'frog brothers' story. The juniper trees always grew at the sides of the road. They resembled pink medlar trees and bore fruit that contained four little seeds. Just as the jay bird in the Alik and Fatik story had said, 'garrkk, garrkk', so did the frog in this story go, 'graak, graak' in reply to the crazy brother who had said to him, 'Tell me, little brother frog, is it milk that you want, because your children are hungry at home?' I would conjure up this crazy brother in my mind's eye. He was a huge man and could lift up a mill stone all by himself and in winter he would take his goats and go right up as far as the peaks of Sultan Baba Mountain. I think the reason that I remembered this story and the juniper tree at the bottom of the road that led to Torut was that the soldiers came to the village whilst my mother was in the middle of telling me the story.

My mother told me so many stories in those days but nowadays I can only remember three of them. Our story time was the point in the day when the sun would start to draw away from the village and the shadows slowly, slowly dip down to the river. During these evenings we would sit outside the village, waiting for the sun to withdraw and I would put my head on my mother's knees and listen to stories. Our sheep seemed to understand too at moments like this. She would come and kneel down next to us and would slowly chew the cud and seem to be sad at the departure of the sun and at all that was going on in the village.

XVII

Early one evening, as my mother was telling me a story under the juniper tree, we suddenly heard Hece screaming, her voice resounding throughout the village. The Military Police had invaded the village. Musa, his wife Hece and their children were caught up between the soldiers. My mother tugged at our sheep's leash and we set off in the other direction, headed for the forest. But the Military Police had got there before us. The whole valley was ringing with Hece's screams. The Military Police were pulling our sheep and my mother along. They brought us back into the village.

Among the Military Police was a woman, dressed in soldier's clothing and sitting on a horse. Afterwards I would see this woman frequently. They called her Fatma Hanım and she knew a few words of Zazaki and Kurdish. We were all gathered there, apart from Perhan and her daughters. There was my mother, a woman called Gare and her two children, another woman called Besik, Musa and his wife Hece. Perhan must have got wind of the soldiers for she had totally disappeared. My mother still held our sheep's leash in her hand. I was nestled between her legs and was shaking life a leaf. One of the Military Police moved towards Musa. At this, his wife Hece leapt upon him in her black sack-cloth, like a hen that's trying to see off a cat that has come for her young. When the other Military Police saw this, they pulled back. Things calmed down a little upon the arrival of an interpreter, who knew my mother a little and who spoke Kurdish and Kermanji. It turned out that the Military Police were looking for Çöyder Hüseyin. It seems he had broken into their headquarters the previous night and had beheaded a soldier. The government were offering one thousand gold pieces for information on his whereabouts. When my mother heard the words 'one thousand gold' she seemed to forget her own violently shaking legs and began to shout in Zazaki and Kurdish at the man who was interpreting for the Military Police.

The man in question was an old refugee from the village of In, near Hozat. He was a strange fellow. All of the refugees looked the same to me. They all had red cheeks and their noses resembled red clown noses. My mother constantly kept shouting, 'Unclean, filthy!' at this man, likening him to the carcass of a dead animal.

'Look at this filthy scoundrel, he's headed up the army and brought them here. My brother, we don't want your money. Take these Military Police and get out of here. If the government wants to hand out a thousand gold, then let them give us our goats back.'

The interpreter replied, 'Fecire Hatun, what are you saying to me? I am an ambassador. I am only repeating what they say. I mean, in this day and age, is it acceptable to speak like that? By God, if the state found out who was feeding Çöyder Hüseyin then they would burn this place to the ground, for real this time.'

My mother grew even more furious. 'Look at this disgusting piece of flesh. So, brother, what is it you want from us?'

The interpreter was clearly uncomfortable at my mother's attitude towards him and started to shout, 'Honestly, Fecire Hatun - why should I bring them here? And anyway, I'm telling you, I'm just repeating what the commander says. I mean, in this day and age, you can't just walk into a Military Police headquarters and cut off the poor soldier's head. Pity for the poor man, don't you agree?'

'Brother, look. The mountain is there and whoever sees the face of that evil one, then let us see it too. He calls himself a Paşa too, covering himself in tin cans, saying, 'I'm a Paşa.'

If was as though my mother had forgotten the Military Police were there. She was chatting away in the same way that she spoke to Musa. The refugee didn't know what to do, but carried on trying to convince my mother, on the one hand of the importance of the state and, on the other, that he hadn't come of his own volition.

As for my mother, she carried on, saying, 'Let them burn everything, brother, go on, tell them to burn everything. Tell that to your state, tell that to Abdullah Paşa, tell him to burn it all.'

I think that my mother was speaking like this to try to overcome her fear. As she spoke her legs stopped trembling, to be replaced by anger and fury.

The refugee went on, 'Alright, Fecire Hatun, I'll tell them that no-one has seen Çöyder at all.'

'Tell them what you like, but take these Military Police of yours and go. Say that dying is better than this, tell that Paşa that death is preferable to this.'

When Musa heard my mother talking like this, he came out from behind Hece's sack cloth dress, where he'd been hiding and threw himself on the floor at my mother's feet.

'Don't do it, Fecire Hatun, don't do it, we have all the children to think of.'

The woman on the horse and the commander of the Military Police looked on in astonishment.

The interpreter said something to them in Turkish and then turned to my mother. 'The commander said that you are from Weroz, aren't you?'

Musa spoke up, 'My brother, Fecire Hatun is staying here, this is her village too. Her husband's sister has taken possession of all her houses.'

The woman seated on the horse dismounted and said a few things in the few words of Kurdish and Zazaki that she knew. 'You have to go to school, you give these girls to me, and take the boys. There is learning...' Then she took out a picture from her saddle bag and showed it to us. I'd seen a similar one in the house of my uncle Kahraman Salih Bey.

She gave it the picture of a man with bushy, upright eyebrows to a soldier to hold up and turned to address us in broken Turkish, 'Look, this is Atatürk, to save you all here is...'

This woman, who was called Fatma Hanim patrolled the villages until I was a young woman. But this was the first time I'd seen her, on this day in Dervişler when my mother was telling me a story by the juniper tree and the soldiers had suddenly overrun the village. Afterwards the lady on horseback went around in clothes just like ours, having taken off her soldier's uniform. She would give out pictures of Atatürk, and gather up the grown children.

A few days after the Military Police had gone Governor Fevzi, the Regional Administrator, suddenly showed up on horseback. With him was the refugee interpreter from Torut village and two mounted commanders accompanied by twenty or thirty soldiers. Governor Fevzi had learned of my mother's situation and was going to take us personally and settle us back in our home in Weroz. My mother had all but given up on the idea of going back to Weroz. But now that Governor Fevzi had suddenly arrived she began to have her doubts. The refugee interpreter was talking, trying to persuade her. But my mother was sitting by Perhan's door, with our sheep's head nestled between her arms, looking for the hidden catch in what he was saying.

'Madam,' said the refugee, 'didn't you come to me every day, pleading, saying "Take me to Deşt, to Governor Fevzi." Now look, Governor Fevzi has got up and come all this way just for you. In fact, I said at the time, Governor Fevzi will sort out whosoever is meddling in this woman's business. Now see, Fecire Hatun, this important government man has got up and come all this way to listen to you.'

My mother, however, was still in a state of great uncertainty. She was afraid that the soldiers would take us away. As Governor Fevzi went on to say something in Kurdish, Musa spoke up, 'Come, Fecire Hatun, up you get. We'll go there together. Weroz is over this way, if it doesn't work out we'll just come back.'

On hearing that Musa would come with us, my mother let the sheep go from her arms, slipped its leash off her arm and tied it to my wrist instead. As Perhan and her daughters were, once again, nowhere to be seen, Musa said to his wife Hece, 'Hece, the child and the sheep are in your charge until Perhan comes back.'

Hece, though, was against her husband leaving. When Governor Fevzi realised this, he said in Kurdish, 'Let him come with us.'

It seemed to me that whenever Governor Fevzi spoke Kurdish everyone felt more comfortable; especially my mother but also Musa, Hece and the other women in the village.

Musa, my mother, the refugee interpreter and the mounted soldiers filed onto the road that led down the hill. But then, even though I hadn't made a noise up until then, on seeing my mother line up and walk off with the soldiers I began to cry. My mother came back, left the sheep with Hece and took me with her. The refugee interpreter ran along the whole way by the side of Governor Fevzi's horse. Every now and then he would turn back and interpret whatever he was saying. What the state wanted from us was to give our children to them so that they may be educated and turned into judges and Paşas.

There was no need any longer to be afraid of the Military Police and whenever they showed up, we were not to run off into the woods. We should not dress up our boys in girls' clothing and register them as female on the census. And, he said, a pardon had been issued and the period of exile for those who had been marched off had been reduced to five years. This meant that the men of our villages who were in exile in other parts of Turkey would return within two years.

We would be allowed to go and join them wherever they were, or they would be able to come back here. The government also wanted every man to join the Military

Police to perform his military service. Governor Fevzi said if it wasn't for the Military Police, who would come and give us back our house? That old era had now come to a close and the time when people would take up arms and take to the mountains was over. And what if we did go into the forests, the state has aeroplanes now and apparently people can die just from the sound of them.

The refugee interpreter kept talking all the way to Weroz. Now and again, he would point out the hilltops before us to Governor Fevzi.

'That's Balıkan Mountain, and you go up this way to the Emirhan Stream and from there you can get up to Yilan Mountain... This road goes to Çet, and from there the road goes beneath Kızılmezra and comes straight out of Karaoğlan and into Hozat.'

After some time, we arrived at Weroz. At that time there were five residences at Weroz. One of these was our former neighbour's, but the other four were occupied by people who had fled here from other villages. My aunt had given each one of them a burned-out house and she'd moved herself into our house. When my aunt saw the Military Police, my mother and Musa she went into her house without saying a word to anyone and came out again with all of her children. The children were terrified and clung tightly to their mother's legs. As my aunt began speaking, they just stared at us. The children pushed themselves closer to their mother, moving left and right, as if they would disappear into a hole in the sackcloth she was wearing, could they find one. I could see myself in the eyes they had pinned on me. It was as if I was there in their place and was looking at myself as if in a mirror. My dress made of black goat hair and the sandals my mother had made out of the soles of my shoes from Erzincan now seemed so alien to me.

What they all said at that time I can't remember at all. My attention was so fully focussed on the children opposite me, the same age as I, that the sounds just boomed in my ears as if a bomb had gone off. Despite the fact that I could see everything around me in the greatest detail I could hear nothing at all. I think that my aunt's children couldn't hear a thing either, for they were just standing there, staring at us. I'd held onto my mother's *shalvar* and they, too, were just snuggling up to their mother. My aunt's hair was once again like a wild bush and so was the hair of the children. Did I look like them too? They were frightened. Their eyes bulged out of their huge heads and were locked on us. They were trying to figure out if I was that child they had pounced upon en masse only a few months ago. They were surprised that I had appeared like this along with the soldiers.

The little boy I guessed was the youngest child was dressed in an undershirt that came down as far as his belly. It was ripped at the elbows and its cuffs were shiny with mucus. His willy was shrunk between his legs and hung there like a tiny scrap of meat. His thumb was thrust all the way into his mouth and he was sucking it as if milk was gurgling from it. As he swallowed his adam's apple, which was stuck out from his thin neck like a rooster's head, would move down and then shoot back under his chin. He too had taken refuge like me by hiding between his mother's legs. As for the girl who still had pale slime running from her nose, she was wearing a sack cloth as a dress, just like Musa's wife. I stood and stared at her for a while, and we nearly came eye to eye for a moment. But she was looking at my feet, in their sandals. This girl had one arm wrapped tightly around my aunt's leg and the other just hung down as if she didn't know what to do with it. With her spare hand she would reach out to a brother or a sister, one at a time and hold onto them, but all the time she didn't know what to do with that hand.

The other two children, boys, were stuck fast behind their mother, looking everyone up and down, the soldiers included, with their big, bulbous eyes. Every time the horses stirred the boys would look left and right in alarm. I looked for a moment at the little boy who was sucking his thumb. A thin dribble of urine was coming out of his shrivelled willy between his legs, but he kept on staring at me and sucking his thumb as if he didn't know he was doing a wee. He would do a few drops and then it would cease again.

My aunt was squabbling with the interpreter and had said nothing to my mother. But when the soldiers went into the house and she saw them take some of the beds of straw and a few sacks outside she began to cry. She looked at them as if they were very valuable items of furniture, wondering whether the soldiers might damage them or not. She would throw herself upon the sacks that the soldiers were throwing outside, holding their noses, and she'd start arranging the sacks on top of one another as if she was unsure of what to do, calling to the children to help her to protect their possessions, to-ing and fro-ing.

'Poor me, where shall I go, poor me, where shall I go?' she began repeating to herself in Zazaki. She was calm, though, almost as if she had expected this. She was calm and utterly helpless, 'poor me, where shall I go, poor me...'

Then with a great cry she began to beat her knees with her hands and beg. *'Sultan Baba, Sultan Baba tu koyta koe Sultan Baba, to cha shia xo onto masero...'*

She threw herself on the ground. She thrashed around on the ground. My aunt's pleading was so heart-rending that I even began to think that the soldiers were listening to her anguished begging, despite the fact that they couldn't understand what she was saying. My aunt was calling out to Sultan Baba Mountain in the same way as my mother would, 'Where are you Sultan Baba Mountain? Why have you cast your shadow over us? Sultan Baba if you don't pity me then feel for these poor fatherless children.' Then she would hit her knees and moan, 'uyy, uyy,' and begin keening and wailing.

'*Uyy Sultan Baba, uyy,* the fire has come and is burning in Yusuf Ağa's house. *Uyy, uyy, lemen, uyy'*, she begged and cried intermittently.

It was as if that house was hers and we had come to throw her out of it. But now, I didn't want to go into this house that the soldiers had given us back. There weren't even any hazy memories in my mind about our beautiful old house, that now lay looking no better than a heap of stones. The only thing I could remember about that old house was my mother running in and out of it on the evening my father was shot.

The interpreter called out to my mother, 'Fevzi Governor says this house is yours now. And no-one can take it off you.'

My mother said nothing.

They walked off along the Hozat road towards the west. When they left, my mother hid her face against the door of the ruined house and began to cry. She was crying very loudly. Musa took her by the arm, to sit down near where my aunt had confronted the soldiers and sat down by her side. Musa took hold of his empty sleeve and wiped her nose with it.

I forgot about my aunt and think she was probably still invoking Sultan Baba Mountain. I don't remember, but I remember that my mother was touching the stones of the fallen house and weeping very loudly.

One minute she was saying, 'Oh Musa! Who has brought our home to this state? Who tore it down and burned it?', and the next minute she was crying at the top of her voice. A little while later she came over to sit with us and began to let out a lament.

Musa went over to my aunt and her children who were sitting on the things that the soldiers had thrown out of the house and said this to her, 'Fecire Hatun says "She can stay here, let her move into Veli Ağa's big house."'

But it was as if my aunt wasn't listening to him at all, she carried on, 'Sultan Baba, I've come to your door with these four fatherless children.'

XVIII

My aunt was sitting there among her possessions with her children, as we went back along the Dervişler road. We walked in silence for some time. Not a word was spoken by Musa or my mother. After we'd gone a considerable way Musa seemed to have an idea and began circling around my mother. All along the narrow path he danced in front of and behind my mother. He was so full of excitement that, in places where the path narrowed, he would walk beside her up on the bank so that he could see my mother's face. The stump of his arm was moving in excitement and causing the layers of sleeves he wore to flutter around like a bird, trying to come out. His breaths were short as he spoke and he kept repeating, 'Fecire Hatun... Fecire Hatun.'

'As if that could happen, first let those who are in exile come back...' When my mother mentioned those in exile, the sleeves of Musa's pullover were fluttering around, he was so out of breath. He didn't know what to say.

'Fecire Hatun. Çet is your village too isn't it? And at least there are two crop fields there. They won't come back, who would return to this hell? I heard it with my own ears at Mameki village. If only you could see, the state has given those in exile huge wide plains by the sea.'

'Musa, it's not possible. The ones in exile will come back. How can I give what is someone else's right, to you?'

When my mother said there was no way, Musa didn't know what to do. 'Fecire Hatun, you say there's no way with Weroz, so then give me something in Çet. You can choose whichever of my goats you like and take it. I'm going to take them to Torut now and put them to the male goat there. I'll take your sheep too. Within six months you'll have both a lamb and a kid goat. Take whichever goat of mine you wish.'

Musa ran around my mother in this manner all the way back to Dervişler Village. He went in front of her, moved back behind her, but no matter what he did he could not persuade her. My mother would not change her mind one iota.

'Alright, Fecire Hatun, don't give me land in Weroz. Instead give me two fields in Çet. You have the deeds to all of these huge villages now. What will come of two fields? And at a hard time like this, would I give away a goat to just anyone? I'd get not just two crop fields but a whole village for a goat right now. I mean, Fecire Hatun, may God convince you of this, each one of those goats give two kilos of milk. Don't just dismiss it as goat's milk either. The fat from it is as white as the driven snow, and it's almost too good just to spread onto bread and eat. And you know, I came all the way to Bend village with you, just out of respect. I came, didn't I? I did, I came with you and if you had said "We're going to Habeshistan", instead of Bend, then still I would have come with you. You know, I did say so, Fecire Hatun, whether we find food or not, I said so.

'I said to myself, her father, Süleyman Salih Bey, sheltered one thousand Armenians and not one of them encountered so much as a nose bleed. And no-one, not even Seyit Riza, could negotiate with the government. He was tricked and called to Erzincan where he was hanged. "Come!" they said, and that great man was fooled and off he went. He went there and they hung him. You know, I always said, if Seyit Riza had listened to the advice of Kahraman Bey then not one soul in Dersim would have had a hair on their head touched. You see, Fecire Hatun, I said, who has been to the government's very door and caused the great administrator of the state to get up and come all the way here, to her very feet. Alright then, don't give me land in Weroz, if you say it will cause your own crop fields to be split up. You say that the crop-sharers will come back, fair enough, I accept that, give me two fields in Çet, then choose whichever of my goats you want and take it...'

By now we had come to Dervişler village. Musa went off to his own house in a state of utter helplessness. My mother, on the other hand, went on about the situation for several days.

'He wants two crop fields for one goat, and what can a person do with those ancient goats of his? If you'd have been a real man, those people at Demenan wouldn't have driven you out.'

When Perhan saw my mother going on like this she asked her, 'What's the matter, Fecire Hatun? Did that asshole say something to you?'

'Perhan, Perhan, he wants to give me one of his old goats and get a village in return. And he makes all these promises to me, as if the goats are really his own. Who was left with any goats? Didn't the army herd up and take away every last one of the livestock? He gave me a constant headache with his pleas of "Let's go there, let's go to Bend village." Said he'd turn that place into paradise. And then as soon as he saw that bogey-man, with his hair all over the place, dishevelled, he ran off with no looking back.'

Perhan's daughter, Goe, couldn't stop herself from laughing at seeing my mother in this state.

'Well, well, didn't you just make Governor Fevzi travel all the way to your feet? No-one can take anything from you now, Fecire Auntie.'

My mother carried on, 'He wants land. I'll say to you then that I want your cow. You're just thinking of your children, what am I supposed to do with your old goats? They haven't even got a tooth in their head. If you saw them! If only his goats were real goats. They can't even climb up this slope. When you talk about real goats, they can climb up a rock face that's as smooth as my palm. Let him give me his cow, Perhan, and I'll give him not two crop fields but half of Çct Village. Whatever I say, he conjures up his cow in his mind, and not just the cow, he imagines it with a calf in its belly too. He thinks he can hoodwink me?'

As my mother was venting her anger like this, I heard the sound of Çöyder Hüseyin's laugh, a sound I will never forget.

'Hahahaha... Fecire Hatun brought the great administrator of the government to her very feet, and there was I, following them all the way from Deşt onwards, saying to myself, "Now, shall I shoot this one, eh?" hahaha... That state administrator pulled Rayber'e Sed Ağa's horse from underneath him and here he is touring the villages of Dersim. Now the fact is, I'm your new Rayber. See how I'm riding our great Rayber's chestnut horse? Anyway, I overtook them below Teştek but I just couldn't settle the matter there. So I went round Seypertek Mountain and there I couldn't catch them up. I mean, I was going to shoot that son of a dog, was going to shoot him and stick that great big medal of his right here.'

Çöyder Hüseyin had appeared out of nowhere like a tornado. He said he'd followed Governor Fevzi from Deşt village. My mother, Perhan and her daughters stared at him in astonishment. He was arrayed from head to foot in diagonally-slung cartridge belts; both sides of his chest were decorated with pieces of tin can; he had two five-cartridge shotguns and was holding a third one.

My mother said, 'Perhan, Perhan, what does this devil want from me? Look at him! He's not even afraid of God, everywhere is pulsing with soldiers, if only he would feel sorry for these villagers, isn't he even afraid of God, leading this great army straight to the doors of these poor villagers.'

Çöyder Hüseyin sidled a bit closer to my mother, as if she had been heaping praises on him. 'Perhan, I'm dying of thirst here, hahaha...'

Perhan's daughter Sede filled a copper dish with water from a wooden barrel and gave it to Çöyder Hüseyin.

'What I'm saying is, Perhan, I went round all the mountains and the infidel fled, I became a bird and flew. I mean, if only I could have settled the scores. If I could have showed him what it means to have taken Kopo Rayber's chestnut horse and be riding around on it. You know, if only I had taken that horse and travelled from village to village around here. If only I'd gone in through Bactria here, and travelled 'til I came out as far as Abasan, Haydaran and Demenan. I mean, it really troubles me, you know, if it wasn't for fear of shooting that horse by mistake, I would have brought him to justice ten times over. That chestnut, it stood there and whinnied just as if it had caught sent of one of its own people. If that infidel had let the horse go, it would have come straight to me all by itself.'

Çöyder, pulled over a stool and sat down on it in the same spot. He leaned back against the wall again and, as he sat back, he let out a huge sigh, as if a great weight had been lifted off his shoulders. He seemed to be tormented in the way of a wolf whose prey had escaped at the last moment.

'You know, I said to myself, that before that infidel reaches the feet of Fecire Hatun I will parade his dead corpse around each and every village. And we'd have made a grave for him, and believe me by God, we'd have had the greatest ceremony ever seen. And we'd have put up an even more majestic memorial to him that he put up to Seyit Riza's son. I mean, the seven worlds would hear news of the great memorial I'd made to him.'

At which Perhan said, 'Çöyder, Çöyder, why on earth would you raise a memorial to him?'

Çöyder Hüseyin tapped the end of the barrel of the five-cartridge gun in his hand on the floor and let out a huge laugh. 'Well, I would, Perhan, I would have made such a memorial to him that all of the seven realms would have heard about it. I would have shown him what it is to go on an inspection tour of all those villages mounted on that fine chestnut. And the grave I would have made for him would have been finer than the one that Seyit Riza made for the twelve soldiers at Orta Mountain. What I mean is, I would show humanity to the man, "You choose!" I would have said to him, "and if it's your wish I will even bury you right up on the holy peak of great Sultan Baba Mountain." I would even have buried him on Bokir Mountain, Haydaran Mountain, Jel Mountain or even Duzgun Baba Mountain...'

'Tovbe! Tovbe! Repent, Çöyder! Why would you bury him at our sacred visitation spots?'

Çöyder began to laugh even more heartily and his tiny eyes shone like glass marbles in the deep recesses of his eye sockets. 'What I mean, Perhan, is that I couldn't bring that man to account. If I had done so, I would have made him a sacrifice to the very horse he took from under the Rayber. I'd have tied him behind it and dragged him around each and every village in front of all these women. What's more, I'd have made a memorial to him, and have dragged him in and out of all these tribes, taking him all the way to Duzgun Baba Mountain and would have built a memorial to him on that holy peak. If I wouldn't have, then let no-one in this Dersim call me Husen-e Çöyder, son of Alo Bom. Let him go and pray to that Rayber's horse. If it weren't for that horse, I would have shot him a thousand times. I mean, Perhan, I've never seen a horse like that. I've travelled the world and I've never seen a horse like that one. And you know what? It got my scent straight away and started to act up under that unbeliever. It started to cry and begged me to save it from him, but I couldn't catch up with them Perhan. I'd come round the hill and they'd gone over it. I'd go over the hill and they'd have gone up the mountain. And if only you saw that horse that belonged to the Rayber, he was whinnying with each step as if he was remembering the earth there. He was almost churning up that holy soil with his feet. and I couldn't bring myself to shoot, if only I had...'

'Perhan, Perhan,' said my mother, 'tell this fiend to get up and clear off. There's a soldier behind every stone on these mountains, and what does he want with us? We have problems of our own that are more than enough for us.'

But even as my mother spoke, Çöyder's eyes, in their dark recesses, sparkled even more brightly. 'Hahahaha... Fecire Hatun, was it me that told you to start fighting amongst each other? Was it me who told Yusuf Ağa to start going about heavy-handedly, shooting and stealing goats from the poor. And me, have I stolen a single person's goat? I mean, it's just not done, is it? Killing livestock just so that the government can't get their hands on them...'

At this my mother picked up a big stone in her two hands in anger. 'Son of a dog, what do you want with women like us? The Hozat Regiment is over that way, Abdullah Paşa will give you a big medal too, just like he gave the others.'

Çöyder Hüseyin, sitting on his stool, bent his head down until his head was between his knees. Then he spoke, striking the back of his neck with his hand, 'Hit me, Fecire Hatun, the stone that flies from your hand and hits me is like a rose from Sultan Baba. It's a gift of high regard from the great scholar, Hıdır Efendi. Ahh, go on! Hit me, hit me wherever you like and see how Abdullah Paşa pays you for it, hahaha,, and you can tell him how you struck this man down all by yourself and brought him to Abdullah Paşa.'

My mother threw the stone she was holding at the ground. 'My brother, those who want to shoot you have shot you, what do you want from poor me? You've taken your own shroud upon your back. May God give you what you wish for. He gave it to Hıdır Efendi too, and to Sahan Ağa. Didn't he give it to Kopo Rayber too, you fiend? Look here, Perhan, he smells of blood, stinks of blood...'

Çöyder shuffled the stool underneath him and puffed out his chest with pride. Then his eyes suddenly darted as if he'd heard a creak from somewhere. When I saw Çöyder like that, I realised that he'd instantly figured out his exit route. He was spooked. He pulled the stool he was sitting on a bit further towards the wall. He stared at the diagonal shadows cast by the evening sun. Perhan and her girls began to giggle as if they could read exactly what was passing through his mind at that moment.

At this, Çöyder's eyes began to whirl with anger and annoyance in their deep sockets. 'You're going to laugh at me, eh?'

'Çöyder, Çöyder,' said Perhan, 'Why would we laugh at you? The girls just forgot themselves for a minute.'

'No, Perhan, Fecire Hatun knows this, when you've taken your own shroud upon your back then you even have to train your own shadow. Hıdır Efendi was a victim of his own shadow.'

'Why would Hıdır Efendi be sacrificed by his own shadow Çöyder, Çöyder?' asked Perhan, 'He strayed into the soldiers' ambush and they got him, the betrayers.'

Çöyder Hüseyin let out a forced laugh, as if he were trying to restore his good mood. 'Hahaha... I've been to that river bed a hundred thousand times. And that clever man threw himself behind the big red rock, but he forgot about the evening sun. I mean, when you're a bandit, you have to know your friends from foes.'

Perhan's daughter Goe wanted Çöyder Hüseyin to talk about how he would shoot Governor Fevzi. But Çöyder's good mood had gone. He took out a huge aluminium tin from the pocket of his parka coat. For a while, he played with it in his hands and then he put it back in his pocket. He made a couple of moves as if he were about to get up and leave.

'What's that, Çöyder?' asked Perhan, 'are you really going to go and leave so many women?'

'Well, I have a long road ahead of me, Perhan. You know, I couldn't bring that man down and that will eat away at me now. If only I'd brought him to justice and, in return, Munzur Baba had seen fit to deny me one palmful of rain on a rainy day. I mean, if only I had shot that dog down, if only I'd stuck that big medal of his right here, and the whole entire world had jeered at me. Have you even seen anything like it, has anyone ever witnessed anything like that, Perhan? To call Sed Ağa into the presence of Kopo Rayber, the great Rayber, most beautiful man of all the world, and bring his horse there too with him. And then, to take a blanket and wrap him in it and bayonet him? You see, my heart just can't accept this, Perhan, how was that great Rayber any different from Seyit Riza? He saw one gallows too many...'

This time, all the other women laughed along with Perhan. 'Çöyder, Çöyder, to hear you, you'd think that the government had met you with a red carpet.'

A comical smile took over his face. 'Well, Perhan, the gallows is an honour. For the one who knows how to die it's the highest honour in God's heaven. Findik Zade's noose broke three times and each time he got up and put it back on his own neck, all three times, and the great government sat there, shocked. You know, they were expecting it. They said to themselves, "the Paşa is coming from Eleziz tomorrow, let him pull the rope of these bandits with his own hand," and they looked and saw that man walking under his own steam up to those gallows. They never would have thought that would happen; never would have said that would be the case, Perhan. And me, I travel the world. I go from Dersim into Bingöl, from Bingöl I end up in Erzurum. I've seen the world, I have, Seyit Riza said so. Tell the Paşa to come tomorrow, tell him to come and see what I've done, because what I've done is to set stone and mountains on fire. I burned them, and see what a helpless gallows tree I've brought you all to now. You know, he did say, "I'm afraid, may the Paşa forgive us..."'

My mother sprang up from her place in a rage and launched a big gob of spit in Çöyder Hüseyin's face. 'Lies! Ha! You liar, I spit on you. The lies you spin have made the stones and mountain go mad, the sacred visiting places have become dusty and blind, and all because of you, you lying demon, spit on you!'

Çöyder Hüseyin's face became patchy with embarrassment. He didn't know what to do. He hadn't been expecting such a thing, nobody had. He wiped his face with his sleeve and got up on his feet with a sudden, angry movement. And then he sat down again.

'Oh, so it's all my fault. Here I am talking to you and it's my fault for thinking of you, and for coming here without complaining about all the stones and mountains I've crossed. I come here asking after you. Are you trying to saying I'm lying, Perhan? Musa, Musa, come here! You can ask Musa here if I'm lying or not.'

Musa was in a world of his own and didn't seem to have heard any of what Çöyder Hüseyin was saying. Çöyder Hüseyin looked at him, but there was no support from Musa. He put the tin of conserved food back in his pocket. He took out the knife out of its sheath attached to his trousers and cleaned the blade by running it through his tightly pressed thumb and forefinger. Then he put it back in its place. Çöyder Hüseyin's eyes had all but disappeared into the dark sockets in which they were set. At that moment, it seemed that not only would a creak not have disturbed him, but the noise of the whole of the Hozat regiment rising up would not have made him stir from where he sat, perched half-on and half-off that stool. He was holding his breath, like a mountain goat that has paused, one foot in front of another, frozen. He looked as if he had pressed himself into the hollow of a tree or rock and was saying, 'come and take me.' He made a sniffling noise and pushed out his lips in a pout. It was as if the man who had laughed with pride and talked five minutes earlier of shooting the high-up government administrator and dragging his body around the villages was gone, and in his place now sat a little boy.

The room was so quiet that we could hear the sound of one of our sheep chewing its cud. Çöyder Hüseyin re-sheathed his knife and got to his feet, using the butt of his shotgun for support.

'Çöyder, Çöyder', said Perhan, 'you brought it all up, we were talking. If we don't talk this world will die of silence...'

'No, Perhan. I'm a man who has fought alongside Hıdır Efendi. All the seven worlds know the value that Hıdır Efendi placed on me. What can I say to this person who won't even give one field to a one-armed man? Hıdır Efendi was a man of great humanity. And how many times did he say to me, "In the whole of this Dersim, there's you and there's my brother Sahan. If it were not for you two then our Dersim would remain with its neck bowed." I mean, there is dying and there is treachery, but who has seen someone raise a hand to a woman in this Dersim of ours? You know, the government didn't understand this, Perhan. They thought they were up against Greeks and Armenians. They got it mixed up. They said to themselves, we'll do the same to the women as we've done to the men, we'll bring them to the military outposts and let them be entertainment for our soldiers. You know, I travelled the hard road with Hıdır Efendi for three days and three nights. For three days and nights he slept and I stood guard. For three days and nights we became each other's confidante and recognised each other as fellow travellers. It just wouldn't have worked, Perhan. If I'd have gone there too, if I'd have made it in time, do you think I could have rescued Hıdır Efendi? He couldn't have been saved. The infidels had set up a machine gun. And even if he had escaped, before you know it one of his own men would have cut off his head while he was sleeping, just like they did to Sahan and delivered it to the state. It's preferable to die, to die is righteous... I said it myself, did I not, I said treachery has befallen this Dersim, and above all, hunger has come. The infidel has identified our weakness and has left us to starve so that we end up eating each other, Perhan.'

As he spoke, he looked only at Perhan. It was as if there was no-one else there but Perhan. Some of his words gave me goosebumps and it was as if he'd drunk an enchanted draught of water because here and there his voice would go quiet and then louder, his eyes would appear and then disappear in their dark sockets. He was writhing in discomfort and you'd think a lion had been put in a cage and the world had come to watch the roaring lion in its helplessness. He was in extreme discomfort at his own state, as if he wanted to tear the cage to pieces and tear off into the forest, roaring. He'd stop and start, going on about the journey he'd made with my father, and the fate of the women he'd been mentioning.

All at once the tone of his voice dropped and he looked about him with a hopeless look, as if he were looking into an abyss. 'You know... you know, Perhan, for three days and nights I....'

'Ha! Tell me Perhan, Perhan, what does this demon want from me?' said my mother, 'Now what have I said to him? He's been nagging on without a break since this morning.'

But at that moment, Musa, who had been crouched down in a corner the whole time, suddenly rushed up out of his place and onto his feet. 'He's right. He's right from earth right up to heaven.' Sparks were flying from his eyes as he spoke. He took hold of his stump in its sleeve with his good hand and wagged it back and forth. 'The Great Creator has given everyone their burden to bear. If this arm of mine was normal and healthy, I wouldn't just sit and take all this.'

His wife Hece pushed her way out from under where all her children had heaped themselves on her and stood up. In her dress made from a goat hair sack she squared up to him, planting herself right at the end of Musa's nose.

'And what would you have done, eh? What was it you would have done, Alover?'

Musa took a step or two towards Perhan. 'Oh, Perhan, take this one away from me. You wouldn't understand. A woman's mind can't take everything in. But I'm right, aren't

I? The great world has been brought to ruins. Is it too much that I ask for a place to dig a grave? I mean, God has given everyone a problem of their own.'

'Musa, Musa, what do you want?' asked Perhan, 'Fecire Hatun has already said, "Let him bring the cow and he can have any field he wants."'

Musa didn't want to hear the words he'd just heard. 'Cow? The cow?'

He couldn't find any words for a moment and just kept repeating the word 'cow' a few times. He turned to the people in the room.

'I'm asking you. At this moment in time, is a human being worth any money? If you gave your best daughter, the most beautiful girl in the village, how many bushels of wheat would you get in return? And the wheat they'd give would be no better than stones and rocks. I'm asking you now, at this time, is a human being worth any money at all? But a cow! A cow, a cow is far and away above a person. A cow doesn't need clothing, cows don't die from being poisoned by foraged plants. Ah, look, Perhan! They're all ill and they can't stop their noses from running. You tell me, Goe. You'd have died, wouldn't you if it were not for my cow? If it weren't for my cow would anyone still be on their feet here in Dervişler village. I would even plough a field with her, but I can't bring myself to...'

While all this conversation was going on, Çöyder Hüseyin got up and left.

Everyone had forgotten him and it was only Perhan's daughter, Sede, and I who saw him leave. For a moment he looked into my eyes with an immense sorrow, but it was for such a short instant, it was as if his eyes peered out of their dark nests and looked into mine for a moment and he was remembering the time that he spent on those three days and nights, travelling with my father. It felt as if he wouldn't be coming back. As he walked off along the path that led into the forest, I felt as though he knew that Sede and I were watching him. As we listened to his footsteps, he disappeared behind the little hill...

XIX

Even though we had been given back our old home, my mother didn't want to go over to Weroz village. If it was up to her, she wanted to take everyone in Dervişler village with her. And, to be truthful, Dervişler was no place to live. As soon as winter came not a drop of sunlight reached the place, whereas Weroz was in full sunlight all day long. Once the wind blew, the blizzard would bring all the snow and heap it onto Dervişler, snowing everyone in. I, too, didn't want to leave all our neighbours and go back to Weroz, not one bit. Perhan, her daughters, Musa and the other neighbours – we were all a big family now. Even so, a week later we packed up and went to Weroz. Along with us came a woman called Geyik and her two children.

Before we'd arrived, my aunt had gone, and had moved into Veli Ağa's big house. This grand house was located on the opposite shore of the stream that bisected the village. It didn't get as much sunlight as our house. I'd never seen the place, not until my aunt's two children died that winter. However, it was almost as if I could see the children sitting around the fire at Veli Ağa's house every day, and its smoke rising from the chimney.

Weroz lived up to its name, which means 'sunny', and was set on an elevation that faced the sun. It saw the sun right through from morning until evening. We were now living on the ruins of the house that my father Hıdır Efendi had built a little higher up than the others. The soldiers had come and destroyed these houses and now we had nothing but a rough shelter on this rubble, topped with branches and scrub. Our neighbours from Dervişler had come with us and our sheep and had settled us into the makeshift house with their own hands, before going back on their way. Geyik and her two children also settled in one of the demolished houses. She had foraged so much plant material for winter supplies that she had far more bags and belongings than we did. The neighbours from Dervişler did not want her to move to Weroz.

I don't think Geyik's heart was really happy to have left Dervişler. She kept saying to herself, 'Well, mother-of-mine, the place gets enough sunshine. When winter comes, the snow-filled mountains will dump their contents on Dervişler in a blizzard. You can't even step outside. How will I keep all these children warm once winter comes? Honestly, I said it already, if we're going to die then let us die alongside Fecire Hatun. For sure, she will at least throw a few spadefuls of earth on top of us.'

Musa also helped us with moving our belongings. Geyik was settled into one of the demolished houses. People worked together to lift up and replace some of the fallen-down stones from the walls and all the scrub and branches that had been gathered up were placed on top. Geyik was happy with her new home. Even though Geyik had moved into this house, Musa set off every day from Dervişler and carried stones with his one arm and together, he and Geyik made a pathway so that it was easier to go in and out of the house.

He didn't speak to my mother, but even so he came to see us every day, lifting up his head and examining the house that my aunt had made. 'You need to weave in a bit of oak leaves over here, because when the rains start, this part will turn into a pool.'

Musa went, without anyone asking him to, and brought oak leaves. He would scatter them on the roof and then throw soil on top of them. On one occasion he asked my mother again for a field of his own in exchange for one of his goats.

My mother replied, 'Musa, Musa, if those fields were mine, I would tell you to take half of the village. But then, see, the pardon would come out and whichever poor person whose field that was would come back from exile and see that his field had been given away. And then what would I say?'

Musa set off again for Dervişler in a state of helplessness and he didn't return for a long time. And, of course, people started coming to see us as soon as they'd heard that Governor Fevzi had awarded all her lands back to my mother. And they all wanted to marry her. Men came from as far away as the villages of Pertek and Kirgan. And all of these people came riding upon oxen. I found the oxen they were riding on much more interesting than the people themselves. The eyes of the oxen were full of sorrow and hosts of flies had nested around the edges of their eyes. Thousands of tiny flies would sometimes rise up from the oxen and come and attack us instead. The oxen, exhausted from their journey, were always tied to a small walnut tree immediately to the western side of our house where they would eat clover that was stuffed into the nosebags put around their necks. A woman called Ceme would collect up their dung. According to my mother there was barley in ox pats. Ceme would wash the dung and pick out the barley that had sunk to the bottom.

Among my mother's new suitors was one by the name of Doğık. He was at least four fingers shorter than my mother and was dressed in brown trousers and a jacket, like a person who's lived in the city. Also, in line with city dwellers, he wore a hat. Doğık had once roamed the mountains along with Pirço's men and then for a while he'd been part of Sahan's outfit and then my father's. He was one of the people who took out an identity card in another name in 1936 and had enrolled for military service. He'd also learned Turkish whilst in the army. When he was speaking, he'd often sprinkle his conversation with Turkish words, to impress the people around him. After using one of these words, he'd add an explanation in the languages of Be-so and Here-were, as we called them, the languages of Zazaki and Kurdish. He thought this gave him more importance.

Because he had done his military service, Doğık was free to travel around the villages. After we'd moved to Weroz he'd come to the village once or twice a week and somehow find a way to try to get close to my mother.

As for my aunt, I could hear her voice, constantly, coming from the other side of the stream. I'd go out in front of our house and watch her. She looked like a ball of bramble, coming and going between the piles of ruined stones of Veli Ağa's house. I heard all her ramblings so many times that I could almost guess what she'd be saying in the morning, who she'd be talking about in the afternoon and who would feature at the end of those declamations in the evening. She even carried on ranting during her morning prayers in the sunshine, cursing someone or other.

'He took the very horse from under Rayber Sed Ağa and came all the way to my door. If you're going to bring a judgement to me, then don't come on the Rayber's horse and maybe I could call you a government official. He brought the whole army with him and came to my door, kicked me out of my own brother's house, Heko, Heko, how great you are. Ana Fatma, you who planted a fig tree in our hearth don't let the labour of Yusuf Ağa be ruined by a man who pitted two brothers against each other. Efe, my girl, why is your little brother crying, you're nothing but trouble, and what fault is it of mine, Sultan Baba, you didn't see fit to grant me a fistful of land? When you call so many servants before you, is it only me that you find so sinful?'

My aunt was the only one who lived over on that side of the river. Why did Veli Ağa build his house on that shady shore? While there was a sunny hillside over here, who would go and build a house on the northern shore of the stream?

My mother now had the government on her side. The great Governor Fevzi had come all the way to her feet, bringing his soldiers with him and he'd roared at the top of his voice to all the villagers knew that these villages belonged to my mother. An administrator of the state had crossed rocks and mountains on horseback to put a prize upon my mother's head and what is more, he'd come all the way to the feet of a woman whose husband was a bandit who had ridden roughshod over the government's soldiers and attacked their military outposts. My mother was an important person. She'd taken the refugee interpreter and gone all the way to the Deşt Regiment and had knocked on Governor Fevzi's door and gone inside. 'Governor Fevzi, Governor Fevzi, you've set the land on fire, abandoned the ones left behind to hunger, is this the greatness of the state?' she'd said. 'Should we women, also, take our guns and flee to the mountains?' and she'd struck Governor Fevzi's table with her hand. And Governor Fevzi had replied, 'Alright, Fecire Hatun, alright, the government has made a mistake.' Then he'd given her the key to the soldiers' provisions depot and said, 'Go! Open it! And take whatever you like.' And my mother had taken a sack of bread and handed it all out by the time she'd travelled from Deşt to Dervişler.

Since we came to Weroz, I'd heard so many things about my mother from the women there that sometimes even I believed them. It was almost as if I could see my mother banging on Governor Fevzi's door and opening it before hitting the table with both her hands. 'Come here, Gülizar', the women would say to me, 'and tell us what Governor Fevzi said when he saw your mother.' But I would run away immediately. I'd listen to what they said but would run away as soon as they asked me something. In 1938, when the villages were burned down, my mother had said to the villagers, 'Don't do anything, let's go to Erzincan, my brother there has signed an agreement with the state.' But no-one believed that Kahraman Bey had signed a contract with the state.

It was impossible to stop that thing we call time. The oak forests quickly began to turn yellow and the leaves of the black poplars began to turn reddish-purple. The whole summer has passed in the blink of an eye and the dark winter stood waiting at the door. Everyone was in a panic. We had to gather acorns. My mother set to work right away. As soon as the day began to warm up, we'd take our woven saddlebag and set off for the oak forests to gather acorns. We'd bring all the acorns we'd found back to our house and store them in a big hole we'd dug in the ground. One layer of acorns, one layer of soil, one layer of soil, one layer of acorns. In this way the acorns would sweeten underground and, if our food supply was to run out in winter, we'd be able to dig up these acorns and toast them in the ashes of the fire. People were important too. The higher the number of people, the better chances you had of getting through the winter. My mother brought a few more of our neighbours back to Weroz; those who had fled the village when trouble had come. Everything seemed to be going well. If we could get through this winter then a new life would begin next year and we'd be able to sow our share of the harvest, a huge bag of barley onto our fields. Perhan's daughters had dried an enormous amount of beetroot. According to my mother, we also had enough dried mushrooms, wild beetroot and knotweed to feed not just ourselves but ten people. Not to mention the buttermilk and dry cottage-cheese that we got from our sheep. As we sat by the fire in the evenings, my mother would start planning things out in her head, and telling what she would do.

'My Butterfly of the Night, tomorrow we will make knotweed soup,' she'd say, showing me the palm of her hand, 'and if we put this much dried cottage-cheese into it, we will be full all day long.'

We'd have baked our acorns in the fire's embers at night, peeled and eaten them. Here in Dersim, the jays and squirrels would survive all winter on acorns. A person who ate acorns, she'd say, wouldn't die easily.

When my mother started speaking like this, I'd remember the woman who live in my uncle Kahraman Bey's stable in Zeranik, who even made bread out of crushed acorns.

'But it's bitter, mummy,' I'd say, 'It's so bitter like this.'

'No, my girl, the earth will take the bitterness out of the acorns. The jay bird hides one acorn a day and he always knows which ones he hid first, to go back and find them one by one.'

The jays and squirrels would eat nothing but acorns all winter and jay birds never got sick from this sole source of food. And if only that Musa had come and moved here with us. That would have been good. Even though he wanted a field, the houses were ready, he could have moved into one and sow and reap any of the fields he wished. And what's more, he was a man, and to hear a man's voice about the place is better.

If you discounted his wife Hece, then there was no-one in the world like Musa. Even though my mother had said all those things to him, he still came and took our sheep to be served by the ram. The male race is merciful; but didn't they all fight against one another over one woman in this Dersim of ours? Weren't Seyit Riza's son, Baba, and Sed Ağa's son, Kopo Rayber, in love with the same woman? Wouldn't the whole world be a garden of roses without women? Was it not women that had brought evil to the world? There were women in Dervişler and they never argued. And yet, here in Weroz there were only three or five women and they were always at each other's throats. If a male voice was heard about the place, they might not argue constantly. According to my mother there should be a man at our head, even if he was disabled, it would be enough if his voice could be heard.

My mother and I would throw wood onto the fire and sit beside it in the house that my aunt had haphazardly thrown together. I'd cuddle up on my mother's knee and stare at the fire. My mother would talk, sometimes to herself and sometimes to me.

She'd talk to whoever came to her mind, sometimes addressing them as if they were there in front of us and sometimes as if she was calling to them. She told me lots of stories too, by this fire. Ones about the frog brothers, Alik and Fatik, and many more. And who didn't she talk about? Musa featured often, whether she was criticising him or praising him. Perhan was also in the wrong, for not having come here with us and also for having taken too large a share of our dried cottage-cheese. But she was still a very good woman, Perhan, saying, 'Take it, Fecire Hatun, this is rightfully yours from your sheep, you can give some to us if you wish, or you can not.' My mother took it and gave her all of it but Perhan said, 'No, that's too much.' As the householder, Perhan had never said, 'I only have a little bread.' She had always put all she had in front of her visitors and it would be wise for the visitor to remember this. But may God praise that woman, she opened her house to us and never once said to my mother, 'Sit here' or 'Don't sit there.' One day my mother had decided not to go gathering beetroot and still they gave their surplus of it to us. They were three people, Perhan and her daughters, they didn't have to share with us what they had foraged. Hece was a good woman too, for following her husband Musa over rocks and mountains. And despite her having four children she was tougher than a man all by herself. To think how she'd thrown herself in front of the soldiers like a hot coal from the fire to stop them from touching Musa. Have you ever seen a man like that? They start trembling for their lives in front of soldiers. The Commander of the soldiers had said himself, 'Musa, you are disabled, should the state take up a man like you and make problems for itself? You can't even hold a gun.'

But even so, he'd shaken and trembled on seeing those soldiers. He'd hidden behind his wife and not spoken a word.

As my mother recounted all this to me, I would stare into the fire in our hearth. Sometimes I would hear my mother's voice mix in with the flames and it would appear that the flames were talking and bickering with one another. Mostly, I would liken the flames in the fire to Musa as the flames appeared to have arms and hands and they'd flutter around like Musa's flapping sleeves. I used to love cuddling on my mother's knee and listening to stories like this, in front of our fire. I heard thousands of tales and hundreds of stories by that fire. When she'd said all she was going to say, my mother would cover over the fire's embers with ash and I'd see her mouthing in a stream of prayers. The embers would sit there under a layer of ash until morning, and then we would get up and throw some more wood on them. My mother also used to tell me a story about three siblings who went off in search of firewood, but, even though I tried hard to remember this story, it is still incomplete.

XX

It was another one of those stories from long ago where two people had been unable to love one another, someone had not listened to someone else, a woman had not known how to behave like a woman and a man hadn't known how to behave like a man. God looked and saw that his servants were unhappy and so he gave his fire to Sultan Baba Mountain. His fire burned for year upon year on Sultan Baba Mountain and could be seen from everywhere, and yet no-one could ever fetch the fire from the mountain and bring it back. In this story, the youngest sibling managed to take hold of the fire and bring it back to the people of the town. If you asked my mother, she'd say once the fire flared up, no-one could pass in front of it and that until it had died down it would burn to ash anything that sat in front of it. My great-grandfather had seen this fire that God had given to Sultan Baba Mountain.

It was difficult for me to understand how God's fire could have been stolen and given to Sultan Baba Mountain and my mother used to get cross with me, but I think it was because she didn't really know the real meaning herself. Whenever I asked, she would say, 'People oppressed one another and forgot how to love.'

'So will he light it again, mummy?' I'd ask.

'Who knows,' she'd say, 'who knows, perhaps he will light it again, my Butterfly.' Then she would stop and stare into space and it was as if she was speaking to the flames in the fireplace. 'He lit it, you know, he lit it, my beautiful girl. What more can he do? He lit it and nobody understood.'

One morning, as she was talking, we heard the sound of Musa. He was driving his cow in front of him and arrived in front of our house.

He opened the door and stuck his head in. 'Take it, Fecire Hatun, take it. You said you wanted to the cow so

I've brought it and come here with it. I said to Hece, "the cow is either ours or Fecire Hatun's. When the cow was ours, what happened? We shared all the milk out equally, didn't we?" We shared it all out and now I've brought the cow to you, Fecire Hatun, and if you like, don't even give me a palmful of earth. Just say to me "Musa, leave the cow and go, especially as you've upset me so much anyway, leave the cow and go", and I swear upon the pilgrimage place of Oriha Hıdır that I'll tie this pale beauty to your door and leave. I said to Hece, "Fecire Hatun's gone and it's just not the same in Dervişler.

"Girl," I said to my wife, "You can't understand it. If that Fecire Hatun is Süleyman Salih's daughter then she won't let us go hungry. She won't deny a sip of milk to our children." Take her, Fecire Hatun, see, I brought her. Now you can say "Musa, you've really upset me, leave the cow and go," and you'd better believe, and let my father in his black grave on Demenan Mountain be my witness, oh, I'll leave her here and go. Say it, Fecire Hatun. Don't give me anything if you like, tell that my cow isn't worth one village, and I'll still leave her here with you, this beauty of the world, my pale girl. I told my wife to shut up. "The men who've been marched into exile will come back and if they do, will it be so easy to find the door of a gentleman's house? Well, it's certain death. We'll die at Fecire Hatun's door." That great administrator got up and came right to her feet and said, "I apologise, Fecire Hatun, if it weren't for your grandfather, the Russian army would have entered Anatolia this way and exited it right on the other side.'

Musa talked on, one moment he was talking about Fecire Hatun's family line and the next he was explaining the bloodstock line of his cow, whom he called his 'pale girl.' He hugged her neck and wept and then repeated again all of her talents and just how precious was her milk.

'I mean, Fecire Hatun, if you only saw her milk, you'd think you had milked a pure Merino sheep, ahh, as soon as you milk her there's an inch of cream on the top. And she's so good-natured, that while she is grazing, you'd think that the Prophet Ali's horse, Duldul, has come down from on high. She's like the mountain goat on Sıncık Mountain, the way she chooses blades of grass one at a time, I've seen it with my own eyes, she won't graze the grass that the soldiers' feet have touched. What can I do, she wouldn't eat it. And she will climb up the banks and pick the buds of the purest flowers, just as goats do. Fecire Hatun, if you take her out grazing in the morning, somehow it's suddenly evening. How many times have I argued with Hece? And her milk smells of the Everlasting flower; just like the milk of the goats that graze on the Munzur meadows. I said, "Girl, Fecire Hatun will look after her better than we will. And she will surely see fit to give a pail of milk for my poor little children." Even if you give no more than a palmful of milk, it will be enough and we can make a soup of it mixed with foraged plants.'

We took the cow and went off with Musa to choose a crop field for him. However, he and my mother couldn't come to an agreement, they argued. Musa became angry and shouted at my mother one minute and took her by the hand the next. But my mother was determined.

'Musa, what more can I do? In exchange for an elderly cow, I am giving you the two best fields of the village. And yet you want the whole village.'

'Well, Fecire Hatun, are you trying to give me two parched fields in exchange for a cow? Fine, give me these two well-watered fields instead and I will say that you are a merciful woman. What I am to do with two dry fields? How will I be able to look Hece in the face?'

The bargaining between my mother and Musa took a very long time. At one point Musa took his cow and set off on the road to Dervişler, but then he came back. They went off to look at another piece of land, but still they couldn't come to an agreement. In the end he set off for Dervişler with his cow in tow, mumbling and complaining all the way.

'Worthy, everything in this Dersim is so worthy. If only the Paşa had wiped out all of the family line of these Ağas, if he had then we would have been saved from this suffering. They deserved it. I bring a great big cow right to your door and you give me a field that's bone dry and boiling with pebbles. I mean, if you were a proper human being you wouldn't have broken the heart of a poor helpless man.'

Musa was making off at such a trot, and shouting at the top of his voice as he went. 'The oppression of these Ağa's has brought these lands to ruin. The poorest of the poor have been oppressed because of their disagreements. If you had been a great man, you would have kissed the hem of his lordship Diyap Ağa and you wouldn't have caused bombs to be rained down on us because one man decided to stand up to all of the seven worlds. I mean to say, a great administrator of the state with his army marching in front of him, came all this way to give the keys to all the villages to a woman, and then he left again. Wherever I decide to take this pale girl, I'd get two villages, not just two fields...'

After all that, Musa turned up again two days later with his wife and two children. He and my mother came to an agreement. They also agreed that the first calf to be born of the cow was to belong to Musa and his family. And anyway, a cow is hardly likely to give birth to a bullock two years running. An ox was necessary too. It was essential to have an ox to be able to plough the fields. And the cow was to give birth in four months' time. Musa took three fields, one of which was quite parched.

He said to my mother, 'Fecire Hatun, if only you could see it, my pale girl is very fertile. As soon as we got to the hill hear Torut she began to run, and it seems that we had made the poor animal suffer by not allowing her to breed more often. If we'd taken her there earlier then my pale girl would have given birth to not one, but two calves within one year. She ran and presented her rear to the bull and I have to say, Fecire Hatun, that those refugees at Torut nearly hit the barn roof in their surprise. They said, "We're livestock owners ourselves and we've never seen an animal like her." They told me that they had difficulty giving their cows to the bull and that they put salt in the cow's vagina so that it would get inflamed and would be more easily inseminated. They also told me that if a cow went in such a docile way to the bull, that the calf would be a heifer.'

And so, along with our cow, we became a family of four. My mother had given away three crop fields and, in return, she had a cow. We immediately made a space for our cow in the corner of our house. We piled up the foraged plants we'd gathered in the back part of the house and we also had a stack of plants outside. Even so, these would not last us the whole winter. My mother made the women gather more plants of various kinds and she gave them a dish of milk in exchange for the plants that they brought her. The cow's milk would decrease in the winter, but it would still be enough for everyone. We hadn't even touched our sack of barley. If we could get through this winter then, next year, we would be able to benefit from nature's bounty and ten to fifteen sacks of barley would enter each and every house.

Musa moved into Uncle Veysel's house. According to my mother, Musa had enough food put by to feed an army and he just kept on bringing it over from Dervişler village.

The weather got cold very quickly. On the morning that the snows fell on the peak of Sıncık Mountain, all of the women and children from Dervişler village turned up at Weroz. Thieves had attacked Dervişler and sacked the village, taking everything that they could find. How could such a thing happen? With winter on our doorstep how could people behave like that? Had they no mercy? Those without enough food to get them through the winter had hit upon Dervişler village and taken every single thing from the village.

Who had done this? Where had they come from? According to Musa, no-one even had a gun in these parts any longer and the mountains were crawling with soldiers.

Last winter, half of the men and boys who had escaped death and the march into exile had died of starvation. After Dervişler village was raided, my mother piled even more logs against the back of the house. But just a few days later our house was set on fire and thieves stole everything we had, including our sheep and our cow. My mother and I managed to get away from the flames, but we were left with nothing. All of our hopes had gone. Everyone was crying about it, cursing and repeating what a terrible thing had happened.

The government had left the thieves hungry and they, in turn, had left us to starve. In this raid, it was only my aunt who was not affected. The thieves did not cross over to her side of the stream. And yet you'd think all this had happened to her and not to us, the way that she threw herself around on the threshing floor in the village, crying and wailing.

'That official, he came here with all his army to my door, why doesn't he go after these thieves then? I ask you, did we even know what thievery was in this Dersim before now? Everyone would leave their door open and go off into the back of beyond. Mother, mother, mother! As soon as that army came and went a heap of stones rained down on our heads and everyone became each other's enemy. Brothers fought brothers and that Paşa just sat there in Hozat with one leg crossed over the other. And you're a Paşa for goodness' sake, have you used your strength to benefit us? Did not your borders stretch over the whole seven worlds? And should we have to suffer all the losses you incurred? Oh mother, to think that three or four people can come in broad daylight and take everything away, take all of our livestock too.'

Musa, Geyik and the other women looked on at my aunt where she lay, collapsed, on the floor. My aunt said that, as my mother knew where all my father's guns were hidden, she should give one to her. And really, what more was there to do than to sing a lament and curse?

The suffering did not end there. The next day Geyik hung herself from a tree in the forest. I don't remember quite how we got news of it. Everyone began singing laments, wailing loudly and walking towards the place where Geyik had hung herself. We went along a path that my mother and I had used frequently before the soldiers had burned the village. There was a wild pear tree along the path that stretched off in a north-westerly direction towards Balıkan Mountain. Geyik had chosen this place, and the wild pear tree, to hang herself. Everyone was crying and the woods were so full of sadness that I imagined that the oaks, black poplars and wild pear trees that grew here and there were hanging their heads and crying for Geyik. Geyik's two small children were holding onto the hem of their mother's dress as she swung from the rope, staring at us approaching them with their empty eyes. I don't think they knew what death was yet. They seemed to be saying to their mother, 'Come on, mummy, come down from there and let's go home now.' The bark had come off the fork in the bough where Geyik had hung herself and her children were looking at the crying women in surprise, wondering what all the fuss was about. What had happened? Where had she found the rope? If you asked Musa, he always carried the rope with him. My mother had had more hope for Geyik once she had moved to Weroz. But Musa had heard her say to her children, when she was angry, 'First I'll kill you and then I'll kill myself.'

'I heard it with my own ears,' he said, 'I was out grazing my pale girl and I looked and saw Geyik. One minute she was gathering wild beetroot and the next she was talking away to herself, saying, "Sultan Baba, why do you not see it fit to just let us die? Take my children to your side, Sultan Baba, winter is coming, which mother can stand to see her child die in front of her eyes? Even the forests have dried up. Before, there used to be such great abundance here in these forests; you could find enough forage to feed a whole army." I heard this with my own ears,' he went on, 'and how many times?' I said to Hece, "Hece, my girl, give that woman a dish of milk, humanity is not dead." And she'd give her some milk. And now my cow, the pale girl's no longer with us either, for if she were still here, I'd say that Geyik could have all of her milk.'

We carried the body to the village. What would happen to her children? And what was going to happen to us? Winter was nearly upon us and we had nothing at all left to eat but acorns.

Once more, we starved. My mother heaped up some oak branches in a corner of our burned-out house and made a sort of bear den for us to crawl into. She closed up the hole with dried weeds. We had cold earth underneath us and I was so hungry that the bitterness of the acorns I ate gurgled in my stomach and echoed up and down inside me like an empty water pipe. The bitterness would repeat on me and travel back down again to my stomach. My mother would take out her breast, again and give it to me. ''Suckle', she'd say, 'suckle.' But there was nothing in those breasts. In the morning we went out to the forest looking for food and we set off along the path towards Balıkan Mountain, past the place where Geyik had hung herself. We saw Musa in the river bed. He was hacking at something with the axe held in his one hand.

'Fecire Hatun,' he said, 'I flushed it out but it's taken refuge in here. It's as big as a lamb.'

'What's that Musa,' asked my mother, 'a pine-marten?'

'A rabbit, Fecire Hatun, a rabbit. I know we're not supposed to eat them, they're forbidden and are dirty food, but after what we've been through...'

He struck the axe into the trunk of the tree. My mother grabbed a dried oak branch in her hand in excitement and poked it into the hole that Musa had been chopping at. But the rabbit suddenly sprang out and ran between the two of them, and escaped. Musa threw his axe to the ground, sweating profusely. 'I knew the damn thing would run away, I knew, but there was hope.'

We walked on further uphill and dug up some thistle roots to eat. In the forest we came across a tree that we called a weeping pear. The tree had lost its leaves but the branches were covered with tiny red fruits, the size a child's little finger. As soon as my mother saw the tree she was overcome with joy. 'Musa, Musa? Vialmuri! Vialmuri! A weeping pear!'

Musa hushed his voice, as if the tree might flee if it heard him. 'Really? Where, Fecire Hatun?'

We came to the base of the tree. Musa thrust his axe at the tree and tried to climb it with just his one arm. He tried once or twice, but each time he slipped and fell back down. He lost his temper and grabbed his axe, saying, 'Wait, Fecire Hatun, I'll fell the damn thing right here.' But my mother wouldn't be beaten and was able to climb up. She kicked at the branches with her feet and made the fruits come tumbling down. The fallen fruits disappeared underneath the dry oak leaves on the ground.

Musa called me, 'Come over to this side, Gülizar, don't tread on these leaves, all the fruit has come down here. Just don't step on the leaves, it's enough, and I will find every single one of those fruits.'

We sifted through every oak leaf with our hands and picked out each of the tiny fruits and put them in the little woven saddlebag that my mother always carried with her. Musa allowed me to eat just a few of them. After swallowing them your mouth felt as if you had really put a willow branch in your mouth and chewed on it. It left a very dry taste in your mouth. It was such an enchanted fruit that within moments your dry mouth would flow with juice that had turned into a honeyed paste.

We were going to boil up the acorns and pour off their bitter juice before mixing them with some of these willow pears and reboiling them.

As we walked along the road, Musa said to my mother, 'Fecire Hatun, the bans have been lifted. Now men are allowed to travel around.'

'No, Musa,' my mother soon, 'No-one can travel anywhere without written papers from the state.'

'Well, that's what I heard,' Musa said, 'They told me when I took the cow and sheep over to Torut. There's freedom to roam again, I heard.'

XXI

We got ready to leave. We were going to go and take Perhan and her daughters with us. We had no idea of where we were heading. But we had to leave before the snows came. As we were making our plans to depart, my uncle Kahraman Bey turned up. He arrived with loaded pack horses, an ox cart full of provisions and about twenty men. This is how we found out that Musa had been right about the restrictions on movement, enforced for the last three years, finally being lifted. In fact, women had always been allowed to move freely and also those who had secured permission from the military authorities. But it had been forbidden for men to travel together in small groups or to go from village to village. My uncle Kahraman had heard that we'd all been robbed, and so as soon as the ban was lifted, he came with all his men. Along with them came my uncle's son, Ağa Cihan, who was ten or eleven years old.

 My uncle came, bringing with him loaded carts full of the provisions that had been collected for the villagers of Erzincan after the earthquake in 1939. They were distributing these goods between all the villages as they went. And what was not among the provisions that they handed out?

 The men of the villages of Ovacık and Erzincan that were under the control of my uncle Kahraman Salih Bey had been going round the villages, as soon as the ban was lifted, with their axes and saws and were building new homes for people. The men who came to Weroz with my uncle, came with ox carts to which were tied axes, sledgehammers and saws.

 It was then that I first understood why my mother had thought it a good thing for us to have men about the place. As soon as they arrived, the men set to work on restoring the houses. Stones were being chosen to build the walls, to the sounds of axes thumping in the forest and great tree trunks began to appear in front of the houses.

As all this was going on, my uncle Kahraman called everyone to the square in the village and began to give out food and clothing.

My uncle's son Ağa took off the rough hair sack I'd been wearing and dressed me in clothes that he had put aside for me. He took out some red and blue sweets from his pocket and put them in my palm. It was obvious that he'd hidden these away to give to me. He even tried to comb my hair.

'Do you recognise me?' he asked. I nodded my head in a 'yes.' My new clothes were beautiful. I had a jumper with white and yellow stripes on it, a thick pair of velvet trousers, a green cardigan and a fur-lined parka coat. It was the first time I'd ever worn clothes like these. The clothes had been worn before, and there was a burn mark on the sleeve of the coat.

After the clothes had been unloaded from the carts and horses, next the wheat, rice, bulgar wheat and flour was taken down and distributed. There were supplies for Dervişler village too. Everyone had forgotten about my aunt. But when we heard shouting coming from the other side of the stream, my uncle Kahraman Salih Bey told Musa to go and fetch her. He did so, but she didn't want to take anything. She turned around and sat down with her back to the things that were offered to her. She told them that my mother had brought the government offical right to her door.

My uncle went up to my aunt, Wae, and said, 'You are almost a sister to me, as I have an obligation to the family of Yusuf Ağa... now is not the time for arguments...'

My uncle and his men stayed for two days at Weroz. In the blink of an eye, they had repaired our house as good as new. What's more, it now resembled a real house. They shored up the other houses too and brought them into a habitable state.

Our new house had two separate parts, one of which was for the animals. It even had holes for windows. These were now filled up with stones, but as soon as winter was over my uncle was going to send his men to fit real windows. On top of the thick stone walls of our new house were planks from the widest of the oak trees that had been felled. Our hearth was still in the same place and was the original fireplace. All but the other walls had been newly built. A sturdy new oak door was fitted to where the old, burned door had stood. This new door was so heavy that I couldn't even move it by myself. When evening came, we would shut this door and secure it further with another solid piece of wood on the inside.

The house was separated in two parts by a wooden partition and we were going to have to plaster the walls with mud. There was certainly soil in abundance and all we'd have to do would be to mix it with water and apply a few coats to the walls. We placed our dried forage and the food that my uncle had given us in this rear part of the house. Now, nobody could set fire to our house from the back. The windows were filled in with stones and my mother had taken yet another precaution. We also had a gun hidden inside the house. The old burnt door had been used in the doorway joining the two rooms. We also had firewood to burn during the winter. There were actually fresh oak logs, but by the time we'd have burned the foremost ones, the ones at the back would have dried to tinder.

My mother told me that, afterwards, my uncle had tried to convince her that he should take us with him to Zeranik. He'd said to my mother, 'Come. We've divided up the land and you can come and eat whatever we eat, with us.' My cousin Ağa had been very moved and had cried, at that age even, and had begged his aunt. But my mother instead asked that she be given a cow. 'Tell your father, I am very grateful to him, and Sultan Baba should likewise be satisfied, but if he wants to give me a cow, then let him do so.'

I think that in all the commotion of the building of our new house, I missed hearing these conversations. But afterwards, whenever my mother complained about all that we were going through she'd say, 'God, how many times did he turn his face to me? He invited me and I didn't go. If we had gone with your uncle to Zeranik that winter, we never would have suffered all of this.'

Another thing happened on the day that my uncle Kahraman's men came and repaired our house. Çöyder Hüseyin appeared again, out of nowhere like a whirlwind. He now only had two guns instead of three. One of them was strung diagonally across his back and the other, five-cartridge shotgun, was in his hand. He studied the men who were repairing the houses, looking them up and down. The men stopped working and looked at Çöyder Hüseyin. He went to sit with my uncle, Kahraman Salih Bey, on the rocky outcrop above our house. They talked and talked for half a day on the rocks where my mother and I had so often sat.

People told me that my uncle had said, 'Çöyder, there's no end to this business. Why don't you come with me and I'll turn you in myself at Erzincan?' But no matter what my uncle said, Çöyder wouldn't accept it.

My uncle gave Çöyder a parka coat belonging to one of the workmen and a sack of flour. They covered over the roof of another of the demolished houses and Çöyder's younger sister, Serayi, and her little girl, who had both escaped during the troubles of 1938 came and moved into the house. No-one knew where Serayi had come from. I think she'd been hidden in a nearby village up until then.

Serayi was tall, just like Çöyder Hüseyin and had even smaller eyes than he did. She sorted through every piece of clothing that my uncle had brought and took some men's clothing from among them.

Once as my uncle had gone, he sent Ali Hüseyin with some more supplies for us. And in those times of great shortage my uncle bought a cow in Erzincan and sent it to us.

There was a large quantity of clothing on the ox cart that Ali Hüseyin was riding. 'Mother,' he said, 'These are the items that were collected for the victims of the Erzincan earthquake. There are clothes here that have come all the way from the Soviet Union and from America. The world is in turmoil. If it weren't for the world war, we'd be drowning in donations for the earthquake victims.'

There was a war on. A man called Hitler had burned and destroyed everywhere. If it weren't for him, perhaps Dersim wouldn't have been burned either.

On hearing these words my aunt said, 'Brother, my brother, you've seen Erzincan and no more, and you'd think that the President of the Republic had sent tidings of the whole world to you.'

'That's how it is, mother. The whole world is talking about Hitler right now. What's this Dersim in comparison, if only you saw it, the man has gone in at one end of the earth and come out at the other.'

'Brother,' my mother said, 'is he setting crop fields on fire too?'

Ali Hüseyin turned to my mother and replied, 'Mother, he is burning them. And how! This Dersim is nothing in comparison.'

'Let him burn them!' my aunt said, 'let him burn them too, let him burn them that this fire here burns them in turn.'

Ali Hüseyin didn't understand what my aunt meant by this. 'Why do you think they would burn, mother? He just sits in his palace and gives orders.'

'So does the Paşa,' my aunt replied.

Ali Hüseyin looked around him. 'Don't say that, mother. Say what you like, but don't talk about the government or say anything about the Paşa.'

'And why is that?' she asked. 'My father ran the whole of this Bactrian region and not one person had so much as a nosebleed. What good is it to sit in a palace, does it suit a leader to sit in a palace and give orders from there? Give them to me, brother, let me have my things and I'll go.'

Ali Hüseyin gave my aunt the things my uncle had sent to her, she took them and left. My aunt and my mother were still not talking but my aunt was often hanging around the houses near ours, and talking.

The white snows up on the peak of Sıncık Mountain crept a little further downhill each day. A few days later, Perhan and her daughters moved from Dervişler village to come and live with us. Everyone had been able to get rid of their old sack-cloth outfits and to wear new clothes. When I saw Perhan's two daughters I didn't recognise them. They had cut up their new dresses and re-sewn them in Dersim's traditional style. Their new dresses suited them so much that when we first stood opposite one-another we could do nothing but stare and giggle.

Goe said, 'Sede, my sister, Gülizar doesn't recognise us. It's us, Butterfly, it's us, little insect. How beautiful you look. If only you'd told your uncle to bring you a yellow skirt...'

I took them by the hand, led them inside and showed them the sacks of flour and bulgur. 'They're all ours,' I said, showing them the sack of wheat, 'and this one is seeds that we'll sow on the fields next year.' Then I took the girls to show them my clothes. Now I had two pairs of shoes. When one of them wore out I would be able to wear the others.

My mother was extremely happy that Perhan and family had come. 'Perhan, it's a big house. And I stayed with you. We've got everything here, and we even had two rolls of canvas. We can cut it and make beds and furniture out of it. I have gathered a sack of dried willow leaves, the whole area's full of dry plants. We can gather them up and fill the canvas, and if you feel it, you'd think it was stuffed with cotton. We can make quilts in the same way.'

In this way Perhan and her daughters moved into our house for the winter.

'Perhan, my mother said, 'now you're here, it's not only thieves who'll be scared to come close; not even a hungry wolf would dare pass near Weroz village. When you put that on top of it, really, this house is like a castle, that's what the master builders said. They said, "Fecire Hatun, Pertek Castle might fall down but this grand house of yours will never crumble." And if you could only see it, they covered the roof with a metre of soil as well.'

'What a shame, what a shame for this house.' Perhan said, 'What it really needs is glass windows. Fecire Hatun, if you and I have each other's backs, then it's not only thieves we could hold off; the whole of Abdullah Paşa's army could rise up and stream down upon us and they'd never get us out of this house.'

My mother began to get excited. 'They couldn't throw us of our here, Perhan. And we have a cow as well. A cow that's with calf! It's such a cow. My brother chose and sent the finest one he could find. Its milk is enough to share with the whole of this Bactrian region.'

Perhan was amazed as she looked around the house. We'd been living in a shack in Dervişler. 'Fecire Hatun?'

'Yes, Perhan?'

'What a shame for this house. They told me and I didn't believe them. This isn't a house, it's a mansion. And what's more, it's Olbeg Bey's mansion. They say it had glass windows and was finer even than Seyit Riza's fine house. If we put glass in these windows, it will be seen from as far away as Hozat.'

'Yes, it will,' my mother said, 'There used to be a two-storey mansion here. If you went out onto the terrace of that mansion, you'd think you were looking out from Sıncık Mountain all the way to Demenan Mountains, it was so spacious.'

My mother took down a half-burned piece of wood from above the hearth and showed it to Perhan. 'See, every piece of wood in the house was as ornamental as this one. Hold it near the fire, can you see? There were mountain goats carved on it, and cranes with their wings spread, flying. Keyrok, the Armenian, spent a whole year carving these in this house. As soon as the master builders spotted them, they pointed them out to Kahraman Salih Bey, saying, "Give them to your sister, they will be a souvenir for her of her husband, she can hang them somewhere."

'Fecire Hatun,' Perhan said, 'Is there anyone in this whole Dersim who doesn't know of Hıdır Efendi's mansion? Kopo Rayber had a mansion too, at Haçeli. Those who saw it would walk past, holding their breath, in front of that place. My father used to tell me, the interior was as large as two threshing floors and each floor exceeded the height of three men. There were murals from end to end on the plastered walls. The master painters had depicted all of the tales and legends there. My late father used to say that you couldn't take them all in in just one day. Lines from the Koran, the Bible and the Torah were painted in between the pictures.'

'That's right, Perhan, and it can be so again. Just let's get through this winter and you'll see. The state has now allowed free movement. Once people can move freely, do you think they will starve? No, they won't. What hit us hardest was this ban on movement, not the exiles and not death. It was this restriction that hurt us the most. Has this Dersim of ours not fallen three times already? And was it not built up again from scratch three times? It was. When Kochgiri was hit, did your father not go there?'

'He did. He went.'

'And they didn't allow a single person to leave. It's this ban that has caused our suffering, Perhan, and once it's lifted there will be no more death and tomorrow, or soon after, those who were in exile will return.'

In order to stop the heat from escaping our house in winter, Perhan, her daughters and my mother thoroughly plastered the wooden partition inside with wet mud paste. We sewed the canvas sheeting and made real beds of it. Perhan found a huge window frame from somewhere and brought it home. The stones were taken out of the window casing and the frame was fitted. This window was the most beautiful thing, because it allowed the daylight to enter our home which had been formerly lit by the fire in our hearth alone. Previously, my mother and I had bedded down among the dried heap of plants and here we now had beds so good that we didn't miss the real thing.

XXII

While all these preparations were going on, the government started a new round of forced exile. However, this time wasn't like the last. Governor Fevzi came, as well as Fatma Hanım, the one who had gathered up the children. There were a lot of officials with them. They spent ages explaining it all to us. Because the government had our best interests in mind, it was sending us to Çorum. There were ready-built houses there. They were houses left behind by the Greeks after they fled and were built well enough to keep out the cold and the snow. The government had filled these houses with provisions, from wood and coal to food and clothing – everything to get you through the winter.

They inspected our identity cards, one by one. My uncle had registered my mother's name as 'Fede Güzel' on hers. The transportation papers had been issued in the name of 'Fecire' but there was no 'Fecire' among the names on the identity cards they collected that day. Çöyder Hüseyin's sister, Serayi, didn't even have an ID card.

Governor Fevzi spoke through the interpreter, 'Ask her. What has she done with her identity card?'

Serayi replied, 'Tell him. Tell him I don't have one. But let them take my daughter and I.'

'That's not possible,' Governor Fevzi said. Later he made an announcement to everyone, telling them that he had had no part to play in ordering the transportation.

'We have had this list in our possession for five years. We can't make these decisions ourselves. I know well enough that Fede Güzel is Fecire Güzel but the government has asked for Fede Güzel and not Fecire.'

Governor Fevzi gave Serayi a report card that he had filled out in place of an identity card. He also registered her daughter. Governor Fevzi had no idea that she was Çöyder Hüseyin's sister.

In this way, my aunt and another woman, whose name I can't remember, were taken off for transportation. There were a lot of people from villages such as Dervişler, Elkaji, Malmes, Sovge, Xerbo and others who were sent into exile that cold autumn in 1940. Many of these people had escaped from the previous transportation convoys. All of the lines of people were brought together and they set off in the direction of Elazig. My aunt managed to escape the convoy with her children near the village of Pertek, and back she came to the village.

This new round of transportations sent Çöyder Hüseyin into a rage. He was seen almost every day in Weroz. He'd come into the village and the soldiers would go out. The soldiers would enter the village and Çöyder would leave.

He'd shout at the top of his voice, 'I mean to say, Musa! You are from Demenan, you'll know. Has this government ever been one you can trust? They wait until the whole summer is over and, when winter is at the door, they take out the old lists they've been hiding and say, "the government wants this and this." Does this state know only oppression? I mean, does this state work only for oppression? I mean, I have a thousand of the state's men on my tail, a thousand of its eyes are trained on my every footprint. And, after all, I am Hüseyin-e Çöyder. I know how to finish off an army that's on the trail of one man up in the mountains. Just as a cat plays with a mouse, it's easy to ride around with a horse underneath you that belonged to Rayber-e Sed Ağa.'

My mother was the one who was most furious at Çöyder's appearing in the village in daytime like this. 'Perhan, Perhan, tell him. Tell him not to go bawling around the village like a Kemah donkey. Serayi, sister, tell him, what does he want from us? Whatever trouble he has, let him take it upon his own head and clear off from here.'

Çöyder Hüseyin and my mother were still fighting like two cockerels at every opportunity.

'Hahaha, Perhan, far from it! Tell her, I'm far from being a Kemah donkey. They get fed with barley and lay in a warm stable. How many people are there in this Dersim who can find a warm stable in which to lay their heads? I mean, the Kemah donkey is a Sultan in Paradise in comparison to us and what we're living. I know as well, how to make a saint of myself, and sit with one leg crossed over the other.'

'Çöyder, Çöyder,' Perhan said, 'if that donkey is a Sultan in Paradise, then you are Sultan of these mountains. Look at all these women who've dropped everything and come to see you as soon as they heard your voice in the village.'

'And come they shall, Perhan. If their husbands had not put their hands up and surrendered to Abdullah Paşa then they wouldn't be missing a man's voice like this. The honour of Bactria is at stake, and the Great Creator has made it my job to pick it up from the floor and raise it high.'

Perhan invited Çöyder to our house. But as Çöyder wasn't expecting such an invitation he hesitated for a moment.

Perhan said to my mother, 'Fecire Hatun, tell him he can come in. Look at how he's shaking with cold, he's come to get warm.'

'The house is over there', my mother said, 'If he wants to go, let him go. Nobody's telling him to do this and do that, anyway.'

'See, Çöyder,' Perhan said, 'Fecire Hatun is saying, "Let him go in and get warm, don't let him stay out in the cold."'

Çöyder laughed, a loud belly laugh. 'Well, Perhan, do you think I don't have a house to go to? If I went to Abashan village over there they'd open their doors wide to me. Kahraman Bey himself said to me, "Come. Come and be my guest." If I went to Kirgan over there, there too all the doors would be open to their widest. I mean, I was born here, my father was born her, and his father was born here. All seven sides of this Balıkan Mountain bore witness to my mother's birthing cries. I know for a fact, that when a person's death is near, they get the smell of the soil of their birthplace in their nostrils, they long for home. You know, when they shot Aleydar, his wound didn't start bleeding until he was on home soil. The Great Creator has provided a death for every person. You have to know how to die. And that's enough, as long as your ashes don't fall into enemy hands.'

My mother looked at Çöyder Hüseyin from underneath her brow, her hands pushed into her armpits to keep them warm. 'Anyone who heard him would think that he was descended from the Prophet's stock, mother-of-mine! His father was hounded out of Kureyşanlı, they kicked him out. And Yusuf Ağa gave him some land at Emirhan River.'

'I mean, I don't need anybody's house, Perhan. Ha! And I have a sister who's as great as a mountain. Serayi, my girl. If you didn't have that child, I'd have taken you with me and we'd have gone in through this here Dersim and come out via Koçgiri. You know, this Serayi, she shot a flying crane in the leg. And I don't mean to say that she's better than you, Perhan, but she could even make a sparrowhawk fall out of a black cloud in the blink of an eye. Girl, Serayi, if this brother of yours happens to die, please don't get upset – it's death. Once you know death, you know it's small. As with Geyik, she went and hung herself from a dried-up pear tree. That too is a death, but treachery is terrible. Treachery is what really confounds a person. It was treachery that took Seyit Riza to the gallows. And a man who was the same age as Seyit Riza's son knew someone who remembers him being born. And what was it that drove that beautiful person of this world, to commit treachery, to make him come and cut off the great Alisher Efendi's head. He cut it off and then went to pieces from the pain of it all, and died. You know, Perhan, if there was no treachery there would be no death in these mountains.'

Çöyder Hüseyin was talking in a strange way. It was as if he was about to go very far away and would never be coming back. It was as if he was saying goodbye.

'Girl, Serayi, girl, be calm within. Look, the whole army came here and no-one remembered your name. You know, there's this, and there's treachery. In this Dersim, after God comes woman. I mean, you should discount the sins of a woman. Even if a woman gives you poison you should drink it, imagining that it is the bubbling water of heaven's Zamzam well. You know, Perhan, tell her not to panic. The Raybers may have fought with the wise men but what she'll be going through is discomfort of the soul. I mean, a person speaks out of pain and if their pain can't be expressed out loud then they go mad, just like poor Geyik. She didn't talk. Had she talked, she could have warded off death. What I mean, Perhan, is tell her that I know a thing or two, I mean, the Great Creator sought to spare me that day...'

When my mother heard these words from Çöyder Hüseyin's mouth, she flew out from where she'd been sheltering on the threshold of our house and stood right under his nose.

'Perhan, this bastard is going to cause problems for us. Get up, you lying devil, get up. Get up and clear off before you land these poor wretches in trouble. Get up and go and do whatever you have to do somewhere else.'

Çöyder's eye twinkled brightly and he smiled. 'Well, Perhan, tell her to hit me. Tell her to hit me while her hand is raised like that and whether she hits me or not, tell her to hit me again, hahaha. I mean, is she the one to decide where I shall and shall not go?'

My mother was moving around Çöyder in circles, striking her knees. 'My Serayi,' she said, 'Tell this dog to get up and go. Whatever he's going to do, let him do it someplace else. All I'm saying is that he comes here every day and shouts his head off in the middle of the village... that's what I'm saying...' Without finishing what she was trying to say she struck her knees again, 'Ooh! Oh, this demon will cause a whole load of trouble for us in the dead of winter. Let him stay then, let him stay and our case will come up on Judgement Day. Let him stay, Sultan Baba, but why would you send us this demon to make more problems for us?"

Çöyder Hüseyin laughed deeply, as if he had somehow won a great victory. 'Well, Perhan, you tell me. Would you take out lists that you've had hidden away and take all of these women and children off into exile in the dead of winter? Would you ride around on Rayber Sed Ağa's horse and cross off one name at a time? I mean, people are in a sorry state already. People have fallen so far. You should bear that in mind... I mean, should this kind of thing happen?'

'Clear off! Get out of here, you demon. If you don't go, I'll crush your head with this rock!'

Çöyder Hüseyin ran to a rock and put his head on it. 'Crush it! Crush it! If you are the daughter of that man of high blood, Süleyman Salih Bey, then crush it, do it and I will call you the mother of the poor!'

My mother threw the stone she'd picked up back on the ground. 'If you'd been a man, you wouldn't have gone all the way to raid that village near Erzurum with Pirço's son, Hıdır, and brought him back. You wouldn't have accustomed that dog's mouth to blood, had you been a real man.'

'Well, I went. I'm not going to say I didn't go. At least I didn't rob the poor here of their very livelihood, stripping them of everything. I went and put a rope around his neck and brought him here, a Captain in the state's army. I brought him here and paraded him from village to village. In other words, I reduced the mighty Paşa of the state to a worthless scrap.'

My mother had turned her back and was heading to the door to our house. But at these words she dashed straight back. 'Ha! Shame on you! Let me go, Musa, let me spit in the face of this lying devil. He was a Captain, that man, oh mother-of-mine! They took that poor soldier and brought him here. And the whole of Dersim rose up in outrage, saying what a shameful thing it was and asking them to let him go. The rocks and mountains here wept for him, that poor soldier. Wept! And this demon puffed out his chest in pride as if he had captured Abdullah Paşa's aide de camp...'

Musa butted in, 'Alright, Fecire Hatun, that's enough. Çöyder's a poor soul too, without even a dry stone on which to rest his head. Let him speak.'

After that, Çöyder Hüseyin really went over the edge. He travelled all the way down to near the Hozat Regiment and got the army onto his trail before heading back this way. Everyone was holding their breath and waiting.

'You know, you shouldn't have done it, Fecire Hatun,' Musa said. 'Çöyder won't be able to take on the army. I'm worried that he'll bring trouble upon you; he'll bring trouble and these children will be left all alone.'

Just as we were expecting the snow, the sun came out and shone for a few days. If Çöyder Hüseyin came down a hill, the army would go up another. Çöyder would come and go around the outskirts of the village but he never came in. If you asked my mother's opinion, he was hiding in the willow scrub in the evenings and sleeping there. He was thirsty for his own blood, my mother would say. One evening, before the cold autumn sun had slipped down over the hilltops, this silence was broken. As the soldiers, who had followed Çöyder Hüseyin up Balıkan Mountain, were making their way back down the mountain, they set an ambush for Çöyder at the river where my father had been shot. The voices of the soldiers, shouting, filled the whole village and a few soldiers ran up to Weroz. The women made hand signals to tell the soldiers that he'd escaped in the direction of Torut. A short while later we heard the sounds of Çöyder's rifles. Then he appeared at the top of a hill and shouted in Zazaki, 'Heyt, Usen-e Çöyder, Alo Bom's son,

Heyt! hey! Duwa-duwa, come! Come! Heyt!' Now and then came the sound of his five-cartridge rifle and the sound of the mauser whistled through the air.

When the light got worse Çöyder Hüseyin came to the village. He was still reading the riot act to everyone. I don't know if he could see us looking at him. It was so hard to make out his face.

Next to his carrysack swung a pair of soldiers' boots. He threw them down in front of Musa. 'Take them Musa. You have a right to these. Take them!'

But at that moment, it wasn't only Musa who couldn't move to take the soldier's boots. We were all so stunned we couldn't even think.

'Take them, Musa! Take them! You have as much right to them as you did to your mother's snow-white milk.'

Çöyder was walking around the village square in a great panic and anyone who saw him would think that he was a horse, whose neck was sweating profusely in the heat of summer, just having come back from the harvest. He couldn't keep still. He'd turn this way and that, as if he didn't know what to do, and then he'd run from one end of the square to the other.

'You know, I spent three days and three nights with Hıdır Efendi, on the road together. Musa, take these boots and put them on. Take a look and see what kind of boots the infidels made for their army.' He struck a stone with the pair of soldier's boots that he was wearing himself, saying,

'The infidel knows the business. They've put iron in the toe-cap. They put it in so that they can crush the poor all the better. It's like saying, Musa, take that wise and learned man, my soul brother, Hıdır Efendi, cut off his head and take it, take it and place it on the upright where they displayed the head of his brother Sahan, that mountain eagle. And you would say, 'Look, how I've cut off their heads. And I'm displaying them here, and how they fled here and there like partridge chicks on hearing the sound of a shotgun. Come,

Perhan, come. And you too, Wae. Come, come, your brother's blood is no longer on the floor. May the seven realms hear me, tell Abdullah Paşa too, tell him that the blood of Sahan Ağa and that learned man, Hıdır Efendi, is no longer on the ground. Tell him to come and get his reward. Tell him not to worry about the head of his commander. I hung it from a beech tree on the Hozat road. Hahaha... so, tell him, Hüseyin-e Çöyder says, "we've learned from you how to cut off the head of a dead man, so here, take this as your medal."'

Nobody spoke. Çöyder Hüseyin's anger still hadn't subsided and he was bellowing like a bull. It looked as if real flames were shooting out of his eyes, which were lost in their dark pits.

Now and then, as he spoke, he addressed my aunt. 'Wae, the blood of your brothers is no longer on the ground. Girl, Serayi, you hear this too. Don't be afraid. If it weren't for this child, I'd take you along with me and we'd roam around the whole of Dersim from village to village. The thing is, if you can't use your strength to fight the state, why would you rob from the poor around you?'

He fished into his woven saddle bag for a tin of conserved food that he'd taken off one of the dead soldiers and threw it into the middle of the threshing floor in the square. 'Here you go. Food from the mouth of the lion. Everyone takes from the mouths of the poor. The state took from you, didn't they? They set fire to your fields, gathered up your livestock and took them away? Didn't they? Why did they take them? So that you'd eat each other. Let the those born of dogs eat one another, they said.'

He stopped and got his breath back. He opened his tiny eyes as if he were dispersing a black cloud, but then he continued to bellow, 'You know, there should be honour among people. I mean, when did you ever expect mercy from the state? There was some compassion, many years ago. When did you ever see a woman get up in public and spit at someone? Oh, that prize of the world, that learned man, Hıdır Efendi, whose head was cut off, my dear fellow traveller. Three days and three nights I travelled with him, Hıdır Efendi...'

He stopped. He stopped as if he had said something bad.

Pointing to my aunt he said, 'And you, you sent that great man Kahraman Bey's sister all the way to the government's gate. You sent this woman off in front of you and you watched her from behind as she walked away. And you said once, "We shouldn't let the granddaughter of Süleyman Salih Bey into Bactria."'

He stopped again and sought out my mother with his empty eyes. He looked at me, where I stood among the others in the doorway, with such sad eyes, as if he were expecting pity of me.

'You know, Perhan, I put my hand on this food here and say that I swore a vow up on top of Sıncık Mountain. I said, "I was not there." Hıdır Efendi fell into an ambush whilst I was up on Balıkan Mountain. I mean, this Dersim has turned against itself with so many lies, with people trying to wipe each other's line out. They came and came to this Serayi of mine, who I've always known as a true, life-long sister of mine, came to her and to Fecire Hatun, sister of Hıdır Efendi with whom I shared the road for three days and nights; the people of Dersim came and said to them both, "Hüseyin-e Çöyder is over there in the woods, but he hasn't reached for his gun yet." I mean, Perhan, this sister Serayi of mine knows, and she is now under your care, that I didn't get as upset when my own father was killed, or when my mother, that beauty of the world, my mother was killed. You know, I am human too. Why would I go and kill those poor soldiers? Why would I cut off that spawn of a dog's head and hang it from that beech tree?'

He stopped again. He was waiting for my mother to come forward, out of the house. Waiting for her to say, 'It's alright, Çöyder, I got angry too. I did it, but there's no reason for you to do it. Who hasn't become angry with someone now and then, is anyone without sin?' But my mother couldn't speak. It was as if the ground had opened up and swallowed her. Perhaps she could hear what was being said but she didn't once put her head out of the darkened doorway and look at Çöyder Hüseyin.

Çöyder collapsed in a heap where he stood, just like a little child. As he fell his hand involuntarily went into his saddlebag that he'd filled with soldiers' provisions. He looked at the soldier's helmet that rested on the floor in front of him, a few paces away. He was worn out, and full of torment. There was a short period of silence. The air around us had the chill of snow.

It looked as if there were nothing left of the Çöyder Hüseyin who'd been bellowing around the square some five minutes earlier, taking on the world.

'Musa?' he said.

'Yes, Wusen?' Musa answered.

'Give me a hand here. I'll carry these weapons as far as that ridge over there... The army will be here tomorrow, breathing down your necks...'

XXIII

Life was merciless in its dealings with us. How quickly the winter had come and how fast the mountains had surrendered themselves to the snow. And why was my aunt's voice, floating from the other side of the stream, so wild? And everything that was driven from blizzard-cloaked Sıncık Mountain and Balıkan Mountain found its way to our doors. Would this pitiless wind never drop? Would it ever drop that we might understand the words my aunt was screaming?

Perhan's daughter, Goe, said, 'Auntie Fecire, I can hear a voice. Sede, did you hear it?'

The little window in our recessed wall was blocked up with snow. We gathered around the window. Perhan went to the door. She got the door ajar but it slammed again. As soon as the doors were opened the wind would blow snow that had drifted there right into the houses. Perhan closed the door again, very tightly.

'Well, I'll be blessed, it seems she's gone mad.'

Goe stuck her head into the recess of the little window, 'Quiet a minute, mother. Well yes, it is your aunt's voice. Did you hear it, Sede? That's your aunt's voice.'

We all went quiet so that we could more clearly hear the voice. Goe spoke again, 'Yes, it is your aunt's voice. She's crying for help.'

The voice that sounded as though it was coming out of a deep well was indeed that of my aunt. It was as though it was not my aunt but the wind itself as it hit the door, crying 'help! help!' There was a blizzard outside. The blizzard wouldn't let us put food outside the door, let alone cross over the stream to my aunt's house. We made our way outside. Perhan told my mother I shouldn't come, that I should stay instead with Musa and his children. But my mother took me up on her back. We couldn't see our hands in front of our faces and the wind was blowing snow dust at us as though it were tiny grains of crystal glass. The powdered snow crystals were stinging us hard.

Serayi called out, 'Come out Musa! Come out! You too will make this journey, and we'll see you do it. Out you come!'

We all lined up closely behind Serayi. My aunt was calling us and she was wailing a lament. This was always the way that death was broadcast. And yes, this was death. The deep of winter had greeted us and, as was always the way, death had come and caught hold of the smallest ones. It was always the helpless that fell prey. And that winter it had started with the youngest.

'Mother! Mother!' my aunt was wailing, 'Only last night she asked me for the story of the Pomegranate Seed; asked me, and I told it to her. Come! Mother, oh mother-of-mine! Tell me that deep winter has come and taken away my little red partridge. Come, my neighbours, come. The earth and the sky, *herdo asmen* have come and taken away my hennaed lamb.'

The first child to die that winter was my aunt's daughter. She'd waited until wintertime to die. All summer long, she had not died from the fluid running from her nose. And just as everyone was thinking that she'd been saved, the snows took her away.

My aunt was cursing herself for having escaped from the transportation line and she saw her daughter's death as her fate being paid back with consequences.

'I didn't go! Blind my eyes, I didn't think she'd survive the journey. Thought she'd die on the road. How was I to know that we escaped only to meet our fate? Come my mother, come! My little red partridge has been taken up by Sultan Baba, and she only asked me for the Pomegranate Seed, just last night. She asked me and her mother told it to her...'

The Pomegranate Seed was a story. I'd first heard it from Perhan's daughter Goe. My aunt was saying that this was the very last story she had told her daughter. The little Pomegranate Seed girl was such a pretty little girl, she had a tiny nose and a heart full of love. She'd run to every sound she heard and hold out her handkerchief to wipe the tears of anyone who cried. Like us, she had been orphaned. Perhaps her father, too, had been killed by the soldiers or had been taken away, to a place nobody knew.

The story was that Pomegranate Seed lived in a tiny village, just like our own, that was hidden behind far away mountains. The tradition there was, when you reached a certain age, the nicest foods would be prepared and you would go to visit a holy place at a rock from which a fountain poured forth. Pomegranate Seed's turn came and she set off on the road with her mother and made for the holy place which would inform her of her purpose in life.

When they arrived, her mother said, 'We have come to you, holy place of visitation. You know the purpose of everyone in life, how many children they will bear, how they will die – this is what you tell us. Speak to us of my girl's fortune and fate. Tell us, so that I will know if my daughter will find her heart's desire.'

The holy rock came to life and spoke, 'Your daughter's vocation is a dead spirit.'

'But you are a great holy station, said the mother, 'you always give good news to everyone.'

The holy rock replied, 'Her fate is a dead spirit.'

The mother and daughter came home in a state of great despair.

The little brother loved his sister and mother very much. When he saw how sad they were, he asked, 'Mother, what's happened? What did the holy place say?'

'What can it say, my son? It's just a dried-up stone. Do stones speak? We left the food we'd prepared at the spot and came away. The insects and creatures can eat it and they will pray for us, because we did not forget them.'

The child saw the pot containing the food had not been opened. It was still covered over with a fine cotton cloth in the basket on his mother's arm.

'Ey wah, Mother!' he said. 'Oh my! If only you had put the food down at the visiting place for the lonesome wild animals, the birds and the little insects with gentle souls to eat. They might have prayed for my sister's soul and changed her fate.'

He took the basket from his mother's arm and set off for the holy spot.

When he arrived, the rock spoke, 'You have come. But you have come too late. Those who were hungry have been and they saw that those who were full had forgotten them and left. People who come to me, who are believers, and they might hear bad forecasts, but no matter what I say to those who come here, they all leave what they brought and then go. In order to know the value of good words, one must first learn not to become angry at the bad. The djinn and the fairy, the wolf and the lamb, plants and insects all drink the same water that burbles from this spring in my shade. But everyone takes what they have wished from me and goes on their way.'

The child spoke, saying, 'Oh great holy station, my mother forgot not through anger, but through sadness.'

'Even if she had been upset, she should have left the offering for the dead spirit and then gone.'

The child was not to know, but every sound on the earth, of every living creature, was a memorial to all humans who had died before attaining their true desire in life. The sounds of the apple in the tree, the crops in the field, this rushing flock of birds were all memorials to people who had suffered an untimely death on earth.

The child saw that there was nothing to be done, so he left the sacred spot.

He said to his mother, 'Mother, I'm going to take my sister far away from here and far away from the terrible fate that awaits her.'

The mother prepared foods for them to eat along the way.

The child intended to take his older sister to a great, big city. They travelled a very long way. They descended four mountains and they ascended four mountains.

From the peak of the fourth mountain, they saw a far-off light, shining in the darkness.

They said to themselves, 'Let's go and spend the night in that house where the light is shining. We'll get up in the morning and carry on our way.' The house was tucked away in the forest and covered with a string of bright lamps. The house was so pretty that a golden light shone out of its windows and almost reached the stars. They approached the house and looked in at the window. Someone was lying on a huge bed covered in silken bedclothes in a huge room. They called out. But no sound came from the man in the bed. They decided to find the front door of the house and to ring the bell.

The little boy said, 'Sister, you stay here and I'll go and try to find the door to this place.'

He went all around the house but couldn't find the door. He came back to where his sister was waiting and he saw that she was not where he had left her.

As he had been looking for the front door, a secret door had opened and Pomegranate Seed had entered. She went into the house and saw that the man on the feather bed wrapped in pink silk sheets was a corpse.

She went to the window and said, 'My brother, this building has no door. While you were trying to help me escape my fate you brought me to meet it with your own hands. Go, and don't wait for me to no avail. I will serve this corpse from now on. My fate was decided. We descended four mountains and we ascended four mountains and little by little we made our way to where this corpse was lying. You go back to our mother and tell her that you took me to a very great city and that I am extremely happy.'

However, the brother stayed outside the house for days and saw that his sister changed the sheets on the corpse's bed every day, lit the candles afresh and sat by the head of the dead man, crying for his fate. She would look, and see that her brother still waited by the window.

Pomegranate Seed came once again to the window and said, 'Go. This is my fate. I've been brought this far just to serve this corpse. You go to our great sacred visitation spot, whose value we have underestimated, tell it that we are sorry for discounting it and believing that it was nothing but a dry stone. Say to it, "We loved you when you sent us rain, we grew angry when we witnessed your flood."

Months went by, years went by. Pomegranate Seed got up every morning and cleaned the house in which the corpse lay. She aired the pillows and quilt, lit the candles and in this way served the corpse.

One day a young woman came to the window and said, 'Sister! You have been serving this dead body for years now. You change its sheets, clean the house from top to bottom and light the candles afresh every evening. Are you not tired of this?'

Pomegranate Seed recounted her story, word for word, to the woman.

The young woman said, 'If that's the case, I will come and help you.'

Pomegranate Seed replied, 'I too would like it if someone came to keep my company, but as you see, there is no door to this building. How can I let you in?'

The woman replied, 'If these stone walls opened up to let you in, then surely they will listen to you again. Give the wall the order to open and I will come in. We can be friends and tell each other our troubles.'

Pomegranate Seed commanded the wall to open and a door appeared. The young woman came in. However, the time had come for the dead soul to awaken. Everything is like this. When its time has come a thing will awaken whether it is suffering pain or even the dry earth, it will wake when its time has come. First it will die and then it will come back to life. When the corpse came back to life and recovered its senses it was surprised to see two women standing there.

'Tell me,' he said, 'which one of you spent more of her time in my service?'

The woman who had arrived just a few days earlier said, 'Why, me, of course sir. It's been years. If I say it's been ten years, you'd say it was more like twenty. Every day I've changed your quilt covers as if you'd been living and each evening I lit the candles afresh. Then I would sit at your head and wail laments for you, tell you stories and my eyes have become blind from crocheting beautiful cloths for you.'

When Pomegranate Seed heard this, she grew red with shame and was unable to say a thing.

The man who had awoken then said, 'In that case you may be my wife and she will be our servant.'

Years went by, Pomegranate Seed served them and said not a word. One day, when the man was going to the city he stopped and said, 'I never ask after this servant of ours. I wonder if she wants something from the city. I will ask her.'

He called Pomegranate Seed and asked, 'I am going to the city, is there anything that you'd like?'

'Yes, sir, you can fetch me a black stone of the highest quality, a knife and a toy doll.'

The man thought about this all the way along the road. Of the knife he said, 'Alright, that might be necessary if she needs to cut something. The doll is fine too, but what of the stone? What does my servant want with a stone? He couldn't get this out of his mind, all the way along the road.'

As his servant had asked, he brought back a black stone, a knife and a toy doll from the city. Pomegranate Seed took these items and went to the shore of a stream.

She told the toy doll of all that had happened to her, saying, 'For years I served a dead soul that was lying in a bed. I aired his bed and quilt, changed his sheets and lit his candles as if he were still living. If you were in my place, what would you have done?'

The toy doll could not resist and she came to life and spoke, 'If that were me, I would long since have died of such trouble.'

Pomegranate Seed turned to the stone and said, 'And you? Had you been in my place what would you have done?'

The black stone replied, 'If I'd been in your place, I'd have smashed on the spot, of exhaustion.'

She asked the knife, 'And you, knife? What would you have done in my place?'

'Had I been in your place,' said the knife, 'I would have stabbed myself.'

On hearing this, Pomegranate Seed grew angry. She took the knife and brought it down towards her stomach. But at this moment, the man, who had been hiding behind a tree, came out and grabbed the knife from her. And so, Pomegranate Seed had been saved.'

XXIV

My aunt's daughter had not survived. Wild beetroot was not only a life saver, sometimes it turned into a pale poison that would then flow from the nose of a person, and leave them as nothing but a bag of bones topped with an enormous head. Above walking bare bones would sit a pair of bulbous eyes that grew even larger as the body grew thinner and that would quietly go out, just as in the folk stories. I often wondered whether these stories were just lies made up to tell us children. Perhaps they were enchanted sounds to make the pain we were suffering seem a little less. They were magic words that made the wind speak, made the stars shine, made snakes come out of their hiding place and speak, gave life to dead souls and showed mercy to hardened hearts. The telling of these stories and the smoke that rose from our chimneys were the only signs of life that proved that we were still alive. Whenever I looked out of the tiny window in our house, I would think of the smoke rising up and the people gathered around the fires within, abandoning themselves to the words of the stories. As they listened, the flickering flames in the black hearth that we called a *locen* would appear and disappear, flashing yellow, red, then green and blue. Were they dancing? Were they fighting? Or did they wish simply to become smoke as soon as they could and mingle with the night?

My aunt was weeping and striking her knees. She was hitting herself and tearing up the clothes she was wearing. She was constantly repeating the same words.

'I didn't go, I ran away. How was I to know that we'd escaped only to come and meet our fate? If only we'd gone and they'd riddled us with bullets. Mother, oh mother! What is our sin that you don't just take our souls that we may be saved?'

These entreaties by my aunt were so heartfelt that it seemed as though she genuinely wanted us all to die and be done with things. She said that she was living only for her children, as Geyik had said too. 'Mother, mother. My hennaed girl has been taken up into Sultan Baba's wings. Now let her mother die for her precious daughter.'

Other women were joining in with these entreaties my aunt was making. It was as if the one who had died was not my aunt's daughter but their husbands, brothers and sisters. All of them were crying out their own story at the top of their voices, telling of how they themselves had been spared, who had died and where, the last words of the dead and sometimes they would pour out their regrets, repeating them over and over.

My aunt's daughter's dead body was the first one I had seen. My aunt had wrapped her in cloths and placed her on a heap of dried plants near the fire. She'd washed the girl's hands and face as if she were going off to school and had combed her hair. She looked as though she had not died, but was only sleeping. It was as though she was listening to the laments that were being sung for her. The women seated around sung out laments in turn. One would finish and the next would start. All of the trials we had suffered were brought up in the laments.

I was sitting on my mother's knee, watching. As the light of the flames played on the face of my aunt's daughter it looked as though her eyes were opening and closing. Then my mother started the lament, telling the story of how we'd fled to Zeranik, telling the story of the children and of how my grandmother had died on the grand wooden bed and how the last thing she had asked for before dying was a cube of sugar.

'Oh enemy, you are not afraid of God, and you will deprive someone of as much as a cube of sugar.'

Then she began mentioning the Paşa. 'The Rayber told us, leave now, if the great God could find his tongue and speak, he'd tell you that the Paşa's army can't be stopped. The Rayber told us to gather up our bundles, that oppression was on the way. Oh, my, my! My mother on that copper bed and the oppressor and destiny at the door.

Then other women would take up the lament, telling their stories.

It was then that I learned that crying at a funeral is not really crying, but the opposite. It's the telling of a life from its very beginning. And there were those who cried really well. They were called *berbiçi* or mourners. Berbiçi would even go and mourn for an enemy as if their closest relative had died. They would wail, '*De vay, vay*' and sing out laments, waving their hands. The day my aunt's daughter died, I found out that Musa's wife, Hece, was in fact a *berbiçi*. Whenever anyone lay on their death bed, they would call Hece and hear their own life story wailing from her lips in a lament before they finally closed their eyes on life. If someone had already died or if a young girl who had grown up in great suffering was to be married then Hece was once again summoned as a '*berbiçi*.'

Hece could wail a lament in two different voices, sometimes more. She would lament and the other women would repeat, '*De vay, vay Ali Kadir*.' Then she went from the story of how Ali Kadir of Haydaran had escaped from the army of İsmail Hakki Paşa's army and from there she passed on to the story of his father. First, she described all of his brothers, one by one, describing their eyes, their height, how they rode a horse, what great shots they were and how bravely they could wrestle. As she told of them it was as if each brother came to life and passed through that dark house. Then Hece's mother and father were the subject of the lament.

Musa said to her, 'Quiet now, girl. Quiet. Everyone has died. And at least the bones of your father were not left under the burning sun. I mean, this poor Fecire Hatun had to put her dead husband Hıdır Efendi's headless body in a grave... Quiet now, silly fool. She's sitting there wailing laments about well-known people. You should be lamenting for orphans, for poor helpless folk who haven't seen the light of day.'

As far as Musa was concerned, you should sing laments for people who had been brought low, and should cry for someone whose legs trembled. Those were the people for whom laments should be sung. Had my mother sung a lament on the death of my father? Musa contested that it was wrong to sing a lament following the death of Seyit Riza. He'd caused a lot of oppression. The great Rayber had gone and burned the village of Sin and left children homeless and even people like himself, like Musa, who never once took a knife in their hands were angry at him. Should a Rayber ever get angry? When you talk of a Rayber, you're talking about the father to all the poor. But the grief of losing a child hit that great man harder than most. He forgot his duties as Rayber but stood firm in the face of death. This was only ever true of brave people, of great people. Laments should be sung for people like Zeynel, who cut off the head of Alisher and took it Abdullah Paşa for a reward of a few coins. Pirço's son, Hıdır, should have laments sung about him too. People should cry over those who have fallen, and laments should not be sung for the brave.

It was a tradition The dead body would be left to remain for one day and then be buried. My aunt's daughter was buried the next day. Sometime later, my aunt's other two children died. They were followed by Serayi's little girl and other children too. If you asked Perhan, this epidemic had sprung from the soup made from dried wild beetroot. The epidemic also put me to bed. I lay for days on end in the bed made of dried plants.

The death of her children frightened my aunt out of her wits. That aunt who had rushed about cursing the administration and the government, looking like a ball of brushwood, was now waiting for the snows to melt so that she could go and surrender to the authorities. As soon as the snows had melted, she was going to walk to Hozat under her own steam and give herself up. She would explain everything that had happened, one by one.

'It's all lies,' she was saying, 'May fire come and burn down this Dersim. One lie in a thousand is a truth. Those who surrender, why would the government kill them? Didn't Doğık go and surrender, go and do his duty in the army and come back? Didn't Yarim Ağa go to Çet and hand himself in? Why didn't the government hang him? They threw him in jail, let them do so! If the government only wants to seek revenge on an old girl like me, let them get on with it. I'll take this poor child of mine and go right to their door and say, 'If you're going to hang me, then hang me.' Sahan was my brother, Hıdır too. The great big state says not a word to Hıdır's wife, are they really going to say anything much to me? Didn't Doğık say, "Don't be afraid, this government is not the old government." Didn't he say that?'

My aunt had escaped from the transportation line and run back to the village. But now, having lost three of her children, she decided to go under her own steam and hand herself in. No matter what anyone said, she turned a deaf ear. Whereas previously she would have been incensed at anyone who surrendered or who even said as much as 'hello' to the soldiers, now she was like a duck that had suddenly pulled in its wings over water and was heading, all by itself, right to the feet of the hunter who'd been pursuing her. She spoke as though it wasn't she who had cursed and sworn at the government just a little while ago.

'Mother-of-mine! If we're going to die, let us die in the transportation line. That government is not going to take this poor child from me. I'll say, 'Drive me off, if you will, like an Armenian into the Egyptian deserts, drive me into Ethiopia. I've come right to your door. A Yazidi is a Yazidi, who fretted over a crane sheltering in its shade, saying "Shame for the bird, put a dish of water in front of it." I'll say that I've come to the door of the government, bringing along my child, as though I am a crane sheltering it in the shade of my wings. I'll say that I've come to take shelter in the government's shade. I'll say that, just as a stone turns to softest cotton under the sword of our Esteemed Prophet Ali, so my neck is thinner than a hair under the blade of the government's sword.'

She turned to Musa. 'It was like that, wasn't it Musa? If you hadn't shown those soldiers the way, would they ever have made their way out of these mountains? And I'll tell the government that I've come to their door for shelter.'

It was so difficult to persuade my aunt otherwise. She was waiting for Doğık and said that, as soon as he arrived, she would take him with her and go to surrender at the Hozat Regiment. Just let the snows freeze a little and Doğık would come right away. Her only wish was that the snows would freeze, because when they did your feet wouldn't get so cold. She was going to take Perhan's boots too and go to Hozat with her son on her back.

'Perhan, I'll give your boots to Doğık and send them back. It won't do any harm, going from here to there, it's not like there will be sharp stones on which to rip them. And if it snows lightly on this frozen snow, you'd think it was cotton. The next day, Doğık can bring the boots back and deliver them to you, and it will look as though not a hand has touched them.'

My aunt also had a silver belt. When she'd been married, her father, Yusuf Ağa had commissioned it far away in Erzurum and had arranged for it to be sent. If it weren't for the snow, she would have dug it up from its hiding place and given it to Perhan in exchange for the boots. For now, it would be difficult to find the hiding place. If it weren't for the snow, she would have sold that belt in Hozat and sent not one pair of rubber shoes but ten pairs to Perhan in exchange for her boots. But the snow was all about.

'Perhan, if it weren't for the snow, I would have taken it out and given you a silver belt in exchange for your boots. And if only you saw what a belt it was, it shines so brightly from one hundred metres that you'd think ten suns had risen. If you saw it, you wouldn't be able to take your eyes off it. You'd think a ball of light had filled your eyes. Yusuf Ağa especially commissioned it from the pure silversmiths all the way over in Erzurum and he counted out a bag of gold coin into the palm of the craftsman. If only you saw what a belt it was. See here, I'm at daggers drawn with Süleyman Salih Bey's daughter. Ask her, ask her. Ask her to tell you what kind of a belt it was. I could ask her too, as God is my witness, but she'd turn a deaf ear to me. My brother Sahan went with Pirço's son and ransacked that beautiful village of Kahraman Salih Bey's. They struck at all the livestock and goods and came away with them. Who didn't do so? There was hunger. It was a time when resentments were taken out by some on others. The government turned all its guns upon us and imprisoned us in these mountains. The tribes fought one another tooth and nail. As God is my witness, when Kahraman Salih Bey saw me, he couldn't hold back the tears. He said, 'Wae, if only Sahan Ağa had lived, may all these worlds be a sacrifice to him. My father went and took all of his goods and cattle and look what happened. And I have piled all of these earthquake donations up on ox carts and brought them. You choose. First choice is yours. Look, my younger sister is here but you choose first. 'I don't have any but, if I had some, I would have given you a pair of rubber shoes.' That's what he said and he took the shoes off Gülizar's feet and gave them to my poor little child.

    Musa, Hece and Perhan were begging my aunt not to surrender.

    Perhan said, 'Alright then, go. No-one is telling you not to go. Let the snows melt, and then go. There hardly any time left until winter is over. But this is death, and whose door has not been visited by death? See, this Sede of mine is a fully grown girl, and how many days has she been ill in bed? "It's *Gağand* in a few days' time, the time of the winter solstice. After that, how many days of winter will be left?

Just wait, when *Gağand* is here, we'll give our dead their due ceremony and then you can go. Who's telling you not to go? Once *the solstice* has passed the cow will give birth, too.

Her belly is just as it should be and she's nearly ready to give birth. Let her do so, after that there'll be no more death. Fecire Hatun said it herself, "If only this cow had given birth, then not one single one of Wae's children would have died."'

My aunt's mind was made up. She was waiting for the snows to freeze and for Doğık to arrive. Once the snows had frozen hard, Doğık, my mother's suitor, would not wait one day to make the journey here.

'Doğık speaks Turkish as fluently as a nightingale,' said my aunt. He'll take me along to the Paşa and I'll say, "Paşa, my lineage is also Turkish and what a high-born line I am from. There's not one person in the whole of Anatolia who hasn't heard the name of Olbeg Bey." I will say that, as soon as I find Doğık, I'll say to him, "quickly, take me to the Paşa, take me so that he can send us to that perfect house that's waiting for us."'

While all of this was going on, not a word came out of my mother's mouth. For days, everyone had been begging my aunt and trying to stop her from going off to surrender herself. It was only my mother who had said nothing on the subject. I think she knew that my aunt had set her mind on going but tried to change her mind when she said, 'Perhan, Perhan, let her go. What will happen, will happen anyway after all this. After this, there is only death. And I even gave her a house and half the village. Let her go. The soldiers aren't going to kill us. We can have our say too. Let her go, for goodness' sake. And let her have my Erzincan boots, let her have them. Tell her that no-one's allowed to board the train to exile without a good pair of boots. She can take them and wear them and not send them back to me. And I've even made a pair of socks to go inside them so that she can wear them too! She'll think that she's put her feet in amongst the warm embers of the fire, even in the coldest month of winter. Let her put them on and see. Army boots are nothing in comparison. With my boots you'd think you were walking on hot sand under blazing sun in the month of the harvest. And tell her, whoever has frozen going from here to Hozat? Even crazy Haskar, in her naked state, manged to go all the way to Hacheli, over Sıncık Mountain. Here, take my boots and give them to her, tell her to wear them well and to get off on her way.'

XXV

It was always this way. It would snow for days on end before the celebration of the *Gağand* festival. My aunt had abandoned Veli Ağa's large house and she and her last remaining child had taken shelter with Serayi. And on that winter's day our population was increased by one more. A woman from Kızılmezra had set out on the road and come to us. Everyone was shocked because it was avalanche season. Never mind the commotion of a person on the paths, if even a hawk had flapped its wings in the Bactrian region the mountain snows would have come tumbling down. And what a coming it was. You'd think she'd been pelted with ten snowballs at once, such snowslides had come off the mountain that she was covered, head to foot. She had pressed on despite the snowslides and taken whatever the weather had thrown at her. People said that my own grandfather, Yusuf Ağa, had been lost in a snow storm with thirteen of his men on a day like this in the winter of 1938. If someone was the victim of an avalanche in Bactria there was no point in searching for them. You would have to wait for the summer months to arrive. Once the snows had melted and the valleys that had been filled by avalanches were clear then it was possible to search for dead bodies, but only in the valleys that had already let down their avalanches. There was a technique used when looking for a man in the snow. People would take long poles and sink them into the snow in the valleys where it had already slipped off the mountainsides. Men would form lines, standing next to one another and move along, feeling under the snow with the poles, almost as if they were working the fields. If the person who'd been covered by the avalanche was near the surface, the body could be detected by probing with the poles. But those who were buried a few pole lengths below the surface would have to be left until the snows had melted in spring.

If it snowed a lot then sometimes snow heaped up on the fallen avalanches in these valleys. And then the snow would take an age to melt. No-one knew what had happened to my grandfather, Yusuf Ağa. On a winter's day like this one, he and his men had taken off, thinking that the soldiers were coming. No-one ever got news of him or his men again. Everyone believed that Yusuf Ağa and his men had been buried under an avalanche. Who knows? There were those who said that perhaps they'd been marched off into exile. But if they were to have fallen into the soldiers' hands, then they too would have been executed at Elaziz.

The woman who walked form Kızılmezra had frost-bitten feet, despite having wrapped them up in rags and her face had frozen black and purple. Even so, she was smiling broadly at having reached Weroz in safety. 'I came over the peaks to avoid the avalanches', she said, 'I came and I said to myself, 'When that dog bit Fecire Hatun, I went from field to field gathering beetroot for her and would she have survived with her leg like that were it not for that beetroot?'

The other women rubbed her feet with snow and then they buried them in some old dung they'd managed to find and put hot ash among it. The best dung for this purpose was that of a sheep or goat, but it could be done with wood ash. The frozen person would be buried in dung and was kept like this for a day or two, or sometimes even a week. The woman was buried in manure in a corner of our house. We would boil up a hot soup of dried plants and feed it to her. As she drank this soup she would heave a deep sigh, 'ohh' and say to Perhan's daughter, Goe, 'May your father rest in peace, my girl, may he rest in peace, ohh.'

And she'd tell us how she'd journeyed from Kızılmezra. 'I said to myself, "I'll go to Torut", but I couldn't see my hand in front of my face. What's more, how are you supposed to scale that mountain? If the mountain had allowed me to, I'd have managed to reach the villages at Kirgin. And they say in Deşt they've never seen the like of it this year. The fields at Sin have given a harvest of forty to one. Every household has poured forty to fifty sacks of wheat into their grain stores. I said to myself, "Let's go. Seeing as you are sitting here waiting for death, let's just go. Should a person wait like this in one place, we've been waiting here all summer." Mother-of-mine, that Fecire Hatun set off on the roads with her leg like that and she foraged for seeds. I said, "Even if we can't be as strong as that, let's get up and go. Governor Fevzi shows everyone the way, he'll surely show us too." But no! Bandits have seized everything. Well, they're people too, the government has brought in a law, so what can they do? Are they supposed to starve in the mountains?'

New cinders from the fire were continuously brought and put on top of the pile of manure in which the woman had been lying buried for two days. Whichever household's fire had built up a bed of cinders, they'd bring them over, still red hot. The kidneys and the feet were most important. The woman didn't stop speaking for two whole days. She appeared to be quite happy with her situation, her only complaint was not being able to go to the toilet. Two days later she came out from the heap and started massaging her feet with cold snow. My mother made her new clothes from the things that my uncle had brought. They matched one thing up with another and dressed her and even though she did look a little comical in her new clothes she appeared pleased, saying, 'God is with us. The clothes I was wearing had rotted. Mother-of-mine, they were a bit worn out by the time winter came and were seething with fleas all over. They'd rotted. One wash and they were disintegrating. Oh, dear God, may you look kindly upon that Kahraman Salih Bey. Now that's what I call a Bey. To who else would it occur to go and get the things collected for the earthquake? Oh, may God turn all that man touches to gold. I said, "If this Kızılmezra was razed to the ground and you were buried underneath it, would such a person stay put on the spot and wait for death?" I said to myself, "It's winter – who will turn us away? Let's get up and go to one of the Pertek villages. Mother! Every village has a hundred houses and if they were to give just a handful of barley flour it would last us a month. We'd mix it up with water and drink it." Let them go die! They're deserving of it.'

The woman, whose name was Zelxe, had chanced everything and travelled here, so she moved into our house as an uninvited guest. And anyway, if someone has come to your house like that, who would tell them to get up and leave? But from Zelxe's incessant talking I came to understand that more people might be leaving their villages and coming. The fear that my mother and Perhan had been harbouring palpably grew. For this reason, everyone forgot that my aunt was intending to go and hand herself in, and everyone fell to worrying about this new situation. It would be *Gağand* in a few days. Once we'd passed the winter solstice, we'd have passed the halfway mark as far as death was concerned.

The *Gağand* festival was a strange affair. My mother had once explained it to me. The day itself was a day to end all days, she'd say. First there would be an impossibly dark night, the moon would not show her face and the dawn would not know how to arrive. On the eve of the festival, day and night would embroil themselves in an unending struggle. Cockerels would crow in the dead of night, and dogs, instead of barking, would howl.

'Why do they howl?' I'd asked.

'They howl, my girl, because they're afraid that the sun won't come back.'

'What would happen if the sun didn't come back?'

My mother would become angry. 'If it didn't come back, good and evil would be mixed up together and the sky and earth would change places.'

This *Gağand* thing was strange. I once asked Goe about it.

'Goe?'

'Yes, my Perperik, my Butterfly?'

'If the sky and the earth were to change places, would we go to the stars?'

'Sede, did you hear that? Gülizar just asked if we would go to the stars if the sky and earth exchanged places.'

'Of course, we'd go,' replied Sede, 'each one of us would become a star.'

'And Sultan Baba?' I asked, 'the good angels that inhabit the mountain's visitation places, would they come too?'

Goe turned to her younger sister, 'Sede, I think they'd come, what do you think?'

'I think they'd stay here and one morning the soldiers would come and see that there was nobody here...'

'And then Çöyder would conquer all of the soldiers,' I said.

Goe looked me in the face, very seriously. 'You're saying that Çöyder would kill all the soldiers? How will he do that? He'll be in the stars, anyway.'

For a moment I thought about Çöyder Hüseyin jumping from star to star with his five-cartridge rifle strapped across his back and his scores of ammunition rounds wrapped diagonally over his chest like ribs. I could almost hear the sound of the tin cans he'd tied to his shoulders and around his neck combined with the sound of the equipment he'd taken off the soldiers and tied to his arms, rattling as he jumped. I remembered how he'd taken off his helmet when he'd argued with my mother and how he'd lain his neck upon that rock.

But actually, there was a different star. Yildiz, whose name meant 'star', was the wife of Çöyder Hüseyin's companion. It turns out that Çöyder would sleep in Yildiz's house in Çet village on relentlessly cold winter days like these.

On the evening of Gağand, when day and night fought their battle, whoever made a wish would see it come true. However, there was a rule regarding this. On the first night, the evening when the sun did not even rise, you had to pray for good to overcome evil. God protect us, what if evil won out and the darkness was victorious over the light – what would happen then? The good outcome is what you had to pray for, to light pieces of kindling wood and to make wishes. And we were not supposed to be afraid as my mother and the other women chanted *'hu hu'* around the hearth. They were calling Sultan Baba. Sultan Baba was making his horse rear up and the Prophet Ali Aleyselam had struck his sword into the middle of the darkness.

The reason for this 'night without end' was also strange. One day, evil powers were trying to prevent the birth of a child into the world. In order to do so they had drawn a cover over the sun so that they could steal the child with whom the mother was in labour. Their aim was to prevent the child from being aware that it was light and that he had come into the world. But the woman somehow wasn't delivering the baby.

Yezid said, 'Ah! The woman has understood that we have drawn a cover over the sun.

'What shall we do?' they asked, 'what shall we do to prevent the child from knowing he's come into the world?'

The evil spirits talked all night, saying, 'If this child is born, sees the light of day and cries, if he makes a noise then Sultan Baba will realise that he's been born.' If that were to be the case, they would not be able to kill the child. So, they were deliberating on how to prevent the sun from rising following the night; how to stop Sultan Baba from realising that one of his own had appeared in the world.

God looked and saw that Yezid had not allowed the dawning of the sun. Then the saintly figure, Hızır, appeared in the guise of one Yezid's men and said, 'O Yezid, there is an easier way. Allow the sun to rise and the woman to give birth to the child. As soon as he is born, we'll say that no-one must let him make a noise. Once the child appears from the birth canal, we'll cover its mouth with ten hands and what is the strength of a child's soul? It will be smothered there and then.'

'That's true,' said Yezid, 'Why are we panicking like this? Is not that which comes into the world just an upside-down bundle of swaddling? We'll close his eyes without him knowing and he'll think he's still within his mother's womb.'

The saintly Hızır Aleyselam said, 'When the time comes, leave it to me to cover the child's mouth, to stop him from crying.'

In this way, as soon as he was born the child let out a cry and with his cry all of the little creatures and animals awoke. The child breathed onto the world. And the breath that we take is the very same one that the child exhaled into the world. When Sultan Baba heard the child cry, he took him up and away in his wings and so prevented Yezid from killing him. Unable to smother the child in this way, Yezid waits for this winter night every year, when the night meets the day and he tries to prevent the rising of the sun. For this is his nature. If the sun were not to rise these snows would remain, the trees would stay bare and the waters of the land would keep flowing underneath the snow.

And even if the day were to show its face, one was not to be fooled by this. Yezid would do this too, making everyone believe that the sun had risen. For this reason, one had to light kindling sticks and pray for three nights in a row. And it was not only we humans, but the animals too who would pray for three days and three nights. The cockerels would crow in the middle of the night and the dogs would howl instead of bark. And so it was too, that our cow bellowed all that night until morning. My mother told me that I should see how the sheep and goats behaved at this time. They would huddle up together and strike the ground with their feet, moving from one side of the barn to the other, backwards and forwards. Poor creatures, they must fear that the day will never dawn.

'And what of God, mummy?'

'My girl, God said, "I divided the darkness from the light but I did not separate them on the eve of *Gağand*. No matter what I did, I could not separate them. No matter how I tried, for one night of the year they come together and merge." This is why they get mixed together.

'And it was Zindik, too, who lied, and who acted like that so as to try to take the place of God. For God had made everything and was resting. He had created everything in partnership with his wife and had separated everything into two so that no one part could win over the other. And God said, "I have divided everything into two, down to a fortieth of a hair's breadth. Female and male; hot and cold; the face of the earth from the sky above. I separated all things from one-another. Now it's up to you. Just as you differentiated between hot and cold, so must you differentiate between good and evil. I gave you knowledge and a mind with which to discern it and I gave you visitation points at which you may commune with me. So that when you argue with one-another, when someone says a bad word about you, there you can sit at the base of that spot I granted you and remember me." And God said, "I left you those visitation points so that you can go there and feel my loneliness."

But Yezid said, 'God is still speaking and there are still some who hear. That must be a lie, for God never speaks. When he blew that breath into the world, did he not say, "From now on, the word is yours." Did he not say, "If you press your ear to the ground you will hear my voice. I speak with the stones, the trees and the flowers. Go to each visiting spot and you'll hear my voice." For if God could speak, why would the wind blow?'

'But what about the saints, mummy, the wise and holy ones?'

'My girl, a Pir is a miracle worker, a Pir is a messenger. If there were no such things as Pirs and Raybers, who would listen to anyone?'

'But the state rounded up and killed all of the true Pirs. There had been Pir Nuri, and Hese Gaj was a saint. If he did not have the essence of a Pir, how could he have played the saz so well and perform the *gulbend* ritual so well? Hese Gaj had a friend called Armenian Mam, he too was a Pir, and when the two of them struck up the saz you'd think that the saz was praying. And they'd sing in many languages, and as they struck the tambour it would come to life and speak.

'Hese Gaj came to our house once, and played. My father asked him, "Hesen, how is it that you play and sing so beautifully?"

'Hese Gaj replied, "Sey Hıdır, once I strike a chord on this saz everything happens by itself, even I do not know what I am singing."

'Hese Gaj was a great *ozan,* and Seyit Riza would listen only to him. In fact, after he burned the village of Sin, Seyit Riza returned and said to Hese Gaj, "Heso. You burned me and may Almighty God burn you. Why do you wail such laments for the son of mine who was killed? You sang such laments that you made me get up and come all this way."

'Hese Gaj sang so well. Had Seyit Riza not listened to the laments sung by him for his dead son then nothing would have happened. The tribes would not have started fighting one-another and the military police would not have seen this as an opportunity and wouldn't have sent so many soldiers flooding into the villages.

'When Hese Gaj was caught, Abdullah Paşa said, "Leave him alone, leave him. If you execute him, you'll be doing him the biggest favour. Let him go, take his saz and let him go. And never give him his saz back again. Send him out into such a world that not only has no saz within it but has no-one there who has ever even heard the name of the saz." Abdullah Paşa said, "It's the saz that makes these wretches go off to fight up in the mountains."

'The prophet Süleyman knew every language on earth. He knew each and every language of the wind, the waters and all the creatures and animals. But one day Almighty God looked and saw Süleyman sitting to one side, thinking. He said, "Oh Süleyman, I gave you everything, but now I see that you're deep in melancholy thought again. You, who understand what the birds are saying, who understand the speech of the flowers, still I see you looking unhappy."

'That great Süleyman replied, "It's true, O most high, I know every language there is, I've made everything on earth find its tongue and speak to me. But then I saw the saz. I saw the saz in the hand of the *ozan*. And until I saw this saz,' he went on, 'I thought I was the only one who could enter into the spirit of a creature and make it sing. But I couldn't understand the miraculous power of the saz in the hands of the *ozan*. I even saw the snake poke its head out of its hiding place and listen to that saz in the hands of the *ozan*. This caused me trouble."

The saz was such a thing that if it were in the hands of a true player, it would become water and flow or would become wind and moan. My mother had seen it with her own eyes, as Hese Gaj had played the saz Pir Nuri, who had been whirling in dance in the room, turned into smoke and drifted up the pipe of the stove and disappeared. When Hese Gaj played the saz the Pirs and Raybers would close their eyes and levitate, houses would shake to their incantations, and when those assembled chanted, 'hu erenler hu', the ashes would take flight. When a pure *ozan* played the saz then first it was the elders who would get up to begin the ritual semah dance, in this way every hand went to the heart and back, was taken from the heart and given. First it was the Pirs and Raybers who would get up to join the cem gathering. If the saz was in the hands of a pure *ozan* and a Pir had appeared in all their perfection, they would have to wait like a loaf buried and proving under a pile of cinders.

One day, Pir Nuri had listened to Hese Gaj at the home of Rayber'e Sed Ağa when he suddenly flew up from his place and said, 'Rayber, make way, I'm aflame! If I don't get up from where I'm sitting within five minutes I'll burn and turn to ash.' Listening to Hese Gaj play the saz had burned him within.

'But mother,' I said, 'why did the man burn?'

'Why, my girl, when the saz is being played, if the Pir does not get up and whirl then he will break apart and die. Once a pure *ozan* has struck the string, who can stay in their place?' If pure *ozans* could roam about playing their saz then there would be no hunger and there would be no such thing as troubles.

These days, celebrating the cem ritual was forbidden. Otherwise, we would have held one on this eve of *Gağand*. Yet if only Hese Gaj could have played the saz now with his Armenian friend Mam, winter would disappear, the barns would be filled with plenty and the trees would bend their necks low to the ground under the weight of their fruit. The whole area is crawling with soldiers now or the gulbend ritual would have been observed as it always has been. At the time of the ritual, the evil powers that had drawn a blind over the sun would have been instantly dispelled and the morning beam of the sun's rays would have burned red like a pomegranate seed and summer would arrive in the middle of winter. But now it was forbidden. The state had outlawed observance of the gulbend ceremony. In fact, if gulbend had not been banned then the tribes would not have come together against the state.

Seyit Riza is supposed to have said to His Holiness Diyab Ağa, "Tell the Paşa that our ceremony should be permitted, let him hang us if he will. If it the ceremony is allowed then there will be no need for him to set his soldiers upon us, as we would go and surrender in Ankara before the military police even arrive. We would say to the Paşa, "You who have allowed us to hold the cem ceremony again, if you will, you may hang us one by one at the door of the Parliament, just as you did to Hasan Hayri Bey. And not one of us will utter a word in contest. We won't even claim that eyebrows sit above eyes. But, if you take the saz from the hand of the *ozan* and the 'hu' from the sung breath of the Pir, then not only will we resist the army, you will not put us off from resisting the whole Russian army falling upon Munzur.'

On the morning of *Gağand,* everyone set off at the same time for the visitation spot in the village's cemetery. Everybody took whatever they had and came to the spot. It was a black poplar tree and we all formed a circle around it. Single pieces of kindling wood were lit at its base and prayers were said as they burned and each person kissed the tree three times and placed their foreheads against it. The helva we had made was placed in the centre of the circle and a piece was given to each person. The same amount that was given to the people gathered was offered also to the black poplar tree.

After this we visited the graves of our relatives, still buried under the snow. And we called out to our close ones underground.

In the evening, everyone brought something along and came to our house. Musa, his wife Hece, my aunt, her only-surviving child – her son, Serayi and lots of other women and children all gathered at our house. When midnight struck the women began to move about, gently tapping their knees and chanting, 'Hu! hu! O Imamsen hu, hu! Sultan Baba hu!'

Perhan took a three-stringed saz from where it had been hidden among the bushes. She touched the strings with her fingers, she struck them again. *'Hu! Erenler hu! huuu,* Sıncık Mountain! Duzgun Baba Rock hu! Away with pains, turn trouble to joy, let enmities be friendships! Hu saints and orphans, hu! Hu the forty, and the seven, hu!'

The raising of the knees and striking them with the hands grew faster and as the hu! was chanted, the hands were raised to meet the lips, parted in the chant of hu! hu! The circle in the centre grew wider and the flames leapt out of the fireplace and licked at the ceiling, hu! hu! All at once, my mother got up from her place and opened her arms out wide, '*huu! O Munzur Baba huu*!' Those gathered chanted and moaned '*halla, halla, huu!*'

The ground moved and the stone wall shook, 'hu! hu!' The heavens seemed to swing back and forth. Musa chanted, '*halla, halla saints, halla halla*, let troubles end, enemies be friends, *halla halla*, Sultan Baba, *halla halla.*'

With the sound of the saz and the sound of hands striking knees, the circle spun faster and the flames in the fireplace grew ever more restless. With an exhalation of hu! their hands left their bodies and struck their knees, the fingers that had been playing the strings of the saz also stopped and the spinning circle suddenly halted in front of the fire and there they prostrated themselves. Their heads bowed low. They rested their foreheads on the floor and laboured breathing from their out-of-breath chests could be heard.

Suddenly the world was plunged into silence and the walls, that seemed to have been flapping their wings and taking off, pulled their wings in close and descended to the ground in the same deep silence. The vault of the skies, which had cracked open now closed upon itself in shame. It was as if a thousand-year sorrow had found its tongue was talking and out of shame at hearing it the rivers had run silent and prostrated themselves. The crackling of the flames as the burned on the cinders in the fireplace slowly subsided like the wheezing of the chests and they too turned into ash and dust.

Those prostrating themselves remained like that for some time. Then with one voice they chanted, 'Halla halla our invocations and our prayers, our love and our supplications, our pain and suffering, our tambur and saz – may they reach to the great seat of the Most High and be deemed fit and accepted, God, God, may the fields be bountiful, the evil forces bathed in light, and may the place of the ill-departed be that of heavenly light, God, God.'

The night had ended and morning had come, the darkness had been defeated and the sun had risen. The hatred in people's breasts had burned up and become the ash of forgiveness. Evil had become holy light and had shone down in bountifulness and the crane that had been captive had flown off to be an envoy in the land of Egypt.

The cem ceremony was such a special thing. When the cem was performed, a person became like the crane, and could take wing and fly. The crane was a pious bird. Only the crane mourned at Kerbela. The crane would never forget its fellow travellers or leave them behind. And if you took a crane and imprisoned it in a cage, it would fall down dead just like that, as a red partridge would. And until it died it would pine for its mate. And neither would it seek another mate. The crane whose mate had died would still fly with the flock, but would fly alone. It would mourn for thirty years. Mecnun mourned for Leyla for thirty years, neither eating nor drinking. And the crane bird was also fond of its fellow-cranes. It wasn't like the crow. These troublesome crows were just like the Dersim tribes, fighting amongst themselves with great determination and, at the crack of dawn, beginning their day with arguments. The crow species were also great thieves. Just like the people of Dersim, they'd go and pillage the nest of their neighbour. If a crow got the chance, he would steal the young from another's nest and eat it. And was the crane anything like that...?

XXVI

The snows froze. My aunt fell in behind Doğık when he'd come from Elkazi and walked off behind him on the Hozat road. She put on the boots that my uncle had brought for my mother from Erzincan and off she went.

She had said her goodbyes to everyone, complaining as she said farewell, and cursing. 'Mother-of-mine, I'm a complainant, I am, a complainant at the highest court in the land. Fires have fallen upon this Dersim, there's not one stone left atop another, but still there's been more knavery and lying than anything at all. May Almighty God weed out and destroy all these tribes. The great Rayber Sed Ağa found out all of their lies. Did they not set nephews against uncles? Well, I am a plaintiff against all of these tricksters, I'm a complainant against all of the people of Bactria who made themselves enemies of the daughter of Süleyman Salih Bey. My case is against the holy men who destabilised the peace and the Raybers who oppressed the poor. The sin will weigh upon their necks for those three poor orphans leaving this world with no direction.'

She took up her place behind Doğık and went off to surrender. My mother, who thought that the soldiers would be coming to take her away, relaxed a lot more when Doğık suddenly returned. According to him, they'd sent my aunt off into exile, to somewhere called Çorum. The Commander of the military police had himself given food to my aunt and her child, as well as new shoes and clothing.

Çöyder Hüseyin was bellowing again. My mother said he was like a crane that had lost direction, the way he was coming and going over the snow, she said there was no logic to it.

As for Çöyder Hüseyin, 'Dog', he said, 'now this race of dogs that this Dersim hound has made appear are being tracked down. Such a hound that he'd die for his owner. And he'd not only keep enemies away from his master, but even wild birds too, and what's happened? Let's ask you, shall we, Perhan? What happened to that pure bred Kangal dog of yours? I mean, wouldn't that dog dart off ahead before your Murtaz had the chance to sling on his shotgun? Really, I'm asking you, Perhan, what happened to that pure Kangal you had? Did he not lick the wound Murtaz got when he was struck by a bullet, for three days and nights? Did that dog not sit by Murtaz's side and mourn for him for three days and nights, that dog shed tears for him, didn't he? What happened to that dog? He became hungry, and went to live with the same soldiers that killed Munzur. And those dogs, they used to fly into a rage not just at soldiers, but at the very smell of them? Then what happened? One by one they went and defected, going to feed off the soldier's refuse pile. The whole lot of those Dersim dogs gathered at the rubbish dump in Hozat and began to attack one another, getting embroiled like a heap of worms and tearing each other apart as if they were pure bred jackals. And this Dersim is just like that line of dogs. Before they'd even dried their tears they'd gone off to find a new door at which to bark.'

As Çöyder Hüseyin was bellowing and shouting like this, Doğık somehow found his way into our house. He closed the door behind him so as not to hear the sound of Çöyder's voice.

It was as if the door that Doğık shut had been slammed in Çöyder's face. Çöyder's eyes, which were spinning like balls of fire, dimmed for a moment like a sparrowhawk recognising it has lost its prey, before they turned back into embers of fury.

'Dog!' he bellowed in rage, 'Dog! Even a dog has some honour. It's not fallen people who are the lesser ones, Perhan, but those who caused them to fall.'

'Fecire Hatun!' he shouted, 'Fecire Hatun, daughter of Süleyman Salih Bey, give me my say, as Sultan Baba is my witness, hear me out!'

He stood there, and banged the rifle he was carrying down hard into the frozen snow beneath his feet, in the same way he had hit the iron helmet of the soldier he had killed. He kicked the snow with the soldiers' boots he was wearing. He was stomping on the spot like an enraged stallion. 'Hoi! You! Yooou!' he shouted as if he wanted to bring the mountains down. 'Before the flesh of our fallen has even rotted in the ground, you swine.'

He was like a tiger in captivity, not knowing what it should do and throwing itself at the bars of the cage in which it was imprisoned. He pulled off the iron helmet he was wearing and slammed it into the ground so that it rang out, the medals on this chest began to swing from side to side as his anger grew.

Something bad was going to happen. Musa jumped up from his place. 'Wusen, Sey Wusen, I prostrate myself at your feet. I have transformed into Sultan Baba and come to your feet. Hece, girl, bring a dish of water for Sey Wusen, quickly, a dish of water. And mix some of that yellow curd from the cow's milk into it. Girl, quickly, bring a dish of water for Sey Wusen.'

Çöyder grabbed hold of Musa's good arm, which in his panic he was flapping up and down like a helpless bird and shook it.

'Don't appear before me, be human. Don't appear in front of me as the one who recites prayers so that our dead may rest in peace.'

Then Çöyder threw himself down on the floor like a little boy throwing a temper tantrum in front of his mother. He began to scream in anger. 'Musa,' he said, 'Musa you are our intermediary between us and God, say this to the daughter of Süleyman Salih Bey, may she set up our gathering with haste. Before this sacred *Gağand* sees the daylight of the holy man, Hızır may our congregation be established with speed. Whoever heard of a bandit being pardoned within just three years? Perhan, tell the daughter of

Süleyman Salih Bey, our congregation should be gathered together without delay.'

Then he calmed down and rearranged the five-cartridge shotgun that had slipped from his back. He checked his cartridge belts. One of the tin cans he called his medals had fallen off and was half-buried in the snow. He picked it up from the floor and looked to see where it had come from on his chest. He put it in his pocket and shouted. The sound he made echoed in the valley as though a hand drum were being struck.

'Perhan! Musa you hear this too. Girl, Serayi, you come too and don't be afraid. Tell the daughter of Süleyman Salih Bey to come so that she may hear too. Is it right to walk, shepherding Wae, the only sister of that dear soul brother of mine Sahan Ağa, in front of you to surrender?'

As he was speaking, he became frightened and his little eyes began to swivel wildly in his eye sockets. 'I mean,' he continued, 'is it becoming of a strong young man who's been a bandit himself and served with the likes of the mighty Sahan Ağa, who's borne arms, is it right for him to set out leading a woman off to the soldiers. Don't let anybody say that Çöyder Hüseyin didn't say so. I mean, I am a merciful man. The daughter of Süleyman Salih Bey got up in front of all our people and spat in my face, and I didn't say a word. Because I'd already said, that woman, who all by herself did that which no-one else had, and carried Hıdır Efendi's headless body on her back all the way here, brought it back and read the Koran over it. So, I'm saying, may the gunpowder in the iron barrel of this gun not touch a single soldier. You know, the poor wretches went weak at the knees when they merely smelled the gunpowder. I looked, and the poor thing couldn't speak, he'd squeezed himself in behind a rock and was crying his heart out. And the poor fellow, I cut off his commander's head and handed it to him. "Take it", I said, "take it and give it to the Paşa."

I mean, he was like a baby that's fallen into the water in this, the coldest month of winter. Go and ask Yarim Ağa who lives in Çet, ask him and say, "Seydali, you're a man who's seen the Yemen. You fell into slavery in the Yemen desert and you're a man who's escaped from slavery. I mean, it just won't do. Hıdır Efendi himself said that things will not end with the killing of soldiers. As long as this race of women exists in Anatolia there'll be no finishing off of the soldiers simply by killing them, will there?'

Nobody knew what Çöyder Hüseyin was on about. But he'd lost a great battle and was now in a state of confusion, as if he couldn't at all fathom how he'd been beaten. He'd lost and he was scared. He was even saying that the dog, the most faithful servant on earth, had been treacherous and what's more, had gone to take refuge with the ones who had thrown stones at his master. Musa had gone over to Çöyder's side and was trying to calm him down.

Çöyder didn't seem to know what to do. He said, 'Musa, you're from Demenan, it's finished. Dersim is finished. This Dersim has become nothing but a hunted race of dogs. Hâshâ, hâshâ Wusen, and a person went and surrendered and all...'

Musa didn't know what to say, 'The thing is...'

'No, Musa, it won't because where treachery has fallen to the ground the seed will never run out Sey Musa. This Dersim has been razed to the ground three times and rebuilt another three times. This Dersim was a protective wing for the Armenians, and Kochi Bey was welcomed with open arms as well. That same Kochi Bey who had one hundred thousand Ottoman soldiers on his trail. His holiness Sarısaltık came here for sanctuary. I mean that he made this Dersim a crown for his head and his sanctuary. That great folk hero Köroğlu came and mixed among the forty on his horse up on Sultan Baba Mountain. It's over now. This Dersim is finished now, Musa. Three times it's been razed and rebuilt. The Hun soldiers saw off the Russian army. But now, the place has drunk the water of treachery.'

As he spoke it was clear that he really wanted to shout. It seemed as if he wanted to fly into a rage, and make the floor ring out by throwing his holed, army helmet upon it. As if he wanted to tear his clothes to pieces, to shout and put the whole world to rights, but instead he was silent, like an innocent man dragged before the court as guilty, he was as quiet as if he had accepted the death penalty that had been set upon his head. Çöyder Hüseyin's anger had become powerless.

XXVII

Eventually the cow that my uncle, Kahraman Salih Bey, had sent us gave birth. As soon as word got around that our cow had given birth, all and sundry began to turn up, showing no regard for the winter weather; crossing the mountains with bowls in their hands.

They wanted milk. The strangest of all who came were two women from Malmes village, a place hidden in a tiny valley at the foot of Sıncık Mountain. The village was at an even higher altitude than ours. In exchange for the milk, they'd brought a pair of fur shoes made from bearskin for my mother. And each of them wore shoes whose fur stood up on end.

My mother said, 'Oh mother-of-mine, what am I to do with your fur shoes? May God let you believe that there is no milk. If there was milk, why would I say that there wasn't? There isn't.' The women continued, alternately begging and then getting mad at my mother.

Musa became angry that everyone had come out and asked for milk. He did take the side of these two women, however. 'Fecire Hatun, you know, these women went out on their own and shot a bear. And look at these shoes, they're hardly like shoes and more like the Istanbul boots that Governor Fevzi wears. Look how beautifully they've stitched them. You know, the bears came down all summer and the women threw a spear at them. Who else had thought of that?'

My mother replied, 'Musa, Musa, the cow is there. There is no milk. A cow has to eat grass to make milk. You've seen it yourself. You go to milk her udder and you'd think the poor thing's lungs are going to detach and come out. The animal's in such pain. There is none. May God make you believe me, there's no milk. No milk! Why would I say there was none if there was some? How can I let that dairy cow die? She's a living soul too.'

The women simply didn't want to hear my mother saying that there was no milk. They were shouting at my mother as if it was their cow she had stolen and tied up in her barn.

'Woman, it's not as if we've come to ask you for the cow herself. Just put a dish underneath so that the throats of all our children may be wet.'

As my mother said no, the women grew more and more angry. It looked as though they would attack her and begin scrapping with her at any time.

'We want what's ours by right. It's as if you think we've come to ask for the cow herself. Give us our due and we'll go. We've set off and walked so far through the snow in deep winter, give us what we're due and we'll leave.'

'Mother! What more can I give you? I gave you the cow's morning milk and you didn't take it. If I give you a week's worth of milk, then what will I give to those who come tomorrow? Do people know the meaning of 'no' these days? Honestly! Everyone who's heard has set out and come here with a cauldron in their hands with no thought as to how it'll be filled. If you see the animal, you'd think it a cow, but it gives no more milk that a goat. You put your hands to the teats to milk her and after two little squirts it's all finished. Tomorrow there'll be people from other villages, so you take the cow, there she is! Take her and you'll be saved and so will I.'

The women had seated themselves by our fireplace and they weren't going anywhere. 'No mother! We don't want anything from you. You've sent everyone who's come here away with a dish full to the brim with milk. And we haven't come empty-handed. We've brought you a pair of pure fur shoes. Put them on and go and climb Balıkan Mountain. Your feet won't even feel the snow. We've only come here to claim our children's due'.

After spending the night sleeping in our house the women took their milk the next day and left. People began to come from other villages. My mother would scream and shout at every newcomer but she would send them on their way with milk. Not to do so was a sin, she said. Their children were on the way out anyway, so at least let no-one think they'd died because of us. And really, new people arrived every two days.

Eventually Perhan said, 'Fecire Hatun, you leave everything to my girls, let them give to whoever they will. Musa can help too. Otherwise, these people will just ridicule you, the first chance they get.'

In this way, we were able to take one glass of milk per day and add it to the soup we'd made. The rest was handed out by Musa and Perhan's daughters. If you asked Musa, it went on for a month, as who would venture outside once fresh snow had fallen on the frozen snow? If any sound hit the snow, it would break free of the mountain and come tumbling down. We would be comfortable now until March. Then, when March came, they could take our cow if they wished. Once the snow melted, nature's bounty would burst forth from everywhere. We had seeds put aside, too. My mother had hidden the barley seed so well that even if we were dying of hunger, we wouldn't be able to get a sniff of a single grain. But now, when spring was to arrive, who was to sew the fields? Without animals how were we to plant these huge fields?

Doğık, having taken my aunt to Hozat, came to Weroz nearly every day, when the snows melted that January. Musa said that Çöyder Hüseyin was watching Doğık like a snake but did not get involved, on account of my mother.

Çöyder told Musa, 'I would have spilled out the guts of that dog, right here, but Süleyman Salih Bey's daughter is caught up in the middle. Otherwise, I would have strung that dog's guts our right here.'

As far as I could understand, Musa didn't like Doğık either.

When Musa began to go on about him, Perhan would say, 'Musa, Musa, you've done the same thing. It's Çöyder who's talking. What could Doğık have done? The woman set her mind to it and said she was going. What was Doğık supposed to do?'

'No, Perhan, Çöyder says, since the day he first came someone has been going and surrendering every single day. Such a thing shouldn't be happening. That's what he says.'

But there was a shortage, a dearth of men. And in the absence of a sheep, a goat becomes as venerated as Abdurrahman Çelebi. There were no strong people left.

Musa said Çöyder also said, 'Sey Musa, I've not told my secret to a soul, until this day. Everyone knows me as a brave man. Having the whole of the Hozat regiment on my tail is also seen as some kind of heroism. When the pardon came out, I really did want to go and turn myself in. Kahraman Salih Bey said to me, 'Come on, let me take you to Erzincan and turn you in. If they get their hands on you here then no-one will even find your corpse.' And you know, Musa, I thought about it a lot. I said to myself, 'If only I'd been there too when Seyit Riza met with the hangman's noose at Findik Zade. A person should go to death alongside mighty people. To die with a valiant person is not death at all.'

Then Çöyder had said, 'I was very sorry about that. When Seyit Riza was caught, I went to the regimental base at Hozat. Me! Bactrian Hüseyin-e Çöyder. I was going to say that I'd come to square up to the government man's noose. But I didn't go. Instead, I dug a hole in the ground just next to the Hozat base and I stayed in the ground there for three days and nights. I said to myself that I'd shoot Pirço's son Hıdır as he exited the main gates with Abdullah Paşa at his side. I set myself up on this little hill by the base and had the soil on top of me, and a bare juniper tree on top of that. Then they passed before me. Pirço on one horse, Abdullah Paşa on the other and cavalrymen around them. I sighted up the gun and held my breath. But just at that moment a turtle dove flew down and perched on the barrel of my five-cartridge gun. That turtle dove is the same one that proved an obstacle to Zaloghlu Rüştem.'

Musa was retelling the stories Çöyder had told him, and he just couldn't stop. He would start recounting the stories at every opportunity. Above all, whenever Doğık was around, Musa was always desperate to talk about Çöyder. And when he told the story he would hold out his single arm as if taking aim with his rifle from his hiding place in the ground, underneath the juniper tree.

'And Çöyder says,' he would continue, 'the juniper tree above me was bare and all that was visible was the barrel of my five-cartridge rifle, I took aim, held my breath. Musa, I began to depress the trigger, but just as I was about to pull it a turtle dove came and landed on the barrel that was sticking out of the ground. It waggled its tail and looked into the hole, right into my eyes. Aha, just like that.'

According to Musa, another matter that upset Çöyder was having hidden the head of the military commander he'd decapitated behind a rock, out of fear, and not handed it personally to one of the commander's soldiers.

Çöyder had said to Musa, 'It wasn't the commander I felt sorry for, but the soldier. He was tucked behind a rock and his knees had given way. His eyes were frozen and cold as ice and his two knees were knocking together and bending like two bows underneath him. He was shivering like a little baby who's fallen into the waters of the Munzur river in the coldest month of the year.

'Musa, I've killed a lot of soldiers. But no matter how many I killed, I couldn't avenge the deaths of my father and brothers. No matter how I tried, I could not quench the fire of anger within me. I took that anger and I plunged it into icy waters in the coldest month of the year, I took it out of there and buried it under the earth. When storms came, I threw it at the storm. But no matter what I do I still haven't been able to quell this anger that's eating me inside. And now I'm at daggers drawn with Fecire Hatun. She got hold of that anger that was burning inside me and she poured a dish of cold water upon it. As soon as she poured it on, there was a sizzling and my insides felt full of smoke. You know how a glowing coal in the fire emits that sound? Well, it was like that. It made a noise as if someone had taken a dish of water and poured it onto the embers in the hearth, here, in my very centre.'

'If I hadn't killed those five soldiers and if I hadn't gone and cut off the head of that commander, cut if off and hidden it behind a rock, and if I hadn't seen that soldier with his knees knocking together then I'd have been hurting even more. But, how could I cut off the head of that commander in front of that soldier, who was shaking to pieces in terror, and hand him the severed head? It was like someone poured a dish of cold water on the flood of rage within me. I've killed that many soldiers. How could I kill that soldier whose legs were banging together like that? I could tell that what he'd seen would always stay with him.'

According to Perhan, Çöyder and Doğık were old brothers-in-arms. What's more, Perhan had heard Çöyder asking Doğık for gun oil with her very own ears. And Doğık had replied, 'No matter what I do, I'll bring you the best and finest gun oil I can find.'

XXVIII

Zelxe, the new woman who'd arrived, was quite strange. Now she'd begun saying that she wasn't going back to Kızılmezra. 'I won't go back, no I won't return,' she'd say, 'Do I have as much as a single field there? I had one son, and God took him. And it's a good job he took him, for what else could he have done? He saw that the boy was dying of hunger, just like me, and he took him. Do I have so much as a nest I could snuggle into in that place I left? I'd be wandering around, living off handouts from other villagers. And whenever someone has knocked on his door in this here Dersim, God has turned that servant away! So, let him turn me away, too.'

Perhan would get angry at everyone. 'Zelxe, Zelxe, you've done it too, wait now, and someday soon the exile period will end. Then the men will come of our prison and will come back from military service, and let me see how you'll be then. Who'd want a woman with a child to make all sorts of trouble. You, you're like a young girl. And your health and strength are all there.'

Zelxe replied, 'Oh Perhan, I've seen what I'll see and I've suffered all that I will suffer. I'll take this saddlebag in my hand and go wandering from village to village. May God mete out his punishment to this Dersim. Once these men return from exile, they'll all be at each other's throats again. And we poor wretches will be the ones that suffer. I'll take myself off, somewhere. Just me. I'll go to that minstrel from Laçinan, like Çöyder did, and I'll ask him to tell my story, too, upon his single-stringed saz. You've played everyone else's, I'll say, now strike out my story on your saz. My voice isn't good, though. If only I had the voice of Hece here, I'd become a *berbiçi,* a funeral singer. Mother-of-mine, whosoever hears that voice, well, they'd never let you go hungry. If only I had that voice, not only would they give me a handful of barley at the doors I knocked on, but every house would sacrifice a goat kid to me. And no ordinary goat kid either, but one that's been raised on a diet of special vetch clover. I'm on my own now, aren't I? I'll take myself off, and go in through Abasan and out through the villages of Haydaran. If that doesn't work, I'll tell stories to the children. And if only you saw just how much children love folk tales. Once the children have heard a story, they'd take me by the hand and lead me by the hand to the most prestigious spot in their house. As soon as the snows have melted, I'll set off by myself. And may God be pleased with Fecire Hatun here, for she's opened her door to me and has given me food out of the mouth of her own child.'

Goe spoke. 'What Zelxe says is true. What good will getting married do, for her? Take your saddlebag and travel from place to place. I say the same thing to my mother, I say, "Mother, how many women are there in Dersim who can play the saz? Take your saz and travel about. You play and Hece can sing." If everyone were to give her a handful of wheat then we'd be stacking up rows of wheat sacks in the house here.'

Doğık, too, was a strange one. He'd set off early in the morning to come here, and return to his home in the evening. He'd put huge snow shoes on in order not to sink down in the snow and that's how he would come. There were times, too, when he'd turn up in the middle of the night. No matter what time Doğık set off from his house and no matter what time he returned, he'd be watched like a hawk by Musa. Doğık came to our house nearly every day. He'd go and fetch wood from the forest and he'd shoot wild animals and bring them to us. Now and then he'd also bring us some bread from the city. What was it that Musa saw in Doğık to make him so suspicious? What was the reason for Musa to become so out of sorts as soon as Doğık showed up? Once Doğık arrived, Musa seemed not to know what to do with himself.

'Fecire Hatun, I gave away my cow in exchange for two dry fields. If they'd have stolen her from my barn, then fair enough. But I gave her to you, and this holy place of visitation is my witness. I drove her in front of me all the way from Dervişler village. Everyone saw, as well. If my pale gazelle were still with me then no-one would have been able to get her away from me; not even if the Paşa's whole army had risen up and come down on me, they would have taken that cow over my dead body.'

Musa's wife, Hece, would get angry at him for saying this same thing, day in, day out. 'Kolo, kolo, and what do you expect Fecire Hatun to do? She swore to you and placed her hand on a piece of bread while she did so. It's 'the cow' when you get up in the morning, and 'the cow' when you go to bed at night. Who was it took your field and gave it to someone else?'

Perhan's daughters, who were hiding in a corner, covered their mouths. But on hearing Musa, they exploded like bottles of carbonated water and began giggling incessantly.

Musa looked at what they were wearing and stared at the torn trousers they had on, which were tied together with pieces of rag instead of being sewn. 'By God, the girls have broken their sewing needles by the looks of it.'

'Laugh', Zelxe said, 'Laugh, you've found a nobody with no-one like me, now laugh.' She began to cry, shaking her thinned-down shoulders. 'Laugh, I won't say anything. Go on, laugh. God has struck me down, now you strike me too. Who's never hit out at a waif? Don't you be any different, go on, take a pot shot at me.' She put her head in her hands and began to sob.

'Oh mother!' Musa said. 'Please! Now what have we done? Zelxe, mother? Oh dear, no-one's been ordering you around, have they? I mean, who hasn't lost children among us? Don't cry sister, don't open up our wounds with your crying.'

When Zelxe heard the others begging her to stop she carried on crying, with sobs as heavy as black clouds full of rain. As she cried, her shoulders heaved and her chest shook so hard it almost rattled.

'Pitiful me,' she sobbed. 'Where shall I go? May God punish that village of Kızılmezra. Where shall I go? Mother! All I had has been taken from me? And what did I have? I would have put my son on my back and gone from village to village. And God thought that having a son was too much of a blessing for me. Abdullah Paşa took one of my sons, but God thought this wasn't sufficient and I had to give my other son to the black earth as well.' As she cried, she began to extend the ends of her words as if she was singing a lament. 'Mother! Mother! I've no place to gooooo! I said to him, "Don't go, Hemo. Don't go. Don't leave us here by this river. No, Hemo, don't go. The soldiers have taken the hilltop. Hemo, don't go and leave me with these two fatherless children."'

Then Zelxe began to recount how her husband had been shot after breaking cover in the little valley where they'd hidden themselves and going to check the surrounding area. She'd told her husband Ahmet the area was safe, but he had decided to mount a small hill to see what was going on. And there he'd been killed by the soldiers. The place where the family had been hiding was a dense forest, a forest of black oak. Every oak reached its topmost branches almost to the clouds. If Ahmet were to look up at the height of the trees, his head would crane so far back that his hat would fall off; so high were the trees. They were so tall that one's head would rest on one's back just trying to see their tops. But Ahmet had gone out from the place where they were hiding and had been shot on the hilltop by the soldiers, with a single bullet.

As she told the story, everyone was shocked. Zelxe was keening a lament for her husband Ahmet as if he had only just died. She had nowhere to go. And who would take on a woman as a crop-sharer?

Musa was sorry that he'd brought up Çöyder's name. He began to humour my mother, saying, 'You're right, Fecire Hatun. He said the same thing to me. He said that he'd learned about the law from spending time with the soldiers. He said, 'Once Fecire Hatun marries, everything will pass to her husband.' And I'm no better off than a pauper. My children's daily bread isn't secured with some red-stamped document from the government. What if they turn up tomorrow and tell me to get out? Now, Çöyder is not here, his God is here. All he said was it's a shame for Süleyman Salih Bey's daughter to be taken advantage of and get peeled like an onion.'

That made my mother get even angrier. 'Mother! Don't let him feel sorry for me, what is it to him? Is he going to oversee all of these villages? When those in exile return, is he going to impose the law? To think he's worried about me! Let him worry about himself, that demon. Tell him! Tell him to feel sorry for himself. Say it. Why don't you go around everywhere gossiping like a fishwife?'

'Perish the thought, Fecire Hatun, perish the thought,' Musa replied. 'He's to be pitied too, if you saw the place where he sleeps, you'd be cut up inside, you would. How can a person live in that stone cave? I mean, he told me so himself, he said, "I feel a pang of sorrow in my heart every time I see that river bed where Hıdır Efendi was shot," and he went on to say, "Musa, I know I've argued with Süleyman Salih Bey's daughter, but..."

I didn't hear what Musa said after that. Instead, I said to myself, 'That means that my mother has got married to Doğık.'

XXIX

My mother had got married to Doğık. When did they get married? When did Doğık become a member of our household? As all of this was being talked about, I sat in between Goe and Sede and tried to understand. I couldn't quite make out just what getting married entailed. I'd only ever known Musa and Hece as being a married couple. Is that what it was? They ran around after the children together, went off to the field together, was marriage that thing between Musa and Hece? A man and a woman speaking to one another as if they were waging a continual war of nerves upon one another?

I looked up and Musa was still talking. Doğık had become a part of our family without anyone really noticing. He came to see us almost every day. He came late in the evening and left in the morning whilst it was still dark. He would sit by the hearth and tell us tales from his military service.

I began to see all of Doğık's adventures come back to life before my eyes but now, instead of Musa's voice, it was Doğık's I heard, 'When I surrendered, they took me and handed me over to the soldiers. We boarded a train. The journey was never-ending. I'd say it lasted a day, you'd say more like a month. There we were in a cold train, one thousand soldiers. The train stops, we get off and walk about. The train gets going again, we start to freeze aboard it. At every stop we let off around five to ten soldiers. Every time the train stopped they'd throw in loaves of bread that were hard as stones. The infidels made fifteen soldiers get out at Çanakkale. And they lined us up, side by side, like nails in a row.'

'As he said this, he'd stand to attention and showed us how a nail would stand up. When he stood to attention, he'd take off the hat he'd been wearing and screw it up in his hand.

'See! This is how we would stand. I mean, Perhan, I know languages. And just as the commander told us to start the roll call, I started by saying my name and surname. And the way I said Hozat, well, the infidel's cuff came down and slapped me on the ear, I thought I'd been struck by lightning and that the earth had cleaved in two. That's how it was. Like my brains were going to fall out of my eyes. "Throw him in jail," he said, "throw this Armenian spawn in prison." They threw me in prison and an infidel came every day to beat me seven times, I looked and their hunger for it wasn't passing, and they locked me up in a lavatory, that was this small, this small!'

Doğık told us that for three years a Captain had locked him in this small lavatory. Until one day a Colonel, who had come on inspection, got him out of there and said, 'Your military service is finished.' Doğık's memories of his military service were so ghastly he recounted them to us nearly every day and we sat there and listened. The Captain who imprisoned him in the lavatory had also apparently killed his very best friend in Dersim.

Whereas I had always been the centre of my mother's attention, now our new life was going to revolve around my mother's third husband, Doğık.

My mother was married. On the day that Doğık took her paperwork to Hozat, Zelxe hung herself and we heard that Çöyder Hüseyin had killed someone in the village of Derik.

Çöyder's sister Serayi howled like a wolf, turned her head to the mountains and began cursing him. 'Çöyder, may the bread that our mother gave you come out through your nose.'

'I told you,' Musa said, 'I told you, Perhan, the Çöyder I know will go into Dersim at one point and reappear on the other side. I mean, don't let anyone say that I didn't tell you so.'

As he spoke, Musa wet his two fingers and made repetitive notch marks on the wall. 'See Perhan! I'm writing it here. Seeing as it's death again, have yourself some death. For every oak leaf in this Bactria, thirty dead bodies have been lined up side by side. And soldiers who know two pennies' worth of the language are being decapitated in our name. He's hanging them up and butchering them, saying that he created these here mountains. I already said it. The Çöyder I know will go into Dersim at one point and reappear right on the other side.'

'Musa, stop,' Serayi said. 'In the name of God, stop. Everyone is saying things about the poor man. Be quiet now, what's done is done. What's Çöyder to do? The twelve tribes came together and even they couldn't impose any law on Dersim. How is Çöyder supposed to do so? The ones who have government paperwork in their hands and know a few words of the language are lording it over us like a Paşa. What's Çöyder to do?'

Musa was almost crying out with joy. He was keeping time with his feet whilst skipping about with his good arm in the air, clicking his fingers as if he was dancing the *halay*. The empty sleeves of his armless side were flying left and right. Whoever he saw, he invited to join him in dancing the *karaçor*.

'Hey! Hey! Come on Goe, come on Sede, my girl, don't sit there all mean like that, up you get. Hey, hey!'

When Perhan came in, he stopped and stood there huffing and puffing, out of breath.

The girls looked up at her as if to say, 'Perhan, what's happening?'

Musa was speaking in fits and starts, jiggling his feet as he spoke. His hand was still up in the air as if dancing the *halay* and *karaçor*.

'Hey, Perhan, hey, la, la.' He was so carried away that he was unaware that his wife Hece had come into the room.

'Hey, Perhan, hey,' He was completely out of breath, 'If only I still had this arm.'

Hece just stared at him in disbelief. 'What would you have done, asshole? What would you have done? And I asked myself what all this noise was. Shameless good-for-nothing, you've been dancing the *karaçor* from morning 'til night. What would you have done? Tell me! What would you have done with that other arm?'

Musa caught his breath in gasps. His good mood had been ruined. He looked around and about as if to say, 'When did she come into the room?'

He turned to Perhan, 'Perhan, what's this? Is it illegal to breathe now?'

Hece replied, 'It's forbidden. Forbidden, asshole! If anyone saw you, they'd think it was the festival of Saint Hızır.'

Musa said nothing to his wife, even though she was berating him like a little child. He moved over to the hearth and sat in the same place that Zelxe had sat every day, as she combed the embers in the fire with the poker.

'Oh sister,' said Musa, 'was there nowhere else to die, that you had to come here and hang yourself? We got used to it, Perhan. But she couldn't get used to it. I mean, that too is a death, she wasn't able to persuade herself. Don't listen to her saying she was going to travel round collecting alms, "I'll go round asking for alms," she said. But no. She was afraid.'

He fished into his pocket and pulled out his curved *simser* knife that was wrapped in cloth. He slowly unwrapped the cloths that covered the blade of the *simser* and began to stroke it along the soot-blackened hearthstone. Then he took the *simser* and squeezed it between his legs. Then he took a piece of wood in his hand and stuck it onto the sharpened end of the *simser*. He wasn't happy with that, so he sharpened it some more on the stone and cleaned the blade once more. He brandished it at the tassels of the goat hair saddlebag hung above the fireplace, then uttered an 'uhh' as if he'd cut his finger on the sharp blade of the *simser*. Then he held the handle of the knife squeezed between his knees as he laboriously began to wind the cloth around the blade, as if wrapping a child in swaddling.

'And this is a new game,' said my mother, 'a new tradition for an old village.'

Musa replied, 'Well, Fecire Hatun, I'm a father to many children too. And of all I hear coming out of Hece's mouth all day, barely a thousandth of it is of any worth. I mean, I too am a human being. Did that poor Zelxe mean any harm to anyone? She just sat here, in the corner of this fireplace and chatted away, what did she have to laugh about? We're all human, we have all poured out our troubles to the standing stones. Is a person not to talk, or to laugh at all? I mean, if a person doesn't talk, how could there be different species of birds in the wild? Çöyder said to me himself, "Sey Musa, in a world devoid of people, there are no birds."'

He took out the *simser* dagger once more, from where he'd placed it in his pocket. Once again, he held the blade between his knees and began to unwind the wrapping cloth. He dragged it along the soot-blackened stone with a grating noise. As he sharpened the knife the lines upon his face were lit up and left dark, flicker by flicker of the flames in the grate. He narrowed he eyes and then opened them wider, again and again. Outside a storm was blowing. The avalanche that had broken away and come down from Sultan Baba Mountain had passed over the Torunoba Valley and hit the Vank Pass.

XXX

The day after Musa had danced the *halay* and the *karaçor* folk dances he plunged into a deep silence. Every day he would go and sit in the corner where Zelxe had sat, next to the fireplace and he'd take his *simser* out of his pocket and slowly unwrap the cloths that covered the sharp blade. He would hold the half-crescent shaped fine and deadly blade and look at it in the flight of the flames, before trying it out on a block of wood. Then he'd test it out on the tassels of the saddlebag hanging above the fire and wonder in amazement at its sharpness. But still, he would sharpen it again with a rasping sound along the soot-blackened hearthstone. He neither spoke nor laughed. No matter what my mother said, he would just reply, 'Tell us, Fecire Hatun.'

His wife Hece was the most disturbed by his state. She'd come in to check on him every two minutes, take a look at him and then go again. All the time she was mumbling to herself and swearing. But no matter what she did, Musa would not open his mouth and say a word. He didn't call her 'fool' or say 'quiet now girl.' Neither did he tell the tale of the Kangal dog that left its master and disappeared.

Musa had also found himself a new friend and that was the new-born calf of the cow that my uncle, Kahraman Salih Bey, had sent us. The little calf, who wandered around the house waving its tail, would leave its mother's side behind the partition as soon as Musa went to sit in Zelxe's place in the corner and would make a beeline for him.

'Come,' Musa would say, 'Come, what would we do without you?'

He would put his index finger into the calf's mouth, as if it were the mother's teat, and the little calf would suckle it just as it would the udder of its mother and would shake its tail and make happy little laugh-like noises, as if it were a person being tickled.

Sometimes Musa would talk to me. 'Do you understand, Gülizar? A person is like that too. They see a dry stone and they expect hope from that stone. Just like this poor little calf. As it suckles, you'd think that pints of milk were flowing from this dry finger in its mouth. My dear departed father had a goat once that died whilst giving birth. The poor little goat kid thought that my late father was its own mother, right up until it grew to be an adult goat. Wherever my father went, the little kid would follow him, just as a baby animal follows its mother.'

'Dear, dear,' he went on, 'They don't say God is great for nothing. They don't say it for nothing. May God not confound us. When a person is thrown off balance, they'll be fooled by anything, just like this little calf. God brought humans into being so that they would believe all that God says. Can a person live without hope? When there's no hope, a person goes mad, just like Zelxe here. They'll go on and on talking about something, believe in it, but then they can't stand it that their belief turns out to be empty, and then they crack.

'Now, if I were to leave my finger in this calf's mouth and not remove it, the calf would keep on suckling and suckling, and then, just like Zelxe, it would get to breaking point and then die. When Melek was running away from the soldiers at Dervişler her breast milk dried up, from fright. Melek's breasts turned to dried-out stone. She saw that her child was getting restless and so she put her finger in its mouth, just as I'm doing with this calf. The child suckled and suckled and died. But, just as with this baby calf, the baby's eyes were smiling as it suckled Melek's finger and it thought that milk was going into its belly. A person without hope cries, and so to stop a person who is crying you have to give them hope.'

'Look,' he'd say to me, 'Gülizar, before I arrive, this little calf stands bellowing here in the house. It comes in front of the partition and wants to suckle its mother, who stands there lowing, but as soon as I appear the calf comes to my side, swishing its tail. And Dersim's the same, Gülizar. Just like this little calf, it mooed and mooed and then it went and suckled the fake teat held out to it by Abdullah Paşa, as if it wasn't the government in the first place who had condemned this place to starvation. Now, if I do not remove my finger from the mouth of this poor little thing, then it will suckle its little lungs out and it will break down and die just like Melek's baby or that poor helpless woman, Zelxe.'

Musa came every single day and sat in front of our fireplace, took out his knife and sharpened it with a scraping noise on the blackened hearthstone. He'd place his finger in the mouth of the cow's little calf and the calf would make a giggling sound as it sucked. He spoke to the calf as if it were a human.

Then he'd turn to me and point to the stool in front of the fire. 'Sit down, Gülizar. Come, that's right, sit here by the fire. You are the only one who doesn't speak, here among us. Even this little calf finds something to say to me. I've heard the voice of every other thing.

'If I sit here in this house, and even if they were to bury me under the ground, and then throw some iron doors on top of that, if someone were to say to me, "Musa, which wind's voice is that, blowing outside?" I'd know it. Just as long as I could catch scent of it, I'd know. If I could smell it, I'd know if it was the evening breeze or the morning breeze; I'd just know. I'd know right away and I'd say, "Aha, this is the wind that blows off Balıkan Mountain." It smells of pure acorn oaks and towards evening it has the faint scent of oak moss. The wind that blows from the direction of the Emirhan River smells of black poplars. If you listen to it carefully, you'll think you can hear the leaves in the black poplar forest as they rustle, rustle, rustle.'

He closed his eyes and sniffed the air in through his nose to show me. 'Aha, that's it. Close your eyes. Once you've closed them, do you hear it? How the poplar leaves rustle? Smell it, go on. Can you smell that one? That one is the wind from the Emirhan River. And if you were able to smell the wind that comes from Sıncık Mountain, you'd never get over it. You'd think that the petals of a thousand and one flowers were being borne before it on the breeze. And, just as the birds sing, so you'd think that a sparrow's feather had dislodged itself from the clouds and was trying to make its way down. It is so silent, that you'd think that when the wind from Sıncık Mountain blows not one single fibre in the world will be disturbed. And you would want it to blow a little more strongly, so that you'd feel as if you'd ascended to the clouds and your lungs had filled with air, and you'd feel so inundated by it.'

    He stopped and looked into my eyes, that had been watching his face the whole time he spoke. 'So that's it, I couldn't figure you out. You follow around after your mother and no-one ever hears your voice. You never speak, and no-one ever knows what you're thinking. Children cry. Have you ever heard of a child that didn't cry? My lot don't stop for a minute, they don't know how to shut up and are always bawling their hearts out.'

    He stopped and looked into my face for a very long time. He stroked my hair with his hand and examined my face closely. His hand smelled of dried oak logs. 'I really don't know why you won't talk. If only you'd talk, say a thing or two now and then? You can't just listen, and go into yourself, now, can you?'

    He took the *simser* knife out of his pocket and looked for a while at the blade end that was swathed in cloth. It was as if he'd lost all his energy and couldn't find enough strength to unwrap those cloths. All of his dreams were in ruins, it was as if he had lost absolutely everything.

    'Çöyder has been killed, hasn't he?' I asked.

    Musa looked at my face in astonishment and his eyes filled with tears. The knife he'd been holding between his fingers slipped out and fell to the floor.

He shouted, 'Fecire Hatun! Fecire Hatun! She spoke! She spoke! Gülizar just spoke, Fecire Hatun, Gülizar spoke.'

Had I really not been speaking? Musa was shouting and was flapping around like a skylark whose young has just fledged and flown away.

'She spoke, Fecire Hatun, she spoke. She looked into my eyes, and I said to myself, this child can speak. I said to myself, "some people talk to themselves and it's only they that hear their voice." That's what I said. Hece, girl! Come! Gülizar just spoke.'

My mother knew all along that I could speak. Perhan's girls knew too. Or at least that's what I think today. They say that I didn't speak at all after the day I saw my father's severed head. But I can't really remember this at all.

This is my last memory of Musa, a man who played a large part in my life. The snows melted and the spring showed its face to us again. Now the fields would have to be sown and we would set up a new life. However, the final round of forced exile began that spring of 1942. They sent Musa, his wife Hece and their children off to exile in Edirne for five years. Musa's crop fields were left to Perhan's daughters. They sowed and reaped them for a few years but the people who returned from exile had worked and saved money which they brought back with them. Doğık sold half of the village, including Musa's two fields to the men who returned from exile. We built one more storey on our house. The World War was over.

And...

One cold winter's day Çöyder Hüseyin went to his comrade Hüseyin's house to warm up. Four people were hiding in the house, lying in wait for Çöyder. Çöyder entered the house and greeted his old companion. He hung his rifle up behind the door. At that moment, the four men piled onto Çöyder. His comrade's wife, Yildiz, was not at home. She had been sent to another house, in advance, and in accordance with their plan. Had Yildiz been there, not just four men, but four hundred men would not have been able to take Çöyder captive.

As the four men began to wrestle with Çöyder, the evening sky was just darkening. Çöyder tried to get his hand on his knife. Had he been able to unsheathe that knife perhaps he would have managed to get away from them, but the four men shouted for all they were worth, 'Hold him! Hold him! If the unbeliever is able to get open his knife, not one of us will come out of this alive.'

Çöyder began to wrestle with all four men. Before long it was midnight. But no, they couldn't take him captive. One moment Çöyder was winning, the next moment the four men were on top. They were streaming with sweat and exhausted. Çöyder's old comrade didn't weigh into the fight for a long time. Instead, he sat in his place and watched. The men asked him for help, 'Hüseyin, if Çöyder manages to get out of this house, you'll be the first one he'll kill.' Eventually, this old companion of Çöyder's, Hüseyin, went to the aid of the men.

Night turned into day, and Çöyder said, 'You've not been able to take me captive and now the lightening sky has been hit by the sun's rays. If dawn breaks upon a bandit, then that bandit is, for all intents and purposes, dead. And now, even if you let me go and told me to get out of here, I wouldn't go.'

He unlocked his hands that he'd had grasped around his knife and the knife fell to the floor. They captured him and tied him up. His medals had been ripped off and his clothing was in shreds following the struggle. One of the army boots had come off his foot. They forgot to put his boot back on him.

There was not a single cloud in the sky and the mountains were pure white. Çöyder began shouting and laying down the law as if all of the mountains had gathered there to listen to him. They climbed up Torut Mountain and saw the Plain of Deşt laid out before them like a sea.

Çöyder began to plead with them, 'Oh, come on, I understand you have no faith nor religion left. I understand that. You're going to turn me in. But have you ever known such a thing? Let me go.' He turned to Doğık, who was one of those who had caught him and said, 'You and I were brothers in arms. We were travelling companions of Sahan Ağa and Hıdır Efendi!' He shouted and he cursed. 'Shoot me!' he said, 'Shoot me. Is there no faith nor religion left among any of you, that you are taking me to deliver me up to my enemy?' He looked at Doğık with pleading eyes, 'Shoot,' he said, 'These others have no faith to speak of, so it's up to you. Shoot me.'

They passed over Seypertek and Doğık said, 'Let's let him go.' But the arrow had already flown from the bow and it was too late. Were they to let him go, they knew full well that Çöyder wouldn't leave a single one of them alive. Çöyder, himself, had now realised there was no turning back, and he went quiet. They swore at him and insulted him but not even a knife could have opened Çöyder's mouth now. One of his feet was bare, it had been sliced by the frozen snow and was bleeding.

They reached lower Teştek. Now they could see the soldiers down on the Plain of Deşt. The huge plain had become a sea of flags that was flooding along towards lower Teştek. It looked as though a huge flock of crows had swarmed over the plain and were undulating like waves. You could see nothing but flags. The men descended to the road where the snow that had come down from the Greyder mountains was heaped up on either side like small ranges themselves. Then they saw Governor Fevzi upon his horse, with his Commander accompanying.

The Commander dismounted his horse with a leap. 'Ooooh! Hüseyin-e Çöyder, you have graced us with your presence! Look! The Republic's entire army has come out to meet you. A warm welcome to you, Hüseyin Bey. Look, these regiments have been waiting days to see you. One thousand soldiers have been making preparations for you for an entire week. How good of you to join us, Hüseyin Bey!'

The Commander laughed loudly and turned to the soldiers. 'Look here! Look! Do you recognise Hüseyin-e Çöyder? Hahaha... Do not be afraid, Hüseyin Bey! Why don't you preach to us all here, imagining you're standing up somewhere on Balıkan Mountain, shout *duwa, duwa duwa* and call us all out! Go on, say it! Hahaha...'

'Look, Hüseyin Bey!' he went on, 'Look, this great army has come out to meet you. This army has never turned out like this; not for the Head of the Republic himself! Hahaha...'

They took Çöyder from the men who had captured him and loaded him onto a horse-drawn cart. His hands and feet were bound and he was surrounded by soldiers. As the cart moved along the regiment of troops silently watched it going by. It was as if a funeral procession were passing and all that could be heard was the sound of wheels of the horse-drawn cart turning. They arrived at the square of the Deşt barracks. Soldiers had formed a ring around the square, three men thick. They were pressing tightly against one another in an effort to see Çöyder.

The Commander shouted, 'Untie him!' They untied Çöyder. However, Çöyder did not get up on his feet. He stared at the ring of soldiers in surprise. He lay there staring at the mass of soldiers who were jostling one another and who had come there to see him. It was as if the soldiers assembled around him were not a regiment but row upon row of snowy mountains. It was as if he had fallen from the sky and landed in a cage full of people and was lying there, just as he had fallen. He seemed to be waiting for some small movement. It was like he was begging for there to be some small stirring among the mass of soldiers pressing and circling around him. Nothing stirred. The clouds themselves seemed to have stopped moving in the sky. He turned, and looked at Doğık, as if he were saying, 'Whatever you do, don't leave me here in this loneliness, and go.' He looked at his old comrade, Hüseyin. No-one could understand what he was thinking. Everyone was gazing at his naked foot that had been cut up by the frozen snows. He looked down at his clothing and his hand went up to the tin medals that had been ripped in half and were still dangling from his chest.

He didn't hear the Commander give the order. A can of petrol was poured all over him, from head to foot. He didn't even move. Doğık's eyes darkened and he saw Çöyder Hüseyin disappearing like a black spot where he lay on the floor in front of him.

He had been turned into a ball of flame within the circle of onlookers. He screamed and heaven and earth quaked. Clouds rushed into one another. He curled around on the floor, in flames, just as a bank of cloud moves among itself in sky, that's how he writhed. He shouted, 'Youuuu!, Youuuu!' and cried out for help. He span around just like a moth circles a flame that's been lit, and a smell of burning meat filled the Plain of Deşt.

XXXI

The train taking people into exile stopped for a break at Kayseri. Musa jumped off the train for a moment and the train moved off again. No-one ever heard from him again. His wife Hece thought that he had returned to Dersim. But when she returned from exile, she learned that Musa had not come back to Dersim from Kayseri.

Years later, Perhan lost her daughter Sede. She then moved out towards Kızılkilise to be near her daughter Goe who had gone there as a bride.

My aunt, Wae, moved into Veli Ağa's fine house when she came back from exile in Çorum. She lived out her days begging for alms.

Çöyder Hüseyin's sister, Serayi, married Mehmet Ali, who was the brother of Hasan Ali, one of the men who had turned Çöyder in to the government. They made a folk song of it and the song spread from tongue to tongue all over Dersim.

Emirhan River, our road the black earth,
I'm a mountain flower on the hillside, the mountains far away

Then she left her husband and ran away to a relative who lived over towards Malatya.

On learning that she really had lost Musa, Hece became a *berbiçi* funeral singer. She attended every death she heard about and turned their stories into laments. She went to every funeral and to every bridal procession and sang laments at all of them.

Fecire Hatun learned from her husband Doğık in person that Çöyder Hüseyin had been caught. She signed over everything she owned, all of her land and possessions, to Doğık. He kept on selling the fields, and eating up the proceeds of all this land he'd gained by deception. Then he brought along a younger bride called Derman as a new wife to take her place above Fecire.

And...

Gülizar, despite receiving quite a number of proposals, did not want to leave her mother. Then a bald man who was at least twice as tall as a normal person, came to ask for her hand. The man's name was İmam'e Lach and he came to ask for Gülizar's hand for his step-son, whose name was Ağa. İmam'e Lach was a minstrel who could play the saz and sing folk songs in Zazaki, Kurdish and Armenian. After gaining the permission of her mother, Gülizar agreed to marry Ağa.

A large train of people on horseback came to take Gülizar away. They decorated the bride in finery and put her on a bay horse. Everything was done in the traditional manner. There were seven drummers and seven wailing singers. The village of Haçeli was half a day's journey away. They threw a multi-coloured cover over Gülizar that was made of pure Yemen silk, with tasselled edges that reached right down to the Erzincan boots that she wore. They put a silver belt around her waist and, on her head, they placed a fez, the tassels of which reached from her forehead right down towards her face. They escorted the bedecked bride out of the door and mounted her onto the horse.

The bridal procession set off along the road to Sıncık Mountain. The drummers were at the front with the procession of men. They walked along the road that wound between the mountains, striking their batons on the drums with a 'boom, boom.' The *berbiçis* wailed laments alongside the horse which bore the bride.

Fecire Hatun did not join the bridal procession on this, her daughter's, most important day. Instead, after saying goodbye to Gülizar, she went and sat at the foot of rock where she and her daughter had always sat, in those early days when they had escaped to the forest.

There was one other familiar face in this bridal procession which sliced along Sıncık Mountain like a knife as it proceeded and that was Hece. Hece walked along at the front for the entire way, singing laments as she went. All they had been through in life was reanimated in those laments as they were sung.

When they reached the peak of Sıncık Mountain the bride, who was covered from head to toe by the silk cloth spoke up. 'Stop!' she shouted.

The procession stopped. Gülizar jumped down from the horse. Yes, this was the place. The voice of her mother still resonated there. There, in between the rocks where she had prayed. The blowing wind was the same and everything was just as it had been. Even their sheep seemed to be there. As she threw herself onto the ground, in the same way her mother had done, the procession went silent.

Gülizar stroked each stone, one by one where they lay, piled one on top of another. What kind of life was this life? What kind of world? She thought of her mother who was sitting at the base of that rock at Weroz, watching the bridal procession as it left. She then understood why her mother had not wanted to be part of the procession. The day would end, and a new day would begin. Her mother would sit by that rock and stare at the road as her daughter disappeared out of sight.

'Mother', Gülizar moaned. It was as if the mountains wanted her to say the name of her mother. 'Mother,' she repeated, 'mother.' She looked around her. She looked for the mountain goat. She listened to the moaning wind.

She heard her mother's voice resounding on the wind, 'Do you see, my little Butterfly, do you see the mountain goats?'

'Yes, mother, I can see them.'

'Their master is Sultan Baba. Look over there, between the heads of those mountains that are wreathed in smoke-like cloud.'

She turned and looked. The peak of Sultan Baba Mountain was, as usual, covered in a mass of pitch-dark cloud.

The pennyroyal flowers, immortelle, and clumps of thyme were bending their heads in the breeze, towards the slopes of the mountain. The wind was once again moaning and whistling in between the smaller stones. It made a noise like a little child who's just learning to whistle and from whose parted lips a noise like, 'uuwww, uuwww' comes forth. A pair of swallows took flight from a clump of giant fennel, their tails fluttering.

'Whoever said,' Gülizar whispered, 'whoever said that stones don't speak? Or that swallows don't watch over the road, whoever said so?' The wind was dragging a dried-out wild liquorice plant between the pebbles. She picked up the red stone under which her mother had placed a strand of her hair and a piece of cloth torn off from her own sleeve. There was something there. It looked, for all the world, like a faded flower.

Zurich, 11th February, 2009

Author's Biography – Haydar Karataş

Haydar Karataş is a Zaza Kurdish novelist, short story writer and activist writing in Turkish. Karataş was arrested as a student activist at 19 and spent 10 years in prison where he wrote several novels. All but one were confiscated. The one that accompanied him in his escape from prison was *Butterfly of the Night*. It was published by İletişim Publishing in 2010 and sold over 200,000 copies. His second novel *Secrets of the 12 Mountains* was published in Turkish in 2012 and *Ejma's Dream* followed in 2017. Karataş's writing has been compared to that of the great folk-literature giant Yaşar Kemal and the keenness of the suffering in this book has been compared to Steinbeck's *Grapes of Wrath*, and Sabatier's *The Safety Matches*. *Butterfly of the Night* was published in German in 2018. Haydar lives in Switzerland with his wife and family.

Translator's Biography – Caroline Stockford

Caroline Stockford is a translator, poet and human rights activist from Barmouth in North Wales. She studied Turkish literature, translation and the history of the Turkish language at the School of Oriental & African Studies, London. Her MA thesis was on the Turkic runiform script of the Orhon monuments. Stockford's poetry and translations have appeared in many online and print journals including Modern Poetry in Translation, the Berlin Quarterly and Turkish Poetry Today. She was a regular attendee of the Cunda International Workshop for Translators of Turkish Literature. Caroline was one of the editors and translators of Turkish poet Haydar Ergülen's first selected works in English, *Pomegranate Garden*, (Parthian, 2019). Stockford is a board member of Wales PEN Cymru and works as Turkey Adviser for PEN Norway, running literary and legal human rights projects.

Palewell Press

Palewell Press is an independent publisher handling poetry, fiction and non-fiction with a focus on books that foster Justice, Equality and Sustainability. The Editor can be reached on enquiries@palewellpress.co.uk

www.ingramcontent.com/pod-product-compliance
Lightning Source LLC
Chambersburg PA
CBHW071559080526
44588CB00010B/962